MW01050100

NORFOLK'S WATERS

To Gene Dixon Jr.,
for blessing Virginia
Beach with the
historic and up-to-date
Mac

For Mary Lee Settle

Norfolk: from
Gosport, Virginia
was painted by
J. Shaw in 1819
from a point just
above the Navy
Yard. From the
Phelps Stokes
Collection. Courtesy,
New York Public
Library.

NORFOLK'S WATERS

An Illustrated History of
Hampton Roads

By William L. Tazewell and Guy Friddell

American Historical Press
Sun Valley, California

Library of Congress Catalogue Card Number: 00-109173
ISBN: 1-892724-16-2

Bibliography: p. 263
Includes Index

The authors gratefully acknowledge permission to quote from
the following:

"Dam Neck, Virginia" from COLLECTED POEMS
1930-1976 by Richard Eberhart
(Copyright ©1960, 1976 by Richard Eberhart)
Reprinted by permission of Oxford University Press

Photos formerly credited to Virginia State Library,
now courtesy, The Library of Virginia.

TABLE OF CONTENTS

INTRODUCTION

A SONG TO THE RIVER

The Elizabeth River, on whose shores Norfolk was born, is the shortest, hardest working river in the United States. It also used to be one of the dirtiest.

It is a ubiquitous river, popping up when you least expect it. In Norfolk you can't walk a few blocks in any direction without coming upon a patch of wetlands that belongs to the sovereign Elizabeth. She is all around and among us.

Its main body of water, bearing navies, is only three miles long, a tidal river fed by the Chesapeake Bay's waters.

A teacher once remarked, "It is the nation's first river named for a woman, Queen Elizabeth, and it is all mouth!" That is a droll, but false notion. It's named for Princess Elizabeth, daughter of King James I.

The Elizabeth's main branches—Southern, Eastern, and Western—extend from Norfolk into three other cities in South Hampton Roads. Each branch is longer, but far slighter, than the mother river.

The Southern Branch is in Portsmouth, across the river from Norfolk. At the century's turn, the Elizabeth River froze. Citizens of both cities walked across the ice, side to side.

When the president of the United States is roused from his sleep at an ungodly hour by word of a crisis abroad, he asks, "Where are my carriers?'"

Six are in California and six are under the Atlantic Fleet Command at the Norfolk Naval Station, the largest naval base in the world, often called the Capital of the Navy.

Installations for other services—Army, Marines, Coast Guard and Air Force—make the Hampton Roads military complex the nation's mightiest.

To know the heart of Norfolk, simply attend the homecoming of a ship from a six month deployment abroad. A gigantic love-in takes place on a cement pier measuring a quarter of a mile long and six lanes wide. Families are as numerous as seabirds crowded onto a long sand bar.

Such welcomes await battleships, cruisers, destroyers, submarines, and even coastal patrol ships with a complement of only 28 on board. The emotions of 100 or so family members yearning for 28 are every bit as intense as those who pack the pier to meet the 6,000 aboard a carrier.

A carrier is a city at sea. You wonder at the first glimpse of the great, gray, clean-edged mass, if she really can be that large. Her sheer towering size, arising in a great arc at the prow, reminds you more of the excesses of nature—a moving wall of rain— than anything man-made.

She keeps getting larger until standing alongside her is like being involved in a giant feature of a landscape, an overhanging cliff, with a huge cave-like cleft in its side.

On September 14, 1967 a special tension attended the arrival of the Carrier *Forrestal*. It had taken heavy damage on July 27 as it sailed in the

Tonkin Gulf off Vietnam. A rocket loaded onto a fighter plane was accidentally launched on the *Forrestal*'s flight deck, rupturing a 400-gallon fuel tank that set off a chain reaction of exploding bombs and ordinance that triggered an inferno and blew a hole 11 decks down.

In the multitude waiting for her in Norfolk, a voice called, "Here she comes!"

And there was the *Forrestal*, growing larger on the horizon, stretching more than a city block, as she paced toward the pier while the tugs hurried to meet her.

But it was as if the persons on the pier were pulling the ship to them, almost visibly, a part of it, remindful of John Donne's "A Valediction Forbidding Mourning." Two souls who, when parted, endure not a breach but an expansion, like gold to airy thinness beat.

And now the gold was contracting, in a rush, into the reunion at the Norfolk Naval Base. As the long gray lance of the ship drew nearer, the watchers could see that the clean edge of her vast flight deck was tufted in white, a fringe of sailors of the *Forrestal* spaced evenly like sentinals around her perimeter.

It looked like snow on a gray mesa.

The sailors were as still as marble caryatids against the blue sky until the ship was turning to dock along the pier, and then the line of sailors on the far side, like a quick wave dashing, ran to join those looking down at the crowd far below.

There, a girl, waiting, suddenly called, '"There he is!" and screamed, "Tom-m-e-e!"

A tall blonde in sunglasses held up a dusty-grey poodle for someone to see, and a father, who could stand it no longer, loosed an anguished bellow, "Mark!" to the white clad sailors high against the sky.

A Marine guard came down the gangplank and a gray-haired woman, who had been holding herself erect, crumpled in tears beside the tall shaft

of her son. The father, approaching, his face alight, said, "Hey-y-y-y-y!" as if the youth, just standing there, was doing something as remarkable as the day he took his first step.

Tearing through the crowd toward the Marine came a tanned, bare-armed girl in a bright orange sheath, her brown hair streaming. She ran, brushing aside anyone between her and the Marine, who caught and lifted her until only a toe touched the ground; when she drew back to look at him, her face was dumb with fierce affection and seeming resentment at their having been parted.

During a brief ceremony, while city officials were trying to put into words what no one could, the reporters went on board, into the huge, crowded hangar deck, where one sailor told another he had seen their wives waiting on the dock.

"Diane's got on a bright green blouse, and your wife's wearing a blue dress."

"Did they see you?" asked the second sailor.

The boy nodded, and swallowed.

"Is it getting to you?"

"Yeah, it is."

Now the dependents were swarming into the hangar. After the first rush came a woman in her '40s, in a dark green and blue plaid, stepping carefully, as a doe entering a glade. Her eyes were searching, and she saw and circled a trim warrant officer, his hair just tipped with silver. Coming up behind him, she said quickly, just before he turned, "Were you looking for somebody?"

To one side of the tumultuous tides of love was a young woman wearing black, a black mantilla over her bright head, merely watching, and waiting for someone who couldn't come.

At the press conference in the senior officer's wardrobe, a reporter was asking the Captain about the conduct of the men during the explosions that ripped the *Forrestal*, destroyed 29 planes, and took 134 lives.

The Captain said, "You read about their bravery?" The reporters nodded, and the Captain said, "They were even braver."

Now, at the deserted end of the pier, where wheeling gulls screamed, one could look down the long grey length of the ship and see the sailors and their families filing off the gangplanks near the bow.

But there was silence around the wounded stern, which was battered and torn as if sledged. No one moved or spoke.

On the deck above the beaten, rusted hulk was a tripod displaying the Stars and Stripes, inexpressibly gay, rippling red and white, straining, and keeping aloft, wind-tossed, as if alive.

Guy Friddell
September 2000

Family members greet the USS Barry as it returns from a six-month deployment, along with the guided missle frigate USS Samuel B. Roberts. The ships were patrolling the northern Persian Gulf in support of Operation Southern Watch, stopping and boarding cargo ships leaving Iraq and searching them. Photo by Ian Martin Courtesy, The Virginia-Pilot.

Jonathan Daniels once called Norfolk "the Hong Kong of the Albemarle." If a Hong Kong the city is, Chesapeake Bay might identify it better than Albemarle, which is a North Carolina sound and region. But Daniels, late editor of *The News* and *Observer* in Raleigh and author of a dozen lively books, linked Norfolk with his state.

Thus he subscribed to a popular notion among Tar Heels. To those in the northeastern counties along the Virginia border, Norfolk is a place to shop, if not emigrate. Tidewater shipyards count hundreds of commuting North Carolinians on their payrolls. A Tidewater joke in the 1960s was that if the Good Lord intended for man to go to the moon, He would create a shipyard there and rely on North Carolinians to reach it. More than a century earlier Norfolk and Portsmouth leaders threatened to petition the North Carolina legislature to annex the Lower Tidewater area because Richmond and Petersburg, on the James and Appomattox Rivers, were blocking the port development of Hampton Roads. Was it any wonder, then, that in 1981 Northeastern North Carolinians, disgruntled at executive inattention and legislative redistricting chicanery, warned that if things didn't improve they would ask Virginia "to take us back in—everything from the Roanoke River through the Chowan River basin"? (Their discontent was voiced by Ron Dill in *Tidewater Review*.)

Whatever Norfolk may be to its neighbors southward, it is other things to other people. To uniformed representatives from far shores to the Supreme Allied Command, Atlantic, headquarters and the Armed Forces Staff College, both near Hampton Boulevard and Little Creek Road, it is a hospitable duty station and gateway to the United States. To the world's mariners—behold their turbans, admire their pom-poms, note the cut of their jackets and mold of their boots, marvel at their polyglotism!—it is a familiar liberty port and sometimes, alas, a dangerous one. To the U.S. Navy it is a principal place for doing business on and beneath the great waters and in the sky; also, it is, for better or worse, home: a house in the suburbs as likely as an apartment on a base, a church more often than a chapel, and a school system, a polling place, and a tax office. The Fleet Reserve Association and the Navy Wives Club are as primary to Norfolk as the Chamber of Commerce and Society of Arts.

Norfolk borough meanwhile remains intact, presided over by families that from the beginning, or so it would seem, have tended a collection of charities, cotillions, and cemeteries—but not, fortunately, to the neglect of fresher institutions and bolder endeavors. If Old Norfolk is outnumbered, it shows no signs of feeling conquered.

Norfolk is advantaged for its cosmopolitanism's exceeding its parochialism, even at its expense of seeming mysterious, like a British crown colony on an Oriental island, to inlanders. In its 300 years it has become used to strangers and their ways. Ideas do not alarm it; change it knows to be as certain as tides. A partial explanation of the late Colgate W. Darden, Jr., the ablest Virginian in this century, whose laugh was as grand as his mind, and whose devotion to fairness was a Commonwealth treasure, is that he was a Norfolkian. The city's courage has had its reflection—and its prodding—in the Norfolk press, which in its best years has been suspicious of conformity and simplicity and guided by compassion.

William L. Tazewell has been a member of that press. As a reporter, political writer, and associate editor of *The Virginian-Pilot*, he recorded and pondered with unusual understanding Norfolk's triumphs and lapses during the physical renewal and social reconstruction periods between the late 1950s and approach of the 1980s. He encouraged the arts. He defended the environment. He joined in a monitoring of authority and watch over justice.

And as a journalist-historian he is in good Virginia tradition—in the Lenoir Chambers, Virginius Dabney, and Douglas Southall Freeman school. At the Pilot he first wrote editorials under Chambers, author of the two-volume *Stonewall Jackson* and of *Salt Water & Printer's Ink: Norfolk and Its Newspapers, 1865-1965*, and was tremendously influenced by his personality and editorship. It was my delight to share editorial offices with both.

Tazewell earned B.A. (1954) and M.A. (1955) degrees at the University of Virginia, and studied also at Ohio State University (Woodrow Wilson Fellow, 1957-58), the School of Letters at Indiana University (summer 1958), and Harvard University (1958-59). He interrupted his newspaper work for a sabbatical at the University of North Carolina (Mark Ethridge Fellow, 1967-68). He was a member of the English faculty at the University of Virginia, teaching a course in nonfiction writing that ought to be called simply a course in *good* writing.

A great-great-grandson of Littleton W. Tazewell, a Virginia governor and United States senator, William L. Tazewell was born into Virginia history. A son and brother of the architects Bradford Tazewell, he was a close witness to Norfolk's structural growth. *Si natura negat, facit indignatio versum*—so observed Juvenal: "When talent fails, indignation writes the verse." Unusual talent guards the author's composure, objectivity, and affection for the city of his forebears, his birth, his hearth, his good works, and his narrative.

ROBERT H. MASON
Editor, *The Virginian-Pilot* 1962-1978
Southern Pines, North Carolina

9

PROLOGUE

This is a book about Norfolk and its surrounding waters, written to celebrate the city's tricentennial. I have sought to write a book for the general reader, yet one that is both faithful to history and responsible to scholarship. I have likewise sought to avoid duplicating familiar works and, as best I could, to integrate the pictures and the text. In retelling the Norfolk story, it has often seemed that I must talk of many other things too. There is a good reason for that.

This is a city by the sea, a city of sailors and traders. It has always looked to the comings and goings of sailing ships and of the great modern vessels. The air blowing in Norfolk has a salty tang. It is a city that was cosmopolitan in outlook when it had not yet grown to be metropolitan in size. The character of the city has made it particularly sensitive to events elsewhere. Fortunes might be made—or dreams dashed—by the decisions of English kings, London merchants, or politicians in Richmond. Always there were extraordinary hazards and opportunities in other people's wars, which have had a tendency to come home to Norfolk. And so I have looked to events elsewhere that affected life by Norfolk's waters.

I have often used those two words, "Norfolk's waters," to describe the region that is now home to more than a million people. Obviously they are not Norfolk's in any exclusive or possessive sense.

If we look at the map, we can be more specific.

The areas of Norfolk, Portsmouth, and Chesapeake that lie within the fishhook of Interstate 64, from Bowers Hill at the hook to the haft at Willoughby Spit, constitute the core city of Tidewater Virginia, watered by the branches of the Elizabeth River and the Lafayette River. Narrowly speaking, these are Norfolk's waters.

The anchorage of Hampton Roads, the harbor's heart, is bounded by the James River Bridge and the tunnels that connects Norfolk to the Peninsula. Norfolk looks across one axis of Hampton Roads to Newport News on the opposite shore. Along the other axis, Churchland faces Fort Monroe at the ends of the great rectangle of sheltered water. It is a second subsystem.

In a cabin cruiser it is about an hour's run from Hampton Roads upstream to Jamestown, where it all started; and you will pass the Newport News shipyard and Fort Eustis on the right, while the countryside to the left is Smithfield ham territory. This is the mouth of the James River, the Newport News waterfront, another distinct subsystem.

A fourth great subsystem is the Chesapeake Bay itself. Here at the Bay's edges are the beaches of Ocean View and Buckroe Beach in Hampton, and from here the inland sea stretches to Baltimore and beyond to the mouth of the Susquehanna. Nowadays the Chesapeake Bay Bridge-Tunnel is the boundary where the Bay empties into the Atlantic Ocean. On the charts of the mariners that may not

Aircraft carrier Shangri-La *was launched at the Norfolk Navy Yard in 1944. Courtesy, Portsmouth Naval Shipyard Museum.*

Family members looks on, as the aircraft carrier USS George Washington departs from Pier 12 at the U.S. Naval Station in Norfolk, VA., in June 2000. The carrier led a battle group deployed to the Persian Gulf and Mediterranean Sea. Photo by Jonathan Kirshner. Courtesy, The Virginian-Pilot.

Battleship Wisconsin *being pushed down the Elizabeth River from the Norfolk Naval Shipyard going to the Norfolk Naval Base. Berthed beside the Museum Nauticus will be the* Wisconsin, *a long, lean, mean battleship, slinking low in the water, prowling for prey. Only the superstructure looms. When the ship enters the river, it appears to be a castle on the water. The 887-foot dread-naught last saw duty in Desert Storm. It pounded Iraqi defenses. Photo by Mark P. Mitchell. Courtesy,* The Virginian-Pilot.

be strictly true, but the miles of trestle are the tangible wall in the water.

From Chesapeake Beach east to Cape Henry, and south to the Back Bay refuge and the Carolina line is the fifth and last subsystem. Here are the bathing beaches, the motel strip, the surfcasting and suntanning territory: Virginia Beach's waters.

Metaphorically, though, these are all Norfolk's waters. The city is the heart of the region today, and there can be no understanding of the history of these waters without the history of Norfolk. Paradoxically, the city of Norfolk has been better served by its historians than by its history, which makes a tale of calamity, frustrated opportunity, and a potential that has seemed to go unrealized until the 20th century.

The city was created by a deed dated 1682, and by 1715 Norfolk was the first real town on the American continent between Philadelphia to the north, the chief city of the colonies, and Charleston to the south. Remember that in 1715 the estimated population of Virginia was 72,000 white settlers and 23,000 slaves. They were living mostly about the shores of Chesapeake Bay and along the rivers of the tidewater. The economy of the region rested on tobacco, a crop that exhausted the land and so tended to disperse the population in plantations, clearings rather than towns.

William Byrd II visited Norfolk in 1728 on his way to survey the "Dividing Line" between Virginia and North Carolina and observed that it "has most the air of a town of any in Virginia." Byrd knew something of urban living; he then was in his mid-fifties and had lived in London for many years. When the Royal Charter of Norfolk Borough was

granted in 1736, the population of the town was about 3,000, By comparison, Baltimore was not founded until 1729 and Richmond remained "still a petty trading post" until the Revolutionary War; its growth really started when it became the capital of Virginia in 1779.

By the eve of the Revolution, in 1775, Norfolk's population was perhaps 6,000. Commerce flourished; merchants thrived. The borough was "a rare place," according to the city's first historian, William S. Forrest, who wrote: "All were busy; a prosperous state of affairs was plainly exhibited on every hand and no one doubted the future greatness of the place."

Then came calamity. The city was burned to the ground at the onset of the war. But Norfolk quickly recovered. By the time independence was won, in 1783, "there were not yet twelve houses rebuilt in Norfolk," as a visitor wrote, yet the census of 1790 showed the population of the town at just under 3,000, rivaling Alexandria, Petersburg, and Richmond, the only other sizable towns in Virginia. The

The Virginia International Tattoo has become one of the most popular events of the month-long Virginia Waterfront International Arts Festival, held each spring. The Tattoo is an extravaganza combining elements of a circus and a Broadway show. It features acts from more than a dozen countries. It has been such a success in Norfolk that it has become a fixture. A local feature is a steel drum band in which high school students from throughout Hampton Roads make music on 50-gallon steel drums abetted by players on pots and pans and a silver snarling trumpet. Courtesy, Virginia Waterfront International Arts Festival.

city continued to grow rapidly. By 1806 Simmons' Directory reported that "the number of inhabitants may be computed at nearly ten thousand and they are characterized by travelers as generally polite, obliging, and hospitable."

Although visitors would go on remarking upon the advantages of the city's geography and its great harbor, Norfolk was entering into what can be seen in history's long perspective as a century of stagnation. It may be conveniently marked off by the Embargo of 1807 and the Jamestown Exposition of 1907. The lucrative West Indian trade withered in the wake of the embargo, the blockade during the War of 1812, and British mercantile policies thereafter. The railroad and the steamship were to revolutionize transportation in the United States between the War of 1812 and the Civil War, but Norfolk remained a relatively small town. It lost out

to Petersburg and Richmond, the cities of the fall line, in the economic and political struggles within Virginia, while the influx of immigrants and the growth of industry that were to change the nation—and ordain the outcome of the Civil War—were events happening to the north of Norfolk. On the brink of conflict in 1860 the city's population was little more than the number reckoned by Simmons' Directory in 1806.

Not only was Norfolk bypassed in the course of economic events, it was also twice visited by disaster. Yellow fever raged through the town in 1855 and, following the moment at center stage during the battle of the *Monitor* and the *Merrimac* in Norfolk's waters, Federal forces occupied the port for the rest of the war.

Norfolk was a generation in returning to what it had been before the Civil War. By the mid-1870s it was enjoying a modest prosperity as a cotton port. In 1883 the first coal train rolled into the city over the Norfolk and Western tracks, an event whose economic significance is all the more pertinent today when a million tons of coal is loaded in a single week. At the turn of the century Norfolk was a provincial seaport with a population of 46,624—about half of Richmond's, less than 1/10th of Baltimore's, 1/12th of Boston's, roughly 1/28th of Philadelphia's, and a bit more than 1/75th the size of New York City. By contrast colonial Norfolk's population had been roughly 1/3rd of Boston's, 1/4th of New York's, and 1/6th of Philadelphia's.

As part of a $4.4 million dollar renovation, three new battleship-related exhibits will be installed with a walkway from Nauticus to the Wisconsin. The navy approached the city about berthing the Wisconsin as a way to free up needed pier space at the Norfolk Naval Shipyard in Portsmouth and to celebrate the long kinship between the city and the navy. The ship will remain on the navy registry preserved at Congress' behest for possible use during an international emergency. Photo by John Whitehead. Courtesy, Norfolk Convention and Visitors Bureau.

Sailors manning the ship during commissioning ceremonies of the USS Harry S. Truman. *Photo by Mark P. Mitchell. Courtesy,* The Virginian-Pilot.

Immigration and industry brought growth and wealth to the big cities of the North; neither was a factor of great significance in the history of Norfolk in the 19th century.

In 1907 two events foreshadowed the changes that were to come to Norfolk as the result of two world wars. One was the Jamestown Exposition and the other was the round-the-world voyage of the Great White Fleet, which sailed out of Hampton Roads on December 16, 1907 and returned a year and 68 days later. Whatever its popular success, the Jamestown Exposition was a financial failure and went into receivership within a week after it

closed down in the fall of 1907. But a decade later the government purchased the site, to turn it into the greatest naval base in the world. The emergence of the United States as a major naval power had been symbolized by the grand gesture of Teddy Roosevelt in sending the Great White Fleet round the world.

Although the history of the Gosport Navy Yard dates from pre-Revolutionary times, the marriage of Norfolk and the Navy was not consummated until the two world wars. Both were boom times for the cities of Hampton Roads and, by 1945, had permanently transformed them. Burdened by civic prob-

The James H. Ricau Collection represents one of the finest concentrations of 19th century American marble sculpture in the United States. *Photo by Scott Wolff. Courtesy of Chrysler Museum of Art.*

lems and the bad name that it had as a sailors' town in wartime, the city then undertook what I have called elsewhere "the making of the new Norfolk." The dramatic postwar renewal saw the demolition of much of the Norfolk that was and its rebuilding in quite a remarkable way, which led in turn to a new sort of civic selfconfidence. The postwar period also saw the annexation battles, the closing of the Norfolk schools during Massive Resistance, and the cycle of change and growth that is everywhere evident around Norfolk's waters.

That is the history that we are living today. The city has been fortunate in its telling. The history of Norfolk was chronicled by Forrest and H.W. Burton in the 19th century and, by Thomas J. Wertenbaker, Marvin W. Schlegel, Peter C. Stewart, Rogers Dey Whichard, Lenoir Chambers, Carroll Walker, and others. If the Norfolk story has been often told, and told well, why bother with its retelling?

The answer is not only that the story should be told upon the city's tricentennial, but that it is also a story with a new twist as we enter Norfolk's 301st year. It has the kind of happy ending that was missing in past years. For now, I think, the city is coming into its own, realizing the visions of William Byrd II and Anne Royall and Matthew Fontaine Maury, the boosters and editors of the 19th century, and those who have contributed to Norfolk's renewal since the end of the Second World War. That may be sensed in Ghent's rebuilding or the downtown Norfolk skyline; the evolution of Old Dominion University and Norfolk State University; the establishment of the

Eastern Virginia Medical School; the coming of, the Chrysler Museum; the development of the Virginia Opera Association, the Virginia Orchestra Group, and the Virginia Stage Company; and in all the activities in the arts and business, commerce and the port, the Navy and tourism, as well as the daily lives of its people that, taken together, are Norfolk in 1982. This is the city destined to grace Norfolk's waters, and the story I have sought to tell.

William L. Tazewell
February 15, 1982

Scope and Chrysler Hall. Photo by David B. Hollingsworth.

Three cranes work to unload the Hapag-Lloyd containership Leverkusen Express, the second ship to call Norfolk International terminals' new north berth. Courtesy, The Virginian-Pilot.

CHAPTER ONE

A NATURAL PARADISE:
1607 - 1682

Chesapeake Bay is a great inland sea that encompasses some 3,237 square miles of water, with a mean depth of 21 feet, and about 4,612 miles of shoreline, scalloped by countless creeks and inlets. It is fed by the four great rivers shaping Virginia—the James, the York, the Rappahannock, and the Potomac—and about 150 lesser tributaries. Where it flows into the Atlantic Ocean between the capes named for two royal brothers—Henry, the Prince of Wales, and Charles, the Duke of York—is one of the greatest harbors in the world, Hampton Roads. Sail 200 miles to the north and you reach the Bay's source, the Susquehanna River. Chesapeake Bay is "new" and "young" in geological terms; it was formed 8,000 to 10,000 years ago by the glacial flooding of the Susquehanna River Valley. The average width of the Bay is 15 miles, but there are stretches where it is more than twice that wide. Its climate is mostly temperate—"the land of pleasant living," in the beer company's commercial tribute—but it can have suddenly treacherous and violent weather, as many have learned to their peril on the water. Ecologically, geologically, topologically, it is an impressive and remarkable body of water. Add the human dimension to the physical setting and you have the historic marriage that led to the cradle of democracy and a new nation, nurtured in Virginia.

More than twenty years before Sir Walter Raleigh's ships landed there, the Spanish sought to colonize the region. In the spring of 1561 Pedro de Menendez de Aviles discovered and explored what he christened the *Bahia de Santa Maria* and took an Indian home to introduce at the court of King Philip II. In 1570 a group of Jesuits landed at Jamestown and planted a mission on the York River that was exterminated by the Indians within a few months. Although the massacre was avenged savagely by the Spaniards in 1572, it was the end of the efforts to establish the flag of Spain as far north as Virginia.

Also before the coming of the English, the French had planted settlements at Port Royal and on the St. Johns to contest for "Florida," as the Spanish termed the American mainland. But the colonizing effort of the French was short-lived and their Fort Caroline fell to the Spanish in 1565. Centuries earlier, some think, Chesapeake Bay was reached by the Vikings or, even earlier, by the Celts in shallops.

If the Celts and the Vikings belong to the realm of legend, we are on the good ground of history with the coming of the English. It was not the Englishmen who landed at Jamestown in 1607, but those who sailed with Sir Richard Grenville in 1585 and established a fort on Roanoke Island who first gave to Chesapeake Bay the Indian name by which we know the region today. In the autumn of 1585 the colonists dispatched an ex-

Pocahontas saved the life of Captain John Smith when he was a prisoner of Powhatan. This chromolithograph depicting the event was published in 1870. Courtesy, Library of Congress.

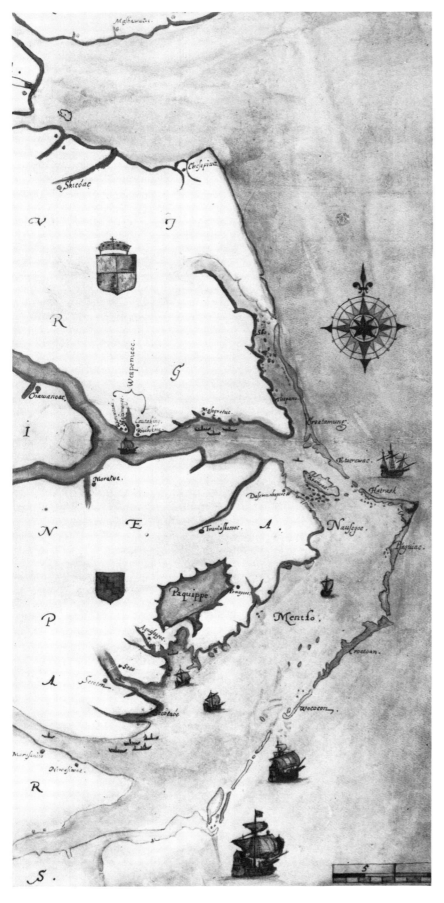

ploring party that followed the coastline north to what is now the city of Virginia Beach and wintered at Chesepuic, the chief village of the Chesepian Indians at the mouth of Chesapeake Bay.

Take the word apart and its Algonquian roots are *che*, or "big," and *sepi*, or "river," with an ending "at," denoting the settlement at the big river. "The English after their custom took it merely as a meaningless label of a town or tribe," George R. Stewart wrote in *Names on the Land*. "They soon transferred it to the broad bay north of the town, so that the bay is called Chesapeake, a name meant for a river."

It hardly matters. The music in the names on the waters is one of the few legacies the Indians left us—Chesapeake, Potomac, Rappahannock; the Appomattox and the Chickahominy; the Piankatank and the Poquoson; the Choptank and the Nanticoke and the Pocomoke; the Patuxent and the Wicomico. The history of the region is the growth of English places by the Indian waters.

By 1606, when a group of speculators organized the Virginia Company of London as a royally chartered joint stock company to finance the planting of a settlement in Virginia, the English knew a lot about the New World. In 1584 Philip Amadas and Arthur Barlow had sailed in Sir Walter Raleigh's ships and landed on what is known today as Bodie Island on the Outer Banks of North Carolina. They remained for five weeks, Barlow sailing straight to England and Amadas going on to Chesapeake Bay, where he found a hostile reception. They brought back to England two friendly Indians, Manteo and Wanchese, and optimistic reports of what they had seen in "Virginia," as Queen Elizabeth permitted Raleigh to call the colony in her honor. Another, bigger expedition sailed the next spring, departing Plymouth on Good Friday, April 9, 1585, and returning to England in the fall, leaving a colony of 107 men under Governor Ralph Lane, nearly all of whom were to come home with Sir Francis Drake's squadron in 1586, in advance of Grenville's relief ships. The fifteen "caretaker" colonists Grenville left vanished—massacred or starved—but another expedition returned in 1587 to establish the "Cittie of Ralegh in Virginia."

These settlers were to become celebrated as the "Lost Colony," though there is good reason to think that Englishmen still survived in the wilderness when Captain Christopher Newport's three ships sailed into Chesapeake Bay in 1607. They would have been Englishmen gone native long since, and Virginia Dare, the first English child to be born in the New World, would have been a young woman of nearly twenty by then. But the colonists of 1587 had intended to land on the shores of Chesapeake Bay, a plan that was frustrated by the Portuguese pilot Simon Fernandez for reasons that we can only speculate upon. Certainly they knew of the English party's staying with the Chesepian Indians, who appear to have been a docile people, in the winter of 1585-1586 and it is easy to imagine the "lost" colonists leaving Roanoke Island, an inhospitable place, and moving north to live near the Chesepians. Perhaps the "Savages" who attacked the first landing party, as Master George Percy reported, and "hurt Captain Gabrill Archer in both his hands, and a sayler in two places of the body" on April 26, 1607, were part of Powhatan's war party; perhaps the "great smoakes" that Percy reported seeing signified a tragedy that Captain Newport and the new settlers did not suspect. In any event, David N. Durant judged in *Ralegh's Lost Colony*: "Their arrival either provoked or coincided with Powhatan's decision to exterminate his neighbors the Chesepians, and the lost colony with them."

Whatever the fate of the Lost Colony, there can be no question that the average Englishman was familiar with Virginia when the London Company's plans were undertaken. The flora and fauna of the New World, and especially the exotic natives to be found there, had been described by Englishmen on earlier voyages and depicted in the drawings of John White. These were reproduced widely in the engravings of Theodore de Bry, issued in editions in four languages in 1590. The "new found land of Virginia" had been described by Thomas Hariot and advertised by the Hakluyts and others in the kind of promoters' prose that echoes familiarly today. To be sure, the information on the New World was tinctured with a great lot of misinformation too. Englishmen preferred to think that there was gold for the taking in Virginia, as the treasures of Mexico and Peru had been plundered by the Spaniards. Thus Ben Jonson and his collaborators gave a gilded speech to Captain Seagull, who instructs Scapethrift and Spendall, the "adventurers bound for Virginia," in the play *Eastward Ho* (1605):

I tell thee, gold is more plentiful there than copper is with us; and for as much red copper as I can bring, I'll have thrice the weight in gold. Why, man, all their dripping-pans and their chamber pots are pure gold; and all the chains with which they chain up their streets are massy gold; all the prisoners

they take are fetter'd in gold; and, for rubies and diamonds, they go forth on holidays and gather 'em by the seashore, to hang on their children's coats, and stick in their caps, as commonly as our children wear saffron gilt brooches and groats with holes in 'em.

Even if Captain Seagull's speech is satire, it gives a good indication of the stories that were common in London at the time that Captain Newport's expedition was being mounted in the summer and fall of 1606.

Its sponsors were more realistic in their view of what awaited the "planters" in Virginia. (The London Company called those who risked only their money the "adventurers," while those who risked themselves were called the "planters." Those who conceived of the project were known, unhappily, as the "undertakers.") "When it Shall please God to Send you on the Coast of Virginia you shall Do your best Endeavour to find out a Safe port in the Entrance of Some navigable River . . . ," ran the London Company's instructions to the settlers. "Let Captain Newport Discover how far that River may be found navigable that you may make Election of the Strongest most Fertile and wholesome place." The settlers were

A lande Crab.

John White recorded the plant and animal life of Virginia as well as the Indians he encountered. Among his watercolor drawings of 1585-1586 are the "lande crab" (above) and an Indian hunter (right). From the Tracy W. McGregor Collection. Courtesy, University of Virginia.

also urged "to Store yourselves of the Country Corn" against the dangers of famine, not to trust "the Country people," that is, the Indians, and to safeguard themselves "That You be not Surprised as the French were in Florida."

Still, when the three tiny vessels under Captain Christopher Newport sailed from London on Saturday, December 20, 1606, fully one-third of the 105 planters were accounted as "gentlemen," and much the same was true of the First Supply (1608), which included a perfumer and six tailors, the Second Supply, and the Third Supply (1609), which was described by Captain John Smith as "this lewd company, wherein were many unruly gallants packed thether by their friends to escape il destinies."

Certainly "packed" is the proper word. The average height of the first settlers was just over five feet, and they had to lie crammed like sardines below decks on their tiny vessels for most of the voyage. With none to wait upon them, unequipped for the wilderness and unwilling to work, the destinies of the "gentlemen" proved to be "il" indeed in Virginia. "When it became known in England that gold mines were not to be found in Virginia and that wealth could be had only by the sweat of the brow, these spendthrift gentlemen ceased coming to the colony," Thomas J. Wertenbaker wrote in *Patrician and Plebeian in Virginia.*

Gentleman or no, what could the Englishman expect to find when he reached Virginia?

It is difficult for today's Virginian—or anybody

living in the late 20th century—to imagine the scene that the first settlers saw when they came to the New World. To make the imaginative jump of 375 years backward in time, we begin by reversing the land's relationship to the water. We are land animals and our automobiles do not swim. So we subconsciously think of the water as an obstacle to our overland travel, a barrier to be bridged or tunneled under. But just the reverse was true when the first settlers sailed into Virginia's waters. The cramped ships that had brought them across the Atlantic Ocean, at great risk and with small comfort, nevertheless represented security. On the ship they were safe from the savages who lurked in the wilderness and beyond the reach of everything else that was unknown, and menacing, in the virgin woods.

The trackless wilderness that awaited the Englishman's foot on the shore was dangerous, impassable, unfamiliar. By contrast, Chesapeake Bay and its great rivers—especially the James and the York, which were domesticated early by the English and given names reminding them of home—were familiar and navigable and safe. Compared to England's gentle rivers and pleasant

White also sketched an Indian soothsayer captioned "the flyer" (left) and an Indian village (below). He was fascinated by the Indians and "the manner of their attire and painting themselves when they go to their general huntings, or at their solemn feasts. From the Tracy W. McGregor Collection. Courtesy, University of Virginia.

the colonists who were dispersed about the shore, staying in close contact with England and their neighbors by water. The rivers and streams served as the central nervous system of 17th century Virginia.

Now that we can see the water as life-sustaining, the means of travel and transportation, and in no sense the barrier it seems to us, what else did the Englishman find in the New World?

Abundance, in a word. There were clams and crabs and oysters and fish and terrapin and waterfowl in or near the waters. The woods were filled with game and offered nuts and berries for the taking. Tall trees awaited felling for houses or for ships' timbers. The land was rich and bountiful in its yield. And endless. There was always land, as much as a man could clear and cultivate, and enough for every man, and more. Much more.

On April 26, 1607, the first morning that the colonists on Captain Christopher Newport's ships saw Virginia, Master George Percy, the eighth son of the Earl of Northumberland, who was to be three times trusted with the command of the colony, from 1609 to 1612, went ashore and found "faire meddowes and goodly tall Trees, with such Fresh-waters running through the woods, as I was almost ravished at the first sight thereof."

A day later he wrote: "We past through excellent ground full of Flowers of divers kinds and colours, and as goodly trees as I have seene, as Cedar, Cipresse, and other kindes. Going a little further we came into a little plat of ground full of fine and beautifull Strawberries, foure times bigger and better than ours in England."

And after the colonists explored the James

streams, they may have seemed strange and vast waters. But to the earliest immigrants they were a defense, even a kind of distant early warning system. "Erect a Little Sconce at the Mouth of the River that may Lodge Some ten men with Whom you Shall Leave a Light boat that when any fleet shall be in Sight they may Come with Speed to Give You Warning," the London Company had instructed them.

As the English settled in growing numbers in Virginia, they came to rely on transportation by water. The English goods that they desired to ease life in the New World were dispatched by water, and the same ship that brought books and dresses and hats and tools and utensils to Virginia would carry home the shipment of tobacco that paid for the comforts they wanted. It was no accident that the first settlers were to build their forts on Roanoke and Jamestown islands, and it was no accident that the colonists continued to live near the water until economic and population pressures pushed the pioneers westward. Think of the Bay and the rivers and the rivulets as the 17th century equivalent of the Interstate highway system or as a great network of railroads serving

River, Percy recounted what he had seen:

It ebbs and flowes a hundred and three-score miles, where ships of great burthen may harbour in safetie. Wheresoever we landed upon this River, wee saw the goodliest Woods as Beech, Oke, Cedar, Cypresse, Wal-nuts, Sassafras, and Vines in great abundance, which hang in great clusters on many Trees, and other Trees unknowne; and all the ground bespred with many sweet and delicate flowres of divers colours and kindes. There are also many fruites as Strawberries, Mulberries, Rasberries, and Fruites unknowne. There are many branches of this River, which runne flowing through the Woods with great plentie of fish of all kindes; as for Sturgeon, all the World cannot be compared to it. In this Countrey I have seene many great and large Medowes having excellent good pasture for any Cattle. There is also great store of Deere both Red and Fallow. There are Beares, Foxes, Otters, Bevers, Muskats, and wild beasts unknowne.

The colonists constructed a fort at Jamestown, where they were to sicken and die in great numbers in the first years. More remarkably, they starved in the midst of the natural paradise. The "starving time" was the winter of 1609-1610, at the end of which, according to Captain John Smith, "There remained not past sixtie men, women and children, most miserable and poore creatures." They died of dysentery and typhoid fever, hastened perhaps by the brackish and contaminated water they used. They drowned. The Indians killed them. The faint of heart pined and perished. Only the hardy were "seasoned" to survive the first year. More than 7,000 colonists came to Virginia between 1607 and 1624, when the London Company was dissolved, partly as a result of the high mortality of the settlers. By the census in February of 1624, just 1,249 still survived.

On March 22, 1622, the Indians had risen and struck at the English settlers, slaughtering 347 men, women, and children. If the inhabitants of Jamestown and the nearby plantations had not been alerted by Chanco, a Pamunkey servant, the toll would have been even larger and the Indian plan of exterminating the English intruders might have nearly succeeded. As it was, Carl Bridenbaugh, the historian of Jamestown, has suggested that "the 'Massacre' of 1622 was probably the most brilliantly conceived, planned, and executed uprising against white aggression in the history of the American Indians."

The London Company did not long survive thereafter. It must be considered a failure in its own terms. It consumed the funds of its investors—£200,000, a staggering sum by the standards of the time—and yielded little or no return. Maybe it is not surprising that the colonists died in the land of plenty. They were ill prepared to live in a new way in a new world. But the paradox is partly psychological. In *American Slavery, American Freedom*, one of the best books on Colonial Virginia, Edmund S. Morgan summarized:

If you were a colonist, you knew that your technology was superior to the Indians'. You knew that you were civilized, and they were savages. It was evident in your firearms, your clothing, your housing, your government, your religion. The Indians were supposed to be overcome with admiration and to join you in extracting riches from the country. But your superior technology had proved insufficient to extract anything. The Indians, keeping to themselves, laughed at your superior methods and lived from the land more abundantly and with less labor than you did. They even furnished you with the food that you somehow did not get around to growing enough of yourselves. To be thus condescended to by heathen savages was intolerable. And when your own people started deserting in order to live with them, it was too much. If it came to that, the whole enterprise of Virginia would be over. So you killed the Indians, tortured them, burned their villages, burned their cornfields. It proved your superiority in spite of your failures. And you gave similar treatment to any of your own people who succumbed to the savage way of life. But you still did not grow much corn. That was not what you had come to Virginia for.

What the colonists did soon start to grow was tobacco. While it had not been the original purpose of the venture, it proved to be the cash crop that was to shape and stabilize Virginia. It was to be the determining factor in the colony's economy and growth, the basis of life around Chesapeake Bay in the 17th century.

Two events at Jamestown in 1619 were to cast long shadows. The first General Assembly was convened in the church at Jamestown on July 30 and adjourned on August 4, complaining of the "extream heat, both paste and likely to ensue." It consisted of the governor, six councillors, and twenty burgesses (the two delegates from Captain Martin's plantation were not seated) and passed a set of "lawes and orders" that can be found in its *Proceedings*. Also in August 1619 some 20 Negroes were brought into the colony and sold there.

While the happenings neatly symbolize what Edmund S. Morgan has termed "the central paradox of American history," the development of the institutions of liberty and slavery side by side in Virginia, we must not mistake the nature of the events themselves.

For the Assembly of 1619 was neither *democratic* nor *representative* in the sense that we conceive those talisman words. The early grandees of the tidewater were as arbitrary and as arrogant as their cousins in England. They conducted the affairs of the colony to suit themselves. They perpetrated frauds to add to their lands and did not scruple to cheat on their taxes. The excesses of officialdom, particularly those who toadied to Governor Berkeley following the Restoration of Charles II to the English throne, were a factor leading to popular uprising in Virginia—the one in 1676, not 1776.

As for the development of slavery, it must be remembered that a condition of servitude was the lot of most Virginians. Slavery was an accepted fact of the time. It existed in Europe. It was commonplace in the West Indies. Sir Francis Drake had been a slaver. The bulk of the evidence is that the black "slave" and the indentured servant were not treated very differently in Virginia until the definition of slavery in statutory terms in the 1660s.

There were only 22 black and about 465 white servants in the colony in 1625. By 1649 the figure was 300 slaves in a population of 15,000. In 1671 Governor Berkeley stated that there were 2,000 slaves in Virginia among about 40,000 inhabitants. As late as 1700 there were only an estimated 6,000 slaves, but by 1715 the number of black slaves and free whites in Virginia was roughly 23,000 and 72,500, a dramatic upturn. The reasons were basically economic. Circumstances first favored indentured labor, but later required slavery to sustain the tobacco economy.

In the first phase of its history, the colony's focus was Jamestown and the hold on the land was tenuous. Disease and savages threatened. Jamestown was a pestilential place and chances of survival improved for the settlers who lived outside its palisades. Between 1625 and 1634 the population of Virginia grew from 1,210 to 4,914 and during the decade the mortality rate was halved. There was another Indian massacre in

23

1644, bloodier than that of 1622, but thereafter the tidewater was the white man's province. By 1700 the number of Indians had been reduced to 2,000 where an estimated 18,000 had lived at the century's start.

The colony's first phase was followed by a period when the continued flow of immigrants and the generally high price of tobacco were beginning to bring a sense of permanence and even a measure of prosperity to Virginia. From the London Company's dissolution in 1624 to the Restoration of the Stuarts in 1660, the conduct of the colony was influenced by the echo of events in England. The Great Rebellion that began in Parliament in 1642 led to the civil war which culminated in the trial and beheading of King Charles in 1649 and Oliver Cromwell's coming to power as Lord Protector. It ended with Cromwell's death in 1658 and Charles II's returning to England and the throne in 1660. But there was no civil war in Virginia and it was a period of prosperity, relatively speaking, succeeded by a time of unhappiness. From 1660 until Bacon's Rebellion in 1676, and thereafter until the Glorious Revolution that brought William and Mary to the throne in 1689, the course of events was characterized by discontent, both economically and politically.

There was a downward trend in prices for tobacco that brought considerable hardship to many planters in Virginia, while the government headed by Sir William Berkeley grew more and more high-handed, oppressive, and unpopular. Berkeley believed it was the duty of the people to obey the king and those who governed in his name. In 1671 he declared in a letter: "I thanke God there is noe free schooles nor printing and I hope wee shall not have these hundred yeares, for learning has brought disobedience & heresaye and sects into the world and printing has divulged them, and libells against the best Government: God keepe us from both."

The antagonists of 1676 are easily stereotyped. Nathaniel Bacon was 27 years old when he came to Virginia in 1674. What became known as Bacon's Rebellion started as trouble with the Indians along the frontier. Berkeley was criticized for inaction and accused of involvement in the Indian trade. Bacon was chosen to lead a force of frontier vigilantes against the Indians, and the backwoodsmen did not much scruple at distinguishing friendly Indians and unfriendly. Berkeley declared Bacon to be a rebel, but offered a pardon to those who followed him if they lay down their arms.

Bacon was popular, Berkeley was unpopular. Bacon first seemed to submit, but soon was master of most of Virginia. After a comic-opera showdown with the governor and his troops, Bacon burned Jamestown on the night of September 19, 1676. He fell ill soon thereafter and died on October 26, presumably the victim of dysentery. Leaderless, the "rebellion" vanished.

Bacon has been characterized as both a demagogue and a democratic hero. Historians tend to agree that Berkeley, who had been a good governor when younger, was despotic and obstinate in his second term. He conducted himself like a king over the ocean until he was recalled by King Charles II, who is supposed to have said: "That old fool! He has taken more lives in that naked country that I in all England for the murder of my father."

Some of the figures from the early history of Virginia, whom we come to know almost as soon as we can read, loom large in American folklore. Although legends surround John Rolfe and Captain John Smith and the Indian princess Pocahontas, we know quite a lot in fact about them. The lives of the three are tangled. Pocahontas was perhaps 13 when she intervened to save Captain John Smith in the famous incident where he was Powhatan's prisoner. Smith had returned to England when John Rolfe fell in love with her at Jamestown five years later. The letter that he wrote to Sir Thomas Dale, the colony's governor, requesting permission to marry Pocahontas survives, and they were wed by Parson Buck in the church at Jamestown on April 5, 1614. The marriage seems to have brought a measure of peaceful coexistence between the Indians and the settlers. Baptized Rebecca Rolfe, she accompanied her husband when he returned with Governor Dale in 1616 to London, where she again met Captain Smith and was received by society. In 1617, just as they were to return to Virginia, she sickened and died and is buried at Gravesend. Rolfe returned to the colony, remarried, and died in 1622. Since he was the first planter to ship tobacco, John Rolfe's role in the history of Virginia is central as well as romantic. He appears to have been a man of admirable character and highly respected.

Captain John Smith was baptized in 1580 and died in 1631. An adventurer in the best Elizabethan fashion, he made his reputation by slaying three Turks in duels while serving as a soldier of fortune in the wars of the Holy Roman Empire. After additional exploits, including an escape from slavery in Turkey, he came home in 1605 and soon was involved in the Virginia venture. He proved to be a dynamic leader, which the colonists needed, but his enemies had managed to maneuver him out of power when he was forced by injury to leave Virginia in 1609. The man of action became a man of letters, publishing a series of works—*A True Relation, Description of Virginia,* and *Generall Historie of Virginia*—which continue to be read today. Enjoying the last laugh on his rivals, he is certainly the hero of his own history of Virginia.

But the colony's early history is less the story of a few great personages than the tale of thousands who are unknown. They came here to labor. It is a good guess that three out of four who came to Virginia in the 17th century were indentured servants. They built the colony, they endured, they really were the first families of Virginia. They and their children and grandchildren, working on the land they had wrested from the wilderness, were to become Jefferson's yeomanry.

Despite the notion that there are cavaliers in every family tree in Virginia, few of the first settlers were considered to be gentry, privileged, or wellborn. The contrary notion that they came disproportionately from the lawless and the low, shiploads of cutpurses and knaves and whores, is also untrue.

Who were the Virginians? By and large the dispossessed, the humble, the jobless, the laboring man, the unskilled, the uprooted. England had a labor surplus and thousands of unfortunates were being driven from the land that had hitherto sustained them. They could go hungry and they could go mad. They could go to the towns. Or they could go to the New World.

Surely there were those who dreamt of making their fortunes in a new found land, who were bound directly for Virginia. But most, one suspects, were unknowing and unlettered. From the countryside they drifted to the nearest town. (London's population was roughly 200,000 when Captain Christopher Newport's ships set sail in 1607. By 1700 the city had grown to 575,000, the biggest in Europe.) When the newcomers arrived in Bristol or Liverpool or London, some found work. Those who did not, the losers in the pitiless struggle, succumbed or drifted on. But many must have been tempted by the middlemen and the promoters—the ship captains and traders—who offered passage to Virginia. Or Maryland, or Massachusetts, or the West Indies. Things might be better there. They probably would not be any worse.

The fortunate were able to pay their way and to debark free men in Virginia. The rest were forced to indenture themselves, to pay for the passage by pledging their labor for a stated time. Beyond their bartered tomorrows was the unknown, a future of hope and hunger and hard work. The determined and the lucky and the strong were the winners. They found what they wanted, a better life than they would have had at home, a sufficiency in the tidewater. From the air-conditioned, comfortable distance of today, it is not always easy to distinguish hardship and plenty. But the indentured servant would be comparing his lot to that of the desperate in England, the peasantry in the shires and the poor in the slums. It was not necessarily such a bad lot in the tidewater.

Ironically, the 17th century in Virginia was the century of the common man. It was the 18th century that was to produce a generation of uncommon Virginians. But in celebrating the Founding Fathers, we ought not to lose sight of those who came first. Aristocrats they were not. Most were plain, rough, and simple: artisans, farmers, small traders, who came mostly as servants. In the 17th century the Virginian was an Englishman struggling to survive in the wilderness. In the 18th century he was evolving into what he would declare himself in 1776—an American and a free man.

Shown here dry-docked for repairs at Colonna's Shipyard in 1961, the Susan Constant *was the largest of the vessels that brought the English settlers to Jamestown in 1607. Replicas of the ships were built in 1957 to commemorate the 350th anniversary of the founding of Jamestown. Courtesy, Colonna's Shipyard.*

THE CULTURE OF TOBACCO

Tobacco was commonly cultivated by the natives of the New World, and among certain Indian tribes there was a ritual significance to its use. Explorers like Francisco Fernandez, who was dispatched to Mexico by Philip II of Spain, brought the plant back to Europe. In 1560 Jean Nicot, the French ambassador to Portugal, sent some seeds to Catherine de Medici and gave his name, *nicotine*, to the weed. It appears to have been introduced into England as early as 1565, perhaps by Sir John Hawkins, who reported the Floridians smoking a dried herb "Which smoke satisfieth their hunger." The habit was promoted by Sir Francis Drake, who brought home a "great store of Tabaco" from the West Indies, and by Sir Walter Raleigh, who helped to make it the fashion of the time. John Aubrey noted that Raleigh "tooke a pipe of tobacco a little before he went to the scaffold, which some formall persons were

scandalized at, but I thinke 'twas well and properly donne, to settle his spirits." Europeans first thought of tobacco as a cure-all, a medicinal substance, an exotic wonder drug for whatever ailed the 16th century gentleman. It was the English who popularized its social use and the habit soon spread throughout the world. By the early years of the 17th century it had reached every continent but Australia, still uncivilized.

Sir Thomas Hariot, who accompanied the expedition Raleigh sent in 1585-1586, described tobacco in *A Briefe and True Report of the New Found Land of Virginia*:

> There is an herbe which is sowed apart by itselfe & is called by the inhabitants Uppowoc: In the West Indies it hath divers names, according to the severall places & countries where it groweth and is used: The Spaniards generally call it Tobacco. The leaves thereof being dried and brought into powder: they use to take the fume or smoke thereof by sucking it through pipes made of claie into their stomacke and heade; from whence it purgeth superfluous fleame & other grosse humors, openeth all the pores

& passages of the body: by which meanes the use thereof, not only preserveth the body from obstructions; but also if any be, so that they have not beene of too long continuance, in short time breaketh them: wherby their bodies are notably preserved in health, & know not many greevous disease wherewithall wee in England are oftentimes afflicted.

This Uppowoc is of so precious estimation amongst them, that they thinke their gods are marveluously delighted therewith: Wherupon sometime they make hallowed fires & cast some of the pouder therein for a sacrifice: being in a storme upon the waters, to pacifie their gods, they cast some therein and into the aire: also after an escape of danger, they cast some into the aire likewise: but all done with strange gestures, stamping, somtime dauncing, clapping of hands, holding up of hands, & staring up into the heavens, uttering therewithal and chattering strange words & noises.

We ourselves during the time we were there used to suck it after their maner, and also since our returne, & have found manie rare and wonderful experiments of the vertues thereof; of which the relation woulde require a volume by itselfe: the use of it by so manie of late, men & women of great calling as else, and some learned Phisitions also, is sufficient witnes.

By 1604 such was the popularity of smoking that King James I was provoked into writing *A Counterblast to Tobacco*, attacking "that vile barbarous custom" and tobacco's users, "like Apes, counterfeiting the manners of others, to our own destruction."

But in 1613 when John Rolfe, who was experimenting with the leaf on his Mulberry Island plantation, shipped some to England from Virginia, it found a ready market. Indeed the price was so high that there was a kind of gold rush in Virginia. Aubrey recorded in *Brief Lives* that tobacco "was sold then for it's wayte in silver. I have heard some of our old yeomen neighbours say that when they went to Malmesbury or Chippenham market, they culled out their biggest shillings to lay in the scales against the tobacco." The colony's governor, Sir Thomas Dale, found it necessary to order the settlers to "set two acres of ground with corn," to guarantee there would be enough to eat, and Captain Samuel Argall, arriving at Jamestown in the spring of 1617, "found but five or six houses, the Church downe, the Palizado's broken, the Bridge in pieces, the Well of fresh water spoiled; the Store-house they used for the Church; the market-place, and streets, and all other spare places planted with Tobacco." In the same year the *George* sailed from Virginia with a cargo of tobacco that fetched five shillings and three pence a pound when it was sold.

Tobacco was to dominate the economy, and to determine the fashion of living, in Virginia. The colony exported 2,500 pounds of tobacco in 1616, nearly 50,000 in 1618, and 552,871 in 1628. A decade later the figure was 1.5 million pounds; it exceeded 20 million pounds by the end of the 17th century and 100 million by 1775. The plant accounted for more than three-fourths of the total value of the Chesapeake colonies' exports in

Rolling tobacco in Virginia. From William Tatham, An Historical and Practical Essay on the Culture and Commerce of Tobacco, *1800.*

The Beſt York River

that year.

The major strains of tobacco were Oronoco and sweet-scented. Oronoco was the stronger, "with a sharper leaf like a fox's ear," noted the Reverend Hugh Jones in *The Present State of Virginia* (1724), "and the other rounder and with finer fibres: but each of these are varied into several sorts, much as apples and pears are." But question a planter on the subject, said William Tatham, who wrote a book on tobacco,

> And he will tell you that he cultivates such or such a kind: as, for example, "Colonel Carter's sort, John Cole's sort," or some other leading crop master; and if the celebrated Linnaeus were at this day to class the characteristics of Virginia tobacco, he would probably discover several divergent species, in which nature and accident might seem to have cohabited sportively.

At first, the trade in the Virginia leaf merely meant that the English could cut down on the import of Spanish tobacco, but by the middle of the

17th century the colonies were growing more tobacco than could be consumed in England. After 1660, when the Navigation Acts (requiring the shipment of tobacco to England, where a duty had to be paid) began to be enforced, the crop glutted the market and the economy in the tidewater was depressed by the falling price of tobacco. Ruin threatened. "Our thriving is our undoing," Governor Culpeper lamented. But by the end of the century two-thirds of the crop was passing through England to European markets and the Chesapeake Bay region was the chief supplier of tobacco to the world.

Although the climate favored the plant, that was not why the region was to become tobacconist to the world. The crop could be grown many places; it flourishes as far north as Canada, Connecticut, and Wisconsin. The advantage of the Chesapeake Bay lay not in growing tobacco, but in getting it to market.

The leaf was commonly shipped in hogsheads holding anywhere from 500 or 600 pounds to twice that weight. As Arthur Pierce Middleton summarized in *Tobacco Coast*:

> The problem of conveying thousands of hogsheads (averaging nearly half a ton apiece) many miles through densely wooded country to a distant seaport would have been insuperable, not only because of the difficulty of road building, but because tobacco was too delicate to be rolled as

Tobacco labels from the Arents Collection. Courtesy, New York Public Library.

THELWALL's
Beft Virginia,
(N° 99.)
Swallow Street,
Hanover Square.

HARRIS, BEEBE & CO.

THE POCAHONTAS CHEWING TOBACCO.

much as twenty miles overland without suffering damage and loss of value. Hence the enthusiasm of the colonists for their "well watered country" where "Planters can deliver their Commodities at their own Back doors," an enthusiasm reflected in Dr. Charles Carroll's observation that but for the convenient water carriage, "it would be impracticable or at least very Expensive to Carry on the making of Tobacco."

Following the Revolutionary War, which forced the planters of the tidewater to shift to wheat and other crops to compensate for the loss of the tobacco trade, there was a major trend in the production of tobacco away from the Chesapeake Bay region to other places, served by other systems of transportation. But the colonial history of the tidewater is based upon the culture of tobacco. Its life relied on the weed.

Although his name is little known, William Tatham is the most interesting personality to be associated with tobacco in Virginia after John Rolfe. He arrived in the colony on his seventeenth birthday in 1769 and lived at various times in North Carolina, Tennessee, and Virginia. At different periods in his life he was a clerk, farmer, lawyer, soldier, and surveyor. An intellectual and a visionary, he was a friend of Thomas Jefferson and other remarkable Virginians. He fancied himself a great man and dabbled at international intrigue, ineffectively, with the English and Spanish. He

lived in London from 1796 to 1805, and was elected a member of the Royal Society of Arts. It was while he was living in London that he published the book by which he is remembered, *An Historical and Practical Essay on the Culture and Commerce of Tobacco* (1800). He returned to the United States in 1805 and was employed by the government periodically under Presidents Jefferson, Madison, and Monroe. But he never really succeeded in earning a living and took to drink in his later years. He died spectacularly in Richmond in 1819, throwing himself in front of the mouth of a cannon just as it fired the evening salute.

From John Rolfe's time to Tatham's, the cycle of tobacco was largely unchanged. About March the planter prepared the seed beds, or *patches*, for receiving the seed by burning brush and rubbish on them, and digging and raking them. In May the seedlings were transplanted to hillocks previously prepared and set about three feet apart from each other. The crop then had to be tended until the plants ripened, and guarded against the "fly" and the "worm." The chief operations required were "suckering," the removal of superfluous shoots from the stalk, and "topping" the plant to five, seven, or nine leaves, said Tatham, "as the quality and soil may seem most likely to bear." Both operations usually were performed by the planter's—or his slave's—thickened and toughened thumbnail.

Tatham continued:

> When the crop is adjudged sufficiently ripe to proceed to cutting, this operation is assigned to the best and most judicious hands who are employed in the culture; and these being provided each with a strong sharp knife, proceed along the respective rows of the field to select such plants as appear to be ripe, leaving others to ripen; those which are cut are sliced off near to the ground, and such plants as have thick stalks or stems are sliced down the middle of the stem in order to admit a more free and equal circulation of air through the parts during the process of curing, and to free the plant, as far as possible, from such partial retention of moisture as might have a tendency to ferment and damage the staple.

Then the crop was gathered into *turns* and taken to the tobacco houses to be cured and, once it was ready for shipping, to be *prized*, or bundled in bulk in hogsheads, usually crafted from hickory, for shipment. A hogshead of tobacco, weighing a thousand pounds or so, was the early equivalent of containerized cargo and anecdotes abound of hogsheads surviving shipwrecks; they were not so successful in protecting the planter against the "depredations privileged by custom," or pilferage, that were an expected part of the tobacco trade.

The annual tobacco fleet then took thousands of hogsheads from the planters' wharves to Bristol or Glasgow, London or Liverpool, and the merchants there who were acting as the agents in England for the planters. A convoy system was developed to safeguard the hundred or more sail of the tobacco fleet. Although it grew more by trial and error than by conscious design, thus was built the basis of the British colonial system, a body of laws and practices that was meant to enrich England and fill the king's treasury, without the colonists suffering unduly.

Customs duties on tobacco were two pence per pound in 1660 and gradually rose to eight and a

third pence in 1758. In the latter years of the colonial period, the duties exceeded the expected price of tobacco in Virginia. (In a bad market the price of tobacco was as low as a penny per pound.) But if the tobacco was re-exported from England, and most was, all but a half penny per pound was refunded until 1723, and the entire sum thereafter. Between 1689 and 1775 the royal revenues from tobacco nearly tripled, and the crop meanwhile was the principal source of revenue for the Chesapeake colonies' governments. Not surprisingly, there was extensive smuggling to evade the laws and levies on both sides of the water.

When the planters prospered, as they did generally until 1660 and again in the 18th century, there was money for English goods and to buy land in Virginia. There was money to buy extra labor too, usually indentured servants in the early period and slaves thereafter. As a result, the flow of immigration rose and fell with the price of tobacco. Conversely, cottage industry increased when cash was short and the colonists had to fend for themselves. In either event, the controlling factor was the tobacco trade. And since tobacco was the main medium of exchange, it served as currency, with the promise to pay x pounds of tobacco under such-and-such terms being as good

as money.

Because the colonists were continually clearing land to grow more tobacco, and because they needed to be near the water, there was a dispersal of population to serve tobacco's wants. Even though there were 100,000 people in Virginia and Maryland by the end of the 17th century, there were no real towns; they developed only slowly in the next century.

Lastly, the economics of tobacco governed the increase in the slave trade. After about 1680 there was a great surge in the number of slaves working in the tobacco fields, and a corresponding dwindling of the number of indentured servants who were hired, or leased, by the planters. Between 1700 and 1730 there was a fivefold increase (6,000 to 30,000) in the black population of Virginia and a comparable growth in Maryland. By 1790 there were nearly 400,000 slaves in the two states. In the time to come, that was to be the highest price of all to pay for tobacco.

CHAPTER TWO

COLONIAL VIRGINIA: 1682 - 1776

If tobacco was the basis of life in the Chesapeake colonies, it also was a crop hungry for land. The ambitious planter was always seeking to expand his holdings so that he could plant more tobacco. That was the way to wealth. A family farm might produce a few hogsheads of tobacco and enough food to sustain those who worked the land. Indeed that was the lot of most planters. But the few who could manage to pyramid their lands into ever-larger plantations were the envy of their fellow Virginians.

While it might be true that debt escalated as the acres multiplied, and often the great planters found themselves to be land-poor as the result, there is no question that theirs was the ideal way of life in pre-Revolutionary Virginia. Thomas J. Wertenbaker wrote in *Patrician and Plebeian in Virginia*:

Though the Virginian who acquired a degree of wealth was no aristocrat, he longed to be one. His grandfather, or his great-grandfather might have been a younger son of an English squire. He envied the honor, wealth, and power landholding brought that ancestor, just as many Virginians today envy the life of the colonial plantation owner. So when he found himself an extensive landholder, he thought of himself as an English squire. He too would build a fine residence, decorate his walls with family portraits, have a formal garden, accumulate a library, and dress in the latest English fashion.

The notion of a squirearchy transplanted to Virginia was not without its pretensions and an American grandee such as William Byrd II would find his comeuppance when he got to London. Nevertheless, those who achieved the ideal, the few leading planters, ran things in Virginia.

Because of the plantation system there were no real towns in the tidewater in the 17th century. There was no need for them. The cash crop, tobacco, was grown on the plantations. The planters shipped the tobacco to England on vessels which came to their own wharves. This was made possible by the geography of the tidewater. The system was convenient and efficient for the planters. So the economy, the geography, and the political system worked together to maintain things as they were.

But the captains of English ships did not like to poke about in the backwaters of the colonies. Often there were dangerous shallows in the unfamiliar waters, the business took time, and the crew of the ship usually were discontented, sullen, and thieving at their tasks. The English sailors hated the mosquitoes and the summer sun, and their clothing was unsuitable to the weather. They

John Murray, the fourth Earl of Dunmore, was the last royal governor of Virginia. He was forced to flee the Governor's Palace in Williamsburg in 1775 and was driven out of Virginia in 1776. He later was dismissed as governor of the Bahamas. Courtesy, Virginia State Library.

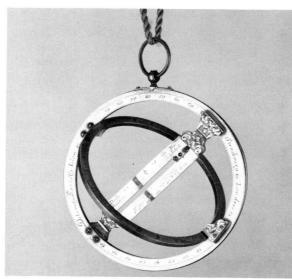

Navigational aids used in the 18th century included such instruments as this circa 1700 French ring dial (right) and circa 1760 Danish tell-tale compass (above). Courtesy, The Peabody Museum of Salem.

the English merchants was frustrated, repeatedly, by the plantation system.

Still the government kept on trying. First in Maryland and then in Virginia, the authorities attempted to plan, or plant, towns on more than 75 separate sites in the tidewater. Norfolk was destined to be one of the few that proved to be more than a paper settlement.

In 1679 the governor of Virginia was instructed to "endeavor all you can to dispose the planters to build towns upon every river, and especially one at least on every great river, as tending very much to their security and profit." In response to the king's wishes, the Assembly did pass an Act for Cohabitation and Encouragement of Trade and Manufacture in 1680. There were to be 20 towns, one in each county of the colony, and all exports and imports were to be shipped through one of the official ports of entry, as envisioned in the law. Each town was to be built on 50 acres of land and the owner was to be paid 10,000 pounds of tobacco for the site. But the merchants objected to the new system; they were accustomed to trading directly with the planters. The commissioners of customs said the traders "would be aggrieved and driven to smuggling," and King Charles II suspended the law's provision that exports and imports be made only through the nonexistent ports of entry.

But the basic idea—that towns were wanted—was not rejected and led to later legislative town-planning ventures. They also came to naught. When towns finally arose in Virginia, the reason was that the settlers were pushing westward, away from the water's edge, and there were new needs to be served by the new towns.

The Act of 1680 designated a tract of land owned by Nicholas Wise as the site for a town in Lower Norfolk County, and the county court promptly responded by ordering a survey of the tract. On October 19, 1680, John Ferebee, the county surveyor, was paid for the work. Exactly one year later another payment to John Ferebee is recorded "as Clerke of the militia & laying out the streets in the Town." Anthony Lawson and William Robinson were appointed as feoffees, or trustees, to acquire title to the tract and, by a deed dated August 16, 1682, the sale of the site by Nicholas Wise, shipwright, was duly recorded. The 50 acres were bounded by the Elizabeth River on two sides, by Back Creek (as it came to be called) on the third, and on the fourth by a row of stakes. The date of the deed, August 16, 1682, has come to be the "birthday" of the city of Norfolk and appears on the city seal, though the Act of 1680 set the events in train and though there was no real town on the tract for quite some time.

were expected to be stevedores when it came time to load the tobacco, which was dirty, heavy work. So the colonies got a bad reputation among the sailors, a reputation that spread from the tales they told in the English taverns when they returned home. Finally, the system was costly to the merchants who were paying for the ships.

Among the English economic interests, then, the plantation system was unpopular. The authorities repeatedly sought to legislate towns into being in the latter part of the 17th century. These towns would be the central points where tobacco was to be gathered for shipment, and where the crown's revenues might be collected more tidily. But the convenience of the crown and

The actual payment to Nicholas Wise "for the towneland" was recorded in January, and the first Norfolkian seems to have been one Peter Smith, a sailor who took title to three lots on October 17, 1683, and is described as living on the land at that time. But the next recorded transaction is not until 1687, when the county clerk, William Porten, received title to six lots in the town.

The General Assembly, attempting to breathe life into the legislation of 1680, passed another Act for Establishing Ports and Markets in 1691. The later law is significant for what it tells us of the earlier one. It describes the 20 sites and shows that only half of the "towns" were established, in fact, following the first law's passage. In the description of "Nicholas Wise's land" in 1691, we are told there are "several dwelling houses and warehouses already built." According to Rogers Dey Whichard, who made a careful record search, there were only five lot owners in 1691: Peter Smith, William Porten, Mrs. Jane Sawcer, William Knott, and William Robinson. A county courthouse was built in Norfolk between 1691 and 1694 (Lower Norfolk County was divided into Norfolk County and Princess Anne County by the General Assembly in 1691), and there are early references to a church and a county jail as well as a ducking stool and a whipping post.

Ferries ran from Norfolk Town to what are now Portsmouth and West Norfolk. According to tradition, the first ferry was instituted in 1636 by Captain Adam Thoroughgood at the junction of the Eastern and Southern Branches of the Elizabeth River, the future site of Norfolk and Portsmouth. It was to be continued by different operators, private and public, until 1955, three years after the opening of the downtown tunnel. Of course, the early ferry was just a skiff manned by a slave. The crossing cannot have differed much from the ferry service that was described by the Duke de la Rochefoucault Liancourt at the end of the 18th century:

The communication between Norfolk and Portsmouth is continual: it is carried on by six row-boats belonging to a company, and by three scows in which horses and carriages are conveniently ferried over. The fare for each passenger is one-sixteenth of a dollar: but, on paying six dollars, a person may become free of passage for twelve months. These boats are managed by negroes belonging to the company. It is not an uninteresting observation to remark that one of those negroes, named Semes, aged from thirty to five and thirty years, has learned to read and write by his own unaided exertions. His conversation announces solid good sense, together with an earnest desire of instruction: and, after having seen him, it is not easy to adopt the opinion of those who refuse to allow the negro race any con-

Rogers Dey Whichard compiled this map of the original site of Norfolk Town, 1680-1736. Back Creek extended to where MacArthur Memorial stands today. Courtesy, Rogers Dey Whichard.

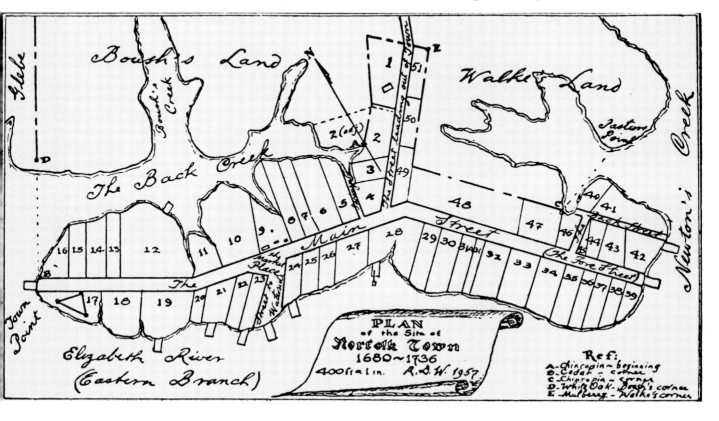

St. John's Church in Hampton was built in 1728, and construction started in the same year on the brick fortifications at Old Point Comfort known as Fort George. From Bishop Meade, Old Churches, Ministries and Families of Virginia, 1891.

siderable portion of intellect.

In 1714 the county court established the prices that might be charged by local tavern keepers (the price, per gallon, of small beer was 7.5 pence, cider 12 pence, and rum 6 shillings), and in 1717 we have a list of eight tavern keepers in Norfolk Town, who were all brought before the court on charges of giving false measure, which the defendants disproved to the justices' satisfaction. It is evident enough that, although there was little to Norfolk as late as 1691, it was recognizably a town by the end of the century.

Norfolk at that time was subsidiary to the settlement at the end of the peninsula that is formed by the James and the York rivers. This was the town of Hampton, or Kecoughtan, as it was called by the first planters, who settled there as early as 1610. The town was given the name of Hampton in 1705, but the Indian name has persisted in local usage and survives today. Although most of the early records were lost when Hampton was burned in 1861, the city's claim to being the oldest continually occupied English settlement in America is undoubted.

"A common ale house" was licensed in Elizabeth City County in 1639 and a ferry patent was granted to Henry Hawley in 1640 near the present town. The Act of 1680 designated land on the Jarvis plantation as the site of the town of Hampton. Apparently there was no survey undertaken, for in 1691 the land is mentioned as owned by William Wilson and in 1692 the three feoffees, Thomas Allamby, Pascho Curle, and William Marshall (who was murdered by sailors the same

year), proceeded to lay out a town. The intersecting main streets were called King and Queen, honoring the sovereigns William and Mary, and lots were surveyed. By the following year 26 had been sold.

In 1716 John Fontaine recorded that Hampton had "one hundred houses, but few of them of any note, and it has no church." Even so, it was "a place of the greatest trade in all Virginia, and all the men-at-war commonly lie before this arm of the river." St. John's Church was built in 1728 and construction started in the same year on the brick fortifications at Old Point Comfort known as Fort George, again honoring the king.

From 1610 on there had been sporadic efforts to fortify Point Comfort, or Cape Comfort. "Old" Point Comfort came later, probably to distinguish it from Point Comfort farther up the bay in Mathews County. But the first forts fell into ruin, since there was no provision for their upkeep, and in any event seem to have been inadequate. At the outbreak of the war between the Dutch and English in 1665, the garrison was withdrawn from Point Comfort to Jamestown, and Dutch men-of-war seized a tobacco fleet of 20 vessels at the mouth of the James River in the spring of 1667. There was another attack by the Dutch in 1673 and the governor, Lord Culpeper, declared the forts to be useless when he inspected them in 1681. Fort George, which was completed in 1732 and demolished by a hurricane in 1749, stood on the present site of Fort Monroe. After the destruction of Fort George there were no further attempts at coastal defense until the Revolutionary War. In 1817 the President was directed by the Senate to survey the harbors and ports of the United States with a view to fortifying them, and Lieutenant Colonel Walker K. Armistead (later to command Fort Monroe) was ordered to Old Point Comfort to supervise the work. A contract for 150,000 "perch" of stone, at the price of three dollars per perch, was awarded in 1818 and the actual construction of Fort Monroe and Fort Calhoun (later Fort Wool), an artificial island about a mile offshore on the Rip Raps, a channel shoal, was started in the spring of 1819. By 1836 Fort Monroe was completed, the chief engineer reported to the Secretary of War. The fortified hexagon looked then as it does today, though the best prospect of the stone snowflake would be reserved to the airborne travelers of the 20th century.

Hampton's primacy soon was yielded to the growing town on the opposite side of the water. In 1728 William Byrd II came to Norfolk on his way to survey the boundary between Virginia and North Carolina in an effort to settle a dispute of long standing. The survey was made in the spring and autumn of 1728, and became the basis of Byrd's *History of the Dividing Line betwixt Virginia and North Carolina,* which was circulated privately but not published until 1841. He found the town a busy place. Here is the description of Norfolk as it appeared to Byrd's eyes on March 1, 1728:

Norfolk has most the air of a town of any in Virginia. There were then near twenty brigantines and sloops riding at the wharves, and oftentimes they have more. It has all the advantages of situation requisite for trade and navigation. There is a secure harbor for a good number of ships of any burden. Their river divides itself into three several branches, which are all navigable. The town is so near the sea that its vessels may sail in and out in a few hours. Their trade is chiefly to the West Indies, whither they export abundance of beef, pork, flour, and lumber. The worst of it is, by importing abundance of rum, which like gin in Great Britain, breaks the constitutions, vitiates the morals, and ruins the industry of most of the poor people of this country. This place is the mart for most of the commodities produced in the adjacent parts of North Carolina. They have a pretty deal of lumber from the borders on the Dismal, who make bold with the King's land thereabouts without the least ceremony. They not only maintain their stocks upon it but get boards, shingles, and other lumber out of it in great abundance.

The town is built on a level spot of ground upon Elizabeth River, the banks whereof are neither so high as to make the landing of goods troublesome or so low as to be in danger of overflowing. The streets are straight and adorned with several good houses, which increase every day. It is not a town of ordinaries and public houses, like most others in this country, but the inhabitants consist of merchants, ship carpenters, and other useful artisans, with sailors enough to manage their navigation. With all these conveniences it lies under the two great disadvantages that most of the towns in Holland do by having neither good air nor good water. The two cardinal virtues that make a place thrive, industry and frugality, are seen here in perfection; and so long as they can banish luxury and idleness the town will remain in a happy and flourishing condition.

In 1736 the "flourishing" town was chartered

William Byrd II of Westover came to Norfolk in 1728 on his way to survey the boundary between Virginia and North Carolina. He wrote of Norfolk, "The two cardinal virtues that make a place thrive, industry and frugality, are seen here in perfection." Courtesy, Virginia State Library.

as a borough by Governor Gooch. In the language of the Royal Charter of Norfolk Borough, dated September 15, Norfolk "hath been very greatly increased in the number of its inhabitants and buildings, in so much that the said town, not being capable of containing all such persons have resorted thereto, divers of our loving subjects have seated themselves upon the adjoining land, so far as to a place called the Town Bridge." The Borough of Norfolk was to be administered by a mayor, "one person learned in the law styled and bearing the office of" Recorder, eight Aldermen, and a Common Council of "sixteen other persons." The first mayor was Samuel Boush, whose family name is commemorated by a downtown

Right
*Captain Edward
Teach was better
known as Blackbeard
the Pirate. He was
killed at Okracoke in
1718, and the
captured pirates
were brought back to
be tried at Williams-
burg. Woodcut from
The History and
Lives of All the Most
Notorious Pirates
and Their Crews,
London, 1725.*

street today.

The eminent Sir John Randolph of Williamsburg was appointed Recorder and came to be sworn on November 18, when the gentlemen of Norfolk "shew'd him all-imaginable Respect, by displaying the Colours, and firing the Guns of the Vessels lying there, and entertained him at their Houses, in the most elegant Manner, for several days," reported the *Virginia Gazette*.

A new parish church was built in 1739, constructed in the form of a Latin cross. It was called "the Borough Church" traditionally, and is known as St. Paul's Church today. According to tradition, which appears to be fanciful, Samuel Boush, the first mayor of Norfolk, donated both the land for the church and the bricks to build it.

The church was burned with the town in 1776 and rebuilt with the original walls after the Revolutionary War. Soon thereafter the congregation split into two factions, each with its own minister, and in 1798 the larger withdrew to a church on the opposite side of the street. Abandoned after 1803, the old building was reconsecrated as St. Paul's Church in 1832 and has been architecturally restored several times.

Norfolk's population was perhaps 2,000 to 3,000 in the 1730s and has been estimated at 6,000 by 1775. According to the city's first historian, William S. Forrest, writing in 1853:

The old borough is said to have been "a rare place," before the disasters of the Revolution. The harbour was almost filled with vessels, many of which were very large. Commerce was exceedingly flourishing; money was plentiful. There was little grumbling about "hard times." The sluggish, lazy, intemperate, or the constitutional grumblers, only, complained; and fortunes were made much more rapidly than at present. Indeed, this port almost monopolized the heavy trade of the West Indies. All were busy; a prosperous state of affairs was plainly exhibited on every hand, and no one doubted the future greatness of the place."

In the 18th century, as Forrest noted, Norfolk was the principal seaport through which the agricultural goods and the natural resources of Virginia and neighboring North Carolina, lacking its own port, were shipped to Europe, the northern states, and the West Indies. Also Norfolk was the center of shipbuilding in Virginia and, at the century's end, the Duke de la Rochefoucault Liancourt reported that "eighty to ninety vessels of different dimensions are annually built at Norfolk." He said the cost "for the hull on coming from the hands of the carpenter" was $24 per ton for ships of above 120 tons, and $47 to $50 "ready for sea."

But business wasn't everything in the life of the town. In 1754 a ceremonial mace, made by a London silversmith, was presented to the Borough of Norfolk by Lieutenant Governor Dinwiddie, with appropriate ceremonies. Benjamin Franklin journeyed to Williamsburg in 1756 to accept the first honorary degree given by the College of William and Mary, and was made an honorary citizen of Norfolk on April 10 when he came to visit.

Answering a complaint that the fees on the five ferries operating on the branches of the Elizabeth River and Tanner's Creek prevented many poor people from bringing their goods to market, the Assembly enacted legislation in 1757 providing for free passage to local residents and establishing rates to be charged others. The Borough was enlarged in 1761 and many names familiar today are to be found on the streets in the survey of 1762: Boush, Bute, Charlotte, Cumberland, Freemason, Granby.

Elsewhere, however, events were beginning to move toward upheaval and the effect was felt in Norfolk. In 1765 a mob tarred and feathered Captain William Smith, who was thought to be a British informant. On March 31, 1766, there was a public meeting at the County Courthouse to organize the local Sons of Liberty to protest the

Stamp Act. The Rev. Thomas Davis, minister of the Borough Church, presided and the meeting passed resolutions with some of the best-known citizens of Norfolk among the 57 signatories. In May the Reverend Davis preached at a special thanksgiving service to celebrate the repeal of the Stamp Act. There was a brawl in 1767, when Captain Jeremiah Morgan of the British sloop-of-war *Hornet* landed one night at Norfolk's public wharf with the intention of "pressing" such sailors as he could catch into His Majesty's service. Captain Morgan and his landing party proceeded to the seamen's taverns, where they knocked down their luckless victims "without ceremony and lugged them away like dogs," according to the *Virginia Gazette*. The alarm was sounded and a number of townspeople, led by a former mayor, Paul Loyall, sought to stop the British at the wharf. Morgan threatened Loyall with his sword, but Loyall was unshaken. The crowd increased and, seeing that his threats were useless, the captain retreated to the ship's tender and abused the Americans "in the most scurrilous language." Finally he jumped into a small boat and ordered one of his sailors to row him out to the *Hornet*. The authorities freed the men the British had taken, jailed some of the landing party, and permitted the rest to return to the ship.

But Norfolk had its own turmoil too. There was rioting in 1768 and again in 1769, prompted by a controversy over inoculation for smallpox and by popular prejudice against Scots. (Many Scotsmen came to America after Britain's Act of Union of 1707 opened the colonial trade to them, and a number settled in Norfolk and prospered.) Although Cotton Mather had introduced inoculation in Massachusetts in the 1720s, it remained suspect. Many doctors and most of the Norfolk population still thought that the procedure only served to infect healthy people with smallpox. In 1768 Dr. Archibald Campbell and a few of his friends, including the leading merchants Niel Jamieson and James Parker, had Dr. John Dalgleish immunize their family members. The news provoked rioting and the inoculated were drummed from their homes by the mob and led to the pesthouse, where they were put under armed guard. Riots flared again when a vessel arrived the following spring with cases of smallpox aboard. Mayor Cornelius Calvert, who owned the ship, ordered the inoculation of three slaves who had been exposed to the disease. A crowd gathered at his house and began breaking windows, then moved on to the homes of several Scots and broke more windows until it was dispersed by force.

When the rioters reached his residence, James Parker wrote: "I opened the Window above and asked their business. They demmanded I should come down, open the door, give them Liqueur, and drop all law Suits I had against them; their Speaker was one Singleton a Carpenter whom we had sued a year ago for Debit. ... The Villains wanted only the Shadow of a pretence to this

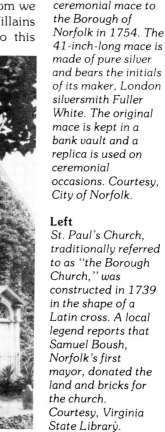

Riot." Here we may see seeds of the sentiment that was to lead to the Americans' burning of Norfolk within a few years.

But even if they mistrusted the "mobility," as Parker termed them, the merchants of Norfolk were optimistic about the passing of political troubles. In 1771 Parker wrote to Charles Steuart suggesting that he dispatch his nephew to earn his fortune in Virginia:

The busines of this Country is very soon acquired, and if he is disposed to push for him self, he'll not want Chances. I have just been thinking of the people in my remembrance who have done anything for themselves, in this place, Pr Anne, Portsmouth, Suffolk, the W. Branch, Smithfield, and the E Shore. Of our Country men, there are some who have made fortunes, Others who have got a sufficiency, with prudent management to get easily through life. ... The Same path is still open and as much probability of Success.

Before moving on to the events that were to bring destruction to Norfolk and eventual independence to the new nation, it would be well to consider the colonies on the eve of the American Revolution. One difference between 17th- and 18th-century Virginia was the growth of towns. Another was the diversification of the economy, noted as early as 1728 by William Byrd. A third was the great increase in the number of slaves—with all the problems that would be involved in the perpetuation of slavery in the new United States.

In the 18th century new towns were planted along the fall line of the large rivers: Fredericksburg on the falls of the Rappahannock, Richmond on the James, Petersburg on the Appomattox, Alexandria at "Hunting Creek warehouse" on the Potomac. Most started as the sites of tobacco warehouses, while the county courthouses nourished other, smaller settlements in Virginia.

By the 1770s the Chesapeake colonies were exporting from 90 million to 100 million pounds of tobacco a year. Even so, the colonies did not depend solely on tobacco, as they had tended to do in earlier times. Planters had started to grow corn and wheat on fields exhausted by tobacco, and had begun to raise cattle, hogs, and sheep. The plantation system actually encouraged domestic industry on a small scale. Cotton, linen, and woolens were woven on the plantations. Leather was tanned. A few homespun garments and rough shoes were manufactured and sold. There were fads of growing flax, ginseng, and in-

digo. An iron industry developed with average annual exports, from 1730 to 1750, of more than 2,000 tons.

Merchants in Norfolk prospered shipping bushels of corn and wheat and barrels of beef and pork to the West Indies, and bringing home molasses, rum, and sugar. With the development of the trade with the West Indies, there was a growth of industries related to shipping and shipbuilding: hemp for rope; hogsheads for tobacco; lumber, tar, pitch, and turpentine. Norfolk's warehouses were crowded with goods of every sort.

But the prosperity rested on the underclass: the convicted felons, indentured servants, and slaves who did most of the manual work. The history of the slave trade is an epic of horror stories. Who can reckon the cost in guilt now, or suffering then?

Before the English ever settled in Virginia, upwards of a million slaves had been brought into the West Indies, and countless more to Mexico and the Spanish colonies in the Americas. Over the course of four centuries it has been estimated that 15 million Africans were carried to the New World in bondage, and millions more were killed by slave traders or died on slave ships.

It may be true that the lot of the ordinary seaman on the slave ships was little better than that of the slaves themselves. White indentured servants were transported to Virginia under conditions of high mortality too, and often met with cruel treatment in the New World. But the basic difference, from the start, was that the children of the white indentured servants would be born free. After 1661 black slaves were to be "perpetual servants" in Virginia, and the laws were made by the owners of slaves to protect their "property" rights.

Certainly the institution was not peculiar to Virginia. There were slaves in all of the colonies, including those of New England, and slavery was legal in all of the 13 colonies when the Declaration of Independence was signed. Almost all of the slaves who were brought into the ports of Virginia came from the West Indies or the colonies to the south. They were employed not only in planting tobacco, but in every kind of skilled and unskilled work. They were the basis of the economic system. As Robert McColley wrote in *Slavery and Jeffersonian Virginia,* "The aristocratic habits of the planters simply could not be maintained without their Negro slaves."

The peopling of Virginia with unfree workers— whether enslaved for life or indentured for a period of time—had a disturbing effect on society. Robert Beverly described Virginia as "the best poor Man's Country in the World" in his

History and Present State of Virginia (1705). He complained of the "slothful Indolence of my Countrymen" saying that "they spunge upon the Blessings of a warm Sun, and a fruitful Soil, and almost grutch the Pains of gathering in the Bounties of the Earth." There was no equivalent of the European peasantry in Virginia. After 1700, however, there began to be a clearly differentiated class structure with a corresponding decline in the status of the poor whites. Thomas Wertenbaker wrote:

> Since they could not purchase Negroes, they were in a sense thrown into competition with them. The enormous increase in the production of tobacco brought down the price and made their single exertions less and less profitable. They were deprived of the privilege of working for wages, for no freeman could toil side by side with Negroes, and retain anything of self-respect. Thus after the year 1700, the class of very poor whites became larger, and their depravity more pronounced.

Another factor that contributed to the disorder of society in 18th-century Virginia was the practice of transporting convicted felons to the American colonies. The English criminal laws were harsh, punishing by death some 300 crimes, even petty theft. As a consequence, the frequent practice was to commute sentences to transportation to the colonies. The Chesapeake colonies had tried to stop the traffic in the 1670s, but in 1718 Parliament passed a law overriding the American feelings in the matter. The transporting of convicts to the colonies was again authorized; they were to be sold into servitude for seven to 14 years by the merchants who contracted with the government to provide the transportation. It is estimated that at least 30,000 felons were shipped to the American colonies during the 18th century, most to Maryland and Virginia.

Besides the convicts and slaves, who came as involuntary passengers, the flow of indentured servants kept up until the Revolutionary War. It did diminish gradually with the rise in the slave trade. But John Harrower came to Virginia as an indentured servant in 1774. He differs from the others only in that he left a journal, so that we know the details of his daily life. Harrower was a family man who was forced by the panic of 1772 to leave his wife and "sweet Infants" in the Shetland Isles to seek work. He journeyed to Scotland and then to London, where on January 26, 1774, he recorded: "This day I being reduced to the last shilling I hade I was oblidged to engage to go to

Virginia for four years as a schoolmaster for Bedd, Board, washing and five pound during the whole time."

He departed on February 7 from Gravesend on a ship "with seventy Servants on board all indented to serve four years there at their different Occoupations." They arrived off Cape Henry on April 27 after a passage that was typical, and on May 16 Harrower noted that two "Soul drivers" came on board the ship at Fredericksburg. "They are men who make it their bussines to go on board all ships who have in either Servants or Convicts and buy sometimes the whole and sometimes a parcell of them as they can agree, and then they drive them through the Country like a parcell of Sheep untill they can sell them to advantage." On May 23 Harrower was indentured to Colonel Daingerfield and soon took up duties as schoolmaster at Belvidera, "verry pleasantly situated on the Banks of the River Rappahannock about seven Miles below the Toun of Fredericksburgh."

It was his hope to earn enough money to bring his family to Virginia. "I yet hope (please God) if I am spared," he wrote his wife on December 6, 1774, "some time to make you a Virginian Lady among the woods of America which is by far more pleasant than the roaring of the raging seas round abo't Zetland, And yet to make you eat more wheat Bread in your old age than what you have done in your Youth." That pretty thought was to be unrealized. John Harrower died in 1777 without ever seeing his family again. He was forty-four years old.

In the 1760s and 1770s, on the eve of the Revolution, Britain's trade with the American colonies was the largest part of its overseas trade, and the trade with the Chesapeake colonies was the most valuable of the commerce with the continental colonies, exceeded only by the Jamaican sugar trade. Added to any calculus of the exports and imports must be the English interest in the human traffic—convicts, servants, and slaves—that was contracted for gain, and often proved to be extremely profitable. The crown had a high stake in the American colonies when crisis menaced the system.

The relations between the crown and the colonies had begun to deteriorate when the government was forced to pay for the Seven Years' War. The French and Indian War, as it was called in the colonies, was part of the global struggle. The passage of the Sugar Act in 1764 and the Stamp Act in 1765 provoked resistance and rioting in

when a band of patriots, well rehearsed and costumed as Indians, boarded three British ships and threw their cargoes of tea into the harbor as a protest against the tax on tea. "The Boston Tea Party was what we today would call guerrilla theater," Page Smith wrote in his history of the American Revolution, "a striking and dramatic enactment of an ideological position, an episode, as John Adams at once discerned, that would capture the popular imagination as few acts in history have."

The action in Boston in December 1773 was emulated, mildly, in Norfolk the next summer. In August the *Mary and John* sailed into port with nine chests of tea in its cargo. The citizens of Norfolk did not throw the tea into the water. They did hold a mass meeting to protest the tax and the tea was not unloaded. The action was an innocent overture to what was to follow in Norfolk's waters.

John Murray, fourth Earl of Dunmore, Viscount Fincastle, Baron of Blair, Moulin, and Tillemot, and an ambitious politician, was appointed governor of New York in 1770 and then transferred to Virginia, against his wishes. He arrived in Williamsburg on September 25, 1771, to succeed Lord Botetourt as governor. Botetourt, who had died in 1769, had been popular with the Virginians. Dunmore was energetic, headstrong, and quarrelsome, qualities that would get him into trouble in Virginia and again in the Bahamas, where he was dismissed as governor in 1796. (He retired to Ramsgate on the English seashore, and died there in 1809.) After Patrick Henry made his celebrated speech to the Virginia Convention at St. John's Church in Richmond on March 23, 1775, events moved swiftly. Dunmore was discredited in the patriot press, rumors spread, and in early June the governor fled with his family and a few followers to the safety of HMS *Fowey* at Yorktown.

He spent the summer in assembling a fleet in Norfolk's waters. He commandeered the merchant vessels *William* and *Eilbeck*, which he renamed the *Dunmore*, and added them to the British men-of-war on station there. There was a skirmish when one of the British ships was grounded off Hampton. On September 30 Dunmore sent a detachment of men ashore at Norfolk to seize the press and wreck the print shop where John Holt published the *Virginia Gazette, or the Norfolk Intelligencer*, a paper started in 1774 that was critical of the governor.

"The public prints of this dirty little Borough of Norfolk has for some time past been wholly employed in exciting, in the minds of all Ranks of People the spirit of sedition and Rebellion," Dunmore reported to the authorities back home.

Above
Lord Dunmore battled American rebels in Norfolk's waters during the Revolutionary War. His armorial bookplate is shown here. From R.A. Brock, Virginia and Virginians, *1888.*

Right
During "Dunmore's War" in 1774, frontiersmen led by Colonel Andrew Lewis tricked Chief Cornstalk and the Shawnees in the bloody massacre at Point Pleasant. From Wills de Hass, History of the Early Settlement and Indian Wars of Western Virginia, *1851. Courtesy, Norfolk Public Library.*

virtually all the colonies. There was a lull when Parliament repealed the Stamp Act, and the Townshend Duties then were enacted and repealed, in turn, as unworkable. Already a hotbed of resistance, Boston was further inflamed in 1770 when five of its citizens were killed by the king's troops. The "Boston Massacre" was kept alive in legal proceedings and anniversary oratory.

So the stage was set for the Boston Tea Party,

Although Editor Holt managed to escape the landing party, the crowd that gathered made no effort to intervene in the seizure, which only served to add to the city's loyalist reputation. By October Lord Dunmore had established his headquarters at Gosport, where Andrew Sprowle, the British naval agent and the governor's close friend, had his shipyard. (Dunmore mockingly styled himself "Lieutenant Governor of Gosport.") In November there was a skirmish at Kemp's Landing (Kempsville now) and the governor issued a proclamation declaring martial law and freeing slaves willing to join His Majesty's troops. Although the emancipation proclamation was carefully limited to those "that are able and willing to bear Arms" and "appertaining to Rebels," it was tactically unwise. It enabled the patriots to play upon the deep fears of a slave uprising. In mid-November Dunmore occupied Norfolk and received a warm welcome. The British began to fortify the town. The colonial forces, or "shirtmen," as they were called, gathered under the command of Colonel Woodford and after some tooing and froing on both sides the battle of Great Bridge was fought on December 9, 1775. Dunmore's forces were put to rout and he prudently withdrew to the British fleet in the harbor, where he was joined by many of the Norfolk tories. There ensued a stalemate for three weeks, while negotiations over protocol and provisions were undertaken.

The deadlock ended on January 1, 1776. In the afternoon, between three and four o'clock, the British fleet started to fire upon the town and landing parties put the torch to wharves on the waterfront. The cannonade continued until the early hours of morning. What the British had started, the Americans finished. There appears to have been considerable drinking and looting among the American soldiery, which is not so surprising, and the buildings that were not burned on the first try were destroyed in February, by order of the Virginia Convention and the Committee of Safety, to deny Dunmore shelter there. Only a desolate stand of chimneys told where the city had stood, and Norfolk would be called "Chimneytown" in the war years.

According to official reports and the best estimates of historians today, the Americans burned roughly 1,300 buildings in Norfolk and the British fewer then 100. That tallies with the account of a British contemporary observer, who blamed

a back-woods mob of American soldiery, who seemed then to carry their unjust, barbarous, and ill-grounded resentments against all the low-country and sea-coast;

having proposed even to spread desolation and throughout the whole, merely because it was within reach and command of the British navy, and because the principles and conduct of the inhabitants were more temperate and liberal than theirs.

Nevertheless, the burning of Norfolk was an American propaganda victory. The news spread quickly and widely. The British were blamed everywhere and Dunmore made the villain. At Belvidera John Harrower recorded in his journal on January 10: "This day we made the Confirmation of Norfolk being reduced to ashes by the Men of War & British Troops under Command of Lord Dunmore. It was the Largest Toun in the Collony and a place of great Trade, it being situate a little within the Capes. Several Women & Childn. are killed." At the end of the month General George Washington wrote to Joseph Reed, "A few more of such flaming arguments ... will not leave numbers at a loss to decide upon the propriety of a separation."

CHAPTER THREE

NORFOLK REBORN: 1776 - 1815

The American colonists who took up arms against the British in 1775 and 1776 were on the other side of an ocean that it normally took two months to cross, sailing west. (The return trip might be made in a month with prevailing westerlies.) The king's ministers were confident that the rebels would not stand up to British redcoats and the British navy's supremacy was unchallenged. Armies might be raised and naval squadrons sent to American waters, but it still would be difficult and expensive to put a stop to the uprising.

Although the Americans were scorned by King George III and by Lord North, the chief minister to the obstinate sovereign, the British had their own problems. The Admiralty was headed by the Earl of Sandwich, a notorious rake who was politically unpopular, and the Secretary of State for the Colonies was Lord George Germain, who had been cashiered for incompetence after the battle of Minden. These were the men who would determine the English grand strategy, if such there was, in bringing the colonists to heel.

When Britannia ruled the waves, her admirals frequently sat as members of Parliament and commands in the fleet more often than not were handed out on the basis of favoritism and politics. The lot of the British tar is dramatically evident in a set of statistics. Between 1775 and 1780 a total of 176,145 men were "raised for the King's

navy," of whom 1,243 were killed in battle by the enemy, 18,543 died of disease, and 42,069 deserted—at the first opportunity, it is safe to say. ("Being in a ship is being in a jail," Dr. Johnson remarked, "with the chance of being drowned.") As for the army, the redcoats tended to be either the rejects of society, or mercenaries the crown hired from German princelings. Because the British commanded the cities in the colonies and controlled the seacoast, the Americans under General Washington were forced to fight a guerrilla war. The elder Pitt, who warned Parliament, "You may ravage, you cannot conquer," was to be proved right. King Louis XVI had little sympathy with the colonists in their uprising. But the enemy of England was the friend of France, and after the British defeat at Saratoga, the first great American victory of the war, the French king was persuaded to enter into the alliance that the Americans had been seeking. The treaty that was signed in 1778 would bring French forces to the American patriots' side at Yorktown. The allied armies and the French fleet that would be brought together, three years later, in Norfolk's waters would decide the outcome of the war.

All of that lay in the future, however, and the future seemed to be anything but bright in the first months of 1776. Norfolk lay ruined. Only a building here and there had escaped the fire, and

The British board the Chesapeake *after the American frigate struck its colors following the brief battle with HMS Leopard of June 21, 1807. American Commodore James Barron had resisted the British demand to search the Chesapeake for deserters. Courtesy, U.S. Naval Institute.*

an army of chimneys was left standing to mourn what had been the chief city of Virginia. After the burning of Norfolk, Lord Dunmore, now reinforced by the British frigate *Roebuck,* and a contingent of marines, moved over the river and established his headquarters at Tucker's Point, where the Naval Hospital stands today. Here he was supplied by local sympathizers until Major General Charles Lee, who was appointed to the command of the American forces by the Continental Congress, moved on Portsmouth in the spring.

Like Norfolk, Portsmouth was a shipping and trading town. Some of the leading merchants maintained establishments on both sides of the river. The land where Portsmouth stands was first granted to Captain William Carver, a shipowner who was hanged by Governor Berkeley in 1676 for his part in Bacon's Rebellion. In 1716 Lieutenant Colonel William Crawford ("Craford" or "Crafford"; the name is spelled variously) was granted a large plantation in the vicinity. An Act of the Assembly in 1752 authorized the surveying of lots on part of the plantation for the town that was to be called Portsmouth, after the British seaport. Nine lots were sold in the first year, and 74 by Crawford's death in 1762. As in Norfolk, many of the early freeholders were Scots who earned a living as merchants and, not so surprisingly, were loyalists at the onset of the Revolution.

The most prominent of the Portsmouth Tories was Andrew Sprowle, who established a shipyard across Crab Creek from Portsmouth. Since the town was called Portsmouth after its sister sea-

port, he gave the name of Gosport to his holdings after the British Gosport, near Portsmouth. There he built large warehouses and many smaller buildings necessary to the shipyard. His property, which was declared forfeit in 1784, was to become the Gosport Navy Yard, and ultimately the Norfolk Naval Shipyard.

Describing Portsmouth as "a hotbed of Toryism," General Lee threatened to burn the town, but contented himself with burning the homes of Jamieson, Sprowle, and a few other prominent Tories. He was reluctant to attack Dunmore at Tucker's Point, and commissioned fireships that he intended to set drifting downriver into the harbor. However, the beleaguered Dunmore thought it wise to abandon his position, and after assembling a flotilla of refugee ships that were crowded with hundreds of loyalists and slaves, and destroying his facilities at Tucker's Point, withdrew to Gwynn's Island at the mouth of the Piankatank River, reaching safety there on May 27. It was a grim haven, short of water and soon to be ravaged by smallpox, and Sprowle was among those who were to die there. In July General Andrew Lewis, Dunmore's one-time subordinate, laid seige to Gwynn's Island and when the bombardment began, Dunmore's people took to their ships for the last time. The armada of motley vessels cleared the capes on August 7 and scattered. Many sailed south to Florida, some went to England, and the rest sailed to New York with Dunmore, who arrived on August 13 and attended a dinner with General Howe the next night to tell his woes. He never returned to Virginia.

Although Dunmore was gone, the British were to return to Hampton Roads several times before the end of the war. In May 1779 Sir George Collier landed troops and attacked Fort Nelson, which was abandoned by its defenders. The Americans burned an almost-completed frigate on the stocks to keep it from enemy hands, and the British burned or captured 137 ships of all sizes in the harbor of Hampton Roads. They pillaged Portsmouth, burned Suffolk, seized a quantity of stores, and put the torch to the Gosport Shipyard, which had been commandeered by the Commonwealth of Virginia. After laying waste to the countryside for two weeks, the British returned to New York without losing a man.

The winter of 1779-1780 was the harshest in memory. According to Forrest, the harbor

was frozen entirely across to Portsmouth, admitting a free and uninterrupted communication between the two towns, on the ice, for several weeks. The Atlantic Ocean was frozen as far out from the shore as the depth of forty fathoms. Chesapeake Bay was so thickly frozen that teams crossed for some time from shore to shore, as far down as the Capes. The ice was piled up along our coast, at some places, twenty feet high, large quantities of which remained as late as the middle of May.

In the fall of 1780 another British fleet sailed into Hampton Roads and landed troops, this time under Major General Alexander Leslie. Hampton

was seized and a garrison occupied Portsmouth, but soon withdrew. In the previous spring the British had taken Charleston, South Carolina, where they had been rebuffed in 1776. The British commander-in-chief, Sir Henry Clinton, returned to New York in June and left Charles, Lord Cornwallis in command in the south. Cornwallis, who is nowadays remembered for surrendering at Yorktown, was one of the ablest British generals in the Revolution. He campaigned through the Carolinas, defeating General Gates, the hero of Saratoga, at the battle of Camden in the late summer and, after the battles of Cowpens in January and Guilford Courthouse in March, he withdrew to Wilmington on the North Carolina coast.

Meanwhile, the British had re-established themselves in Hampton Roads. A detachment led by Benedict Arnold, the turncoat, landed on December 30, 1780, and pushed up the James River to Richmond. In January Arnold occupied Portsmouth and began to fortify the town, where he was reinforced in March by Major General William Phillips with another 2,000 troops. Cornwallis moved north and the two British forces joined on May 1 at Petersburg. The American troops in Virginia were commanded by the Marquis de Lafayette. He had left France at the age of 19 and was commissioned by the Continental Congress the next year. The Americans were unequal to the British combined forces and Lafayette sought to avoid battle for the next several weeks. Phillips was dead of the fever by this time and Arnold had returned to New York. Cornwallis was left in the south. In July he was in Portsmouth, preparing to embark his own troops, when he was ordered by Clinton to stay in Virginia. In August the British evacuated Portsmouth and withdrew to Yorktown. The stage was now set.

To the north Washington was contemplating a joint operation utilizing the French troops who had landed at Newport, Rhode Island, under the Comte de Rochambeau and the fleet of the Comte de Grasse in the Indies. After flirting with plans to attack Clinton in New York, the allied army at midsummer turned toward Virginia, while a feint was mounted at New York.

Able to cover only 15 to 20 miles in a day's march, the Americans and French moved slowly south. Clinton in New York was informed of the army's progress by his spies. Cornwallis in Virginia was mindful of the danger, and expected to be rescued by sea. But the Americans and French hoped to spring the trap. "Should a French fleet now come to Hampton Roads," Lafayette wrote to Washington on July 31, "the British army would, I think, be ours."

The Marquis de Lafayette left France at the age of 19 and was commissioned by the Continental Congress the next year. The boy general of the American Revolution returned to the United States on a triumphal tour in 1824-1825. From James Thacher, Military Journal of the American Revolution, *1862.*

FRANCOIS JOSEPH PAUL DE GRASSE

THIS STATUE, A GIFT FROM FRANCE, IS PLACED HERE OVERLOOKING
THE WATERS WHERE ADMIRAL COMTE DE GRASSE SUCCESSFULLY
ENGAGED THE BRITISH FLEET ON SEPTEMBER 5, 1781. THE "BATTLE
OFF THE CAPES" PREVENTED CRUCIAL REINFORCEMENTS FROM
REACHING CORNWALLIS, THUS HASTENING HIS SURRENDER.

DEDICATED IN GRATEFUL REMEMBRANCE OF THE DECISIVE
CONTRIBUTION OF ADMIRAL DE GRASSE TO THE WINNING OF
AMERICAN INDEPENDENCE

OCTOBER 17, 1976

The French fleet was the key to the operation, and the critical decision was made by Admiral de Grasse. After receiving letters from General Rochambeau by a French frigate in July at Martinique, he determined to go north with his 24 ships of the line. If he could join with the French squadron under Admiral de Barras, he would command a combined fleet more powerful than any available to the English in those waters. In retrospect, the Americans and French were lucky, the British unlucky. But the allies chose to gamble and the British chose to sit tight. Boldness is its own reward.

On August 29 Cornwallis was informed that a considerable French fleet was in Virginia waters.

By midday August 30 General Washington had arrived at Philadelphia, to confer with Congress and to be feasted there. Four French frigates anchored in the river below Yorktown on September 1 and, belatedly, that same day the British fleet departed New York under the command of Admiral Sir Thomas Graves, a brave but dull-witted sailor.

Action came on September 5. Running before the wind, the British fleet sailed into the capes of Virginia and lookouts spotted the French fleet lying in Lynnhaven Bay. The French were superior in guns and number of ships, but many officers and sailors were ashore and the ships were unready. The alarm was sounded. The classic, cumbersome ritual of forming a line of battle was begun on both sides.

It was not until quarter past four or so in the afternoon that the battle started; the firing stopped about six-thirty in the evening. A comparatively few ships on each side sustained the bulk of the damage. The British lost 90 killed and 246 wounded; casualties in the French fleet totaled 209.

The battle had been indecisive, or so it seemed then, and both fleets made ready to resume the fight with the coming of daylight. Dawn found six of the 19 British battleships in poor shape; one of them, the 74-gun *Terrible*, was to be abandoned and burned a few days later. The British commanders, Admiral Graves and Admiral Sir Samuel Hood, started to wrangle at a conference on the flagship on the morning of the 6th—a dispute over the responsibility for the battle that was to be carried forward, in and out of Parliament, for years.

Admiral de Grasse, for his part, was cautious and kept sailing southward, still uncertain of the whereabouts of Admiral de Barras and his squadron. He wanted to draw the British away from the Capes of Virginia. By nightfall on September 7 the fleets were nearing Cape Hatteras, a hundred miles to the south, and continued jockeying for position until Admiral de Grasse ordered his ships to come about at nightfall on September 9 and return to the Chesapeake Bay. There he found the French squadron waiting. Admiral Graves was informed by a British ship on September 13 that the combined French fleet was in Lynnhaven Bay. The British limped on to New York. Admiral de Grasse was master of Norfolk's waters. Cornwallis was doomed.

The Battle of the Capes, as it came to be called, is a curiosity. Harold Larrabee described it in *Decision at the Chesapeake*:

One of the greatest naval victories of all

sailed "in the Brig Alexander bound to New York."

As the architect Latrobe said, there was a continual danger of fire in Norfolk. There was an extensive fire in 1799, and much of the town was destroyed by another blaze in 1804. At the time Mrs. Anne Ritson, an Englishwoman who had married an American, was living in Norfolk. After the death of her husband she returned to England and published *A Poetical Picture of America* in 1809. The fire of 1804 was started, she wrote, when a candle ignited a cask of rum at "a jovial party." She described what happened in her inimitable verse:

The alarm bell rung, the town was rais'd
Th' adjoining stores with fury blaz'd;
The shipping mov'd with haste away,
Being dang'rous near the shore to stay,
As two large ships had caught the flame,
And dropp'd for safety down the stream.
The fire impetuous raging o'er
The warehouses upon the shore,
The streets along the wharfs soon caught,
The inhabitants their safety sought,
And hardly cover'd, fled away,
In frighten'd terror and dismay.
All night the fire incessant burn'd,
Its rage on Main-Street quickly turn'd;
Up Market-Street it bent its way,
And soon that part in ashes lay:
The town devoted seem'd to be,
To that most cruel enemy;
When the wind fell, and gave the hope,
They might prevent its further scope,
By blowing up some houses near,
And leave a space from fuel clear.
Perhaps you'll ask me, where were then
The engines, and the engine-men?
But, if I must the truth relate,
They were not in a proper state.
Two engines I believe they had,
But they were small, and very bad,
And could not easily be got
To play upon the proper spot;
So the old fashion'd modes were try'd,
Wet blankets on the roofs apply'd,
While negroes on the chimnies stand,
Receiving buckets hand from hand,
With water from the pumps below,
Which o'er the roofs they constant throw,
Trying to slake the raging flame,
When it too near the dwelling came.

"Till noon the fire incessant rag'd," she concluded, a few lines later, "And then its fury was assuag'd."

But despite the fires, the high cost of living, the stench, and the yellow fever, the city continued to grow. According to *Simmons' Directory* of 1806, the inhabitants "may be computed at nearly ten thousand, and they are characterized by travelers as generally polite, obliging, and hospitable."

The good times were about to come to an end for Norfolk and for the United States. American prosperity had been relatively steady since the Revolutionary War. Norfolk's remarkable recovery testified to that. Anglo-American commerce had not only resumed, it had swelled to the point where Americans were Britain's best customers, purchasing roughly a third of British export goods. Almost half of American exports, in turn, went to British buyers, often for resale.

But the counting house view was to be overruled by the play of passions and policy. From 1805 on, events tended toward the war which, almost as an anticlimax, was declared in 1812. In 1805 Thomas Jefferson was entering upon his second term in the White House. British mastery of the seas was assured by Admiral Nelson at the battle of Trafalgar that year. And following Napoleon's victories at Austerlitz, Jena, and Friedland and the peace signed with Czar Alexander on a raft at Tilsit in 1807, the continent of Europe lay under the French emperor's sway. For a decade, from Trafalgar to Waterloo, the British and Napoleon were locked in a death struggle.

Lawyer William Wirt was among many people attracted to Norfolk by the town's prosperity. In 1804 he wrote to a friend: "In the Borough of Norfolk every drone feels the pressure of business." Wirt later served as Attorney General under Presidents James Monroe and John Quincy Adams. Courtesy, Virginia State Library.

American merchants, who hoped to profit from peaceful trading in time of war, were caught in the middle of the European hostilities. The British made a practice of "impressing," or forcibly seizing, seamen from American merchant ships to serve in His Majesty's navy. (In 1812 Secretary of State James Monroe stated that the British had impressed no fewer than 6,257 American seamen in the previous 10 years.) The British feared and hated Napoleon; they scorned the United States. That was the attitude generally of the king's ministers and the attitude held on the navy's quarterdecks. In 1807 an incident in Norfolk's waters nearly brought the two nations to war.

It is hardly surprising that there were British deserters to be found in Norfolk, which was a busy seaport, or that the authorities protected them. One such was Jenkin Ratford, who had signed on the American frigate *Chesapeake*, provoking Sir George Cranfield Berkeley, the admiral on the American station, into issuing an order to his squadron to stop and search the *Chesapeake* in the event of meeting the American frigate on the high seas.

The *Chesapeake*, one of the six ships that were authorized by Congress in 1794, the first of the new United States navy, was destined to be unlucky. She had stuck on the builder's ways when she was launched at the Gosport Navy Yard in December 1799. When the *Chesapeake* had sailed for the Mediterranean in the spring of 1802, she leaked and rolled so that her mainmast had to be replaced at Gibraltar, and she had come home in 1803 without firing a single shot at the Barbary pirates. In 1807 the frigate was in Norfolk to be refitted; James Barron had been named as commodore of the Mediterranean squadron with orders to sail as soon as the *Chesapeake* was ready for sea.

When she weighed anchor on the morning of June 21, among the crew members were Jenkin Ratford, who had enlisted under the name of John Wilson, and Daniel Martin, John Strachan, and William Ware, who had deserted in February from the British frigate *Melampus*, then at anchor in Hampton Roads. About four in the afternoon the *Chesapeake* was courteously hailed by the British frigate *Leopard* and a lieutenant boarded the American ship to deliver a letter with Admiral Berkeley's order that the *Chesapeake* be searched for deserters. Barron responded that he would not permit the crew "to be mustered by any other but their own officers."

The British lieutenant left the ship. Then the *Leopard* fired a shot across the bow of the *Chesapeake*. Broadsides followed in quick succession. The American frigate was unready and the crew largely untrained. The action was brief and one-sided. The *Chesapeake* fired a single shot, for honor's sake, and Barron ordered the flag to be struck. Three men were killed on the *Chesapeake* and 18 wounded; the commodore himself sustained seven wounds.

A British boarding party returned and took the three deserters from the *Melampus*, who were immediately recognized. Ratford was found hiding in the hold of the ship. The four were dragged off to the *Leopard* by the boarding party. Ratford was soon to be hanged from the yardarm in Halifax. The others proved to be American citizens and escaped execution; one died and the other two ultimately were returned to the United States.

As soon as the *Chesapeake* had limped into Norfolk and the affair became known, the nation reacted with patriotic zeal. The citizens of Norfolk and Portsmouth voted to stop supplies to the Brit-

55

56

ish squadron. The British were denounced everywhere in meetings and patriotism raged up and down the land. "The probability of war is very strong," Wirt wrote.

But the British prudently withdrew their squadron from Norfolk's waters. Diplomatic noises were uttered in Washington. The crisis passed. Ironically, there was far less provocation when war came, finally, five years later.

Captain Stephen Decatur was ordered to take command of the *Chesapeake*. Barron was brought before a court-martial on board the frigate in 1808 and suspended from service for five years, without pay. The bad blood between Barron, who was made the scapegoat, and Decatur, who criticized him openly, was to linger on. Finally, Barron felt himself provoked into challenging Decatur and a duel was fought. That was not until 1820, however, when the two were middle-aged men. They met at Bladensburg, near Washington. When all the ceremonies of the duel were done, they exchanged simultaneous shots. Both were wounded. Decatur died; Barron survived to serve as commandant of the Gosport Navy Yard.

The American government sought to counter the British and French policies with its own trade weapons. The Nonimportation Act of 1806 had not worked. The Embargo Act of 1807, which became law on December 22, was meant to be stronger stuff. Its effectiveness was questionable at the start. Merchants quickly sent ships to sea, and the Embargo only seemed to stimulate smuggling. As the enforcement of the law grew stricter and it began to pinch, the prohibition against trade grew more and more unpopular. The President sought "to cure the corns by cutting off the toes," the acidulous John Randolph remarked. American exports fell from $49 million in 1807 to just $9 million in 1808, with consequent distress to American merchants, American shipping, and the American seaports, such as Norfolk, that depended on its trade. The British did not fall to their knees as a result. The Embargo's failure was apparent by the end of 1808 and on March 1, 1809, the law was repealed, three days before Jefferson left the White House.

There was a reprise of the affair of the *Chesapeake* and *Leopard* in 1811, this time with an American twist. Reacting to a series of impressment incidents, the frigate *President* sailed from Norfolk under Commodore John Rodgers in early May, and on the 16th of the month chased and captured the English sloop of war *Little Belt*. Americans were delighted, the English enraged. In August 1811 HMS *Tartarus* took two merchantmen off Norfolk and then brazenly sailed into port. The captain immediately was warned by the British consul to get to sea to escape the gathering mob.

What was characterized by an American diplomat in London as "our temporizing & cringing policy" plainly was not working, and in 1812 opinion slowly tacked toward war in Washington. The congressional War Hawks were resolute, the rest uncertain. The declaration of war was voted in June, five days after the British rescinded the Orders in Council.

"The War of 1812" is an American term; the British saw the conflict as a footnote to the Napoleonic wars. (Had the collapse of Napoleon been foreseen, President Madison later was to say, the United States would not have gone to war in 1812.) Americans of a belligerent stripe talked of taking Canada, and maybe the West Indies. The British were confident, naturally, of punishing the upstart Yankees.

Both would be disappointed. The American campaign against Canada collapsed at every turn. But the infant navy, which was disparaged by a London journalist as "a few fir-built frigates, manned by a handful of bastards and outlaws," was to embarrass the English in a series of duels at sea. Within the year, as Winston Churchill in his role as Anglo-American historian later noted, the bastard frigates "had won more successes over the British than the French and Spaniards in two decades of warfare."

The naval odds seemed uneven. Only five frigates in the American navy were seaworthy at the outset of the war; the British fleet numbered nearly 700 men-of-war and roughly a third of those were either frigates or ponderous, powerful ships of the line. But the British battleships were in European waters and the squadron on the North Atlantic station was no stronger than the American fleet. And the American frigates proved to be splendid ships that could outgun the British frigates and outrun the ships of the line.

American naval tradition would be built upon their victories: *Constitution* versus *Guerriere*, *United States* versus *Macedonian*, *Constitution* versus *Java*. But the *Chesapeake*, still unlucky, was lost to HMS *Shannon* in a fight off Cape Ann in 1813, with Captain James Lawrence, mortally wounded, uttering the famous order: "Don't give up the ship." The captured frigate later was sold off. Many of her timbers were used to build houses in Portsmouth—the British seaport, not the one in Virginia—and a mill in the nearby village of Wickham, which is still standing.

The American frigates' victories were not sufficient to offset the weight of British sea power. In 1813 a British squadron—four ships of the line, six frigates, and smaller vessels—under the command of Rear Admiral George Cockburn sailed into Virginia waters. The British blockaded Chesapeake Bay, seizing several ships, and alarm spread throughout the tidewater. The American frigate *Constellation* retreated upriver to Norfolk, where she was to remain for the duration of the war. Soon there was a formidable force in Norfolk: the militia mustered, reinforced by the *Constellation*'s crew and sailors from other ships in the harbor, plus Virginia volunteers. The British decided not to challenge the guns of Fort Norfolk and Fort Nelson, which protected the approaches to the city on either side of the Elizabeth River.

Admiral Cockburn's fleet sailed up the Chesapeake Bay, plundering the smaller waterways as they went. The British established a base on Tangier Island, which is approximately at the Bay's midpoint, that they kept until the end of the war. Cockburn harassed shipping and burned Havre de Grace and the twin towns of Georgetown and Fredericktown, all in Maryland. But he did not have sufficient troops to attack the bigger cities—Annapolis, Baltimore, and Washington—and in June withdrew to the Bay's mouth, where the fleet was joined by more men-of-war and troop transports.

An attack on Norfolk was expected imminently, but the city was well defended. Craney Island, five miles downriver from the harbor, was fortified with a battery manned by the *Constellation*'s gunners and companies of light artillery, militia, and riflemen. There were 20 gunboats mounting one or more 18-pounders in the river and, beyond

them, Fort Nelson, on the site of the Naval Hospital, and Fort Norfolk, near Smith's Creek (called the Hague now), protected the approaches to Norfolk and Portsmouth, where a considerable force was mustered under General Robert B. Taylor. The British fleet moved to the mouth of the Nansemond River on June 21, 1813, and the attack came at dawn the following morning.

The British meant to assault the Americans by land and sea. A body of troops was landed near Captain George Wise's plantation, while two columns of barges loaded with marines and sailors approached Craney Island from the water. The British troops were repulsed by "a brisk fire of grape and canister-shot," in Forrest's telling, "with a loss of many killed and wounded." The barges got an even hotter reception. Several were sunk "and many others so shattered that it was with difficulty they were kept afloat." The barges retired with their wounded, and in the afternoon the landing party returned to their vessels—after "shooting hogs, sheep, &c., breaking furniture, cutting open beds, &c., in the dwelling-houses near which they landed." The British lost 200 men; the Americans did not lose one. Norfolk was saved, but Hampton was occupied and sacked three days later.

In August, after another defeat on land at St. Michael's in Maryland, the British operations in the Bay ended for the year. In 1814 Napoleon was overthrown and exiled to Elba (whence he was to escape and return to his final defeat at Waterloo) and Britain's power was freed to turn against the Americans. Admiral Cockburn returned in the summer of 1814 to burn Washington, and was beaten back at Baltimore, while Francis Scott Key watched the bombs bursting and the red glare of the rockets over Fort McHenry.

The British blockade was now telling. American commerce had been largely throttled. But American privateers seemed suddenly to be everywhere on the oceans, with crews hungry for prizes, and British ships were being captured in home waters and as far away as the East Indies and the Indian Ocean. American free enterprise found that war too was profitable.

So the Anglo-American war, which neither party really wanted, was brought to an end at Ghent, where a peace treaty was signed on Christmas Eve in 1814. It was several weeks before the news reached the United States. In January, meanwhile, the frontiersmen of General Andy Jackson had massacred General Pakenham's redcoats at the battle of New Orleans, but it was not until the end of February that the British finally sailed from Tangier Island and abandoned Chesapeake Bay for good.

Facing page
The frigate USS Constellation, defender of Norfolk and Portsmouth in the War of 1812, returned a century later and was photographed in Portsmouth in June of 1914. Courtesy, U.S. Naval Historical Center.

58

Forty-two bonfires lit the opposite shore, where Portsmouth showed its welcome. The general was honored at a banquet for 300 persons on Saturday, and conducted to church on Sunday by "the largest Masonic procession Norfolk has ever witnessed." Then he visited Fort Monroe, and on Monday returned to Portsmouth and the Navy Yard and a ball in the evening at the customs house in Norfolk on Water Street.

From time to time there were other distinguished visitors, including Louis Napoleon, later to be Emperor of France, who stayed at French's Hotel in 1837, and a number of Presidents, ex-Presidents, and would-be Presidents of the United States (Andrew Jackson, Martin Van Buren, Henry Clay, John Tyler, Millard Fillmore, Franklin Pierce, General Winfield Scott). The celebrated violinist Ole Bull came to Norfolk in 1853, accompanied by Adelina Patti, then a child of eight, and the great actor Joseph Jefferson played the town in 1860.

A less well-known visitor was Mrs. Anne Royall, who published an account of her travels in 1828. She was pleasantly surprised by what she found in Norfolk:

> I expected to have seen an old, dirty-looking, gloomy, clownish town, inhabited by barbarous tuckyhoes: on the contrary, the houses looked fresh, and the citizens polite and hospitable; on the score of refinement and taste, it has more than any town in Virginia; in this respect, it resembles Boston. The houses are large and elegant, and many of them surrounded with beautiful trees; the water, however, is not very good. Norfolk stands on Elizabeth river, which, at this place, forms a beautiful basin, a mile in

width. It contains three banks, a courthouse, a jail, an academy, three insurance offices, an orphan's asylum, an atheneum, containing 6000 volumes of well-chosen books, and seven churches; none of the churches in the Southern States have anything that can be called steeples. It contains 11,000 inhabitants. . . .

Mrs. Royall was impressed by finding in the market on April 25, "ripe strawberries, peas, potatoes, green beans, cucumbers, and all sorts of vegetables in the greatest perfection and abundance," but considered the Negroes tending them to be insolent and insufferable. She visited Littleton Tazewell in Norfolk and Commodore Barron at the Gosport Navy Yard. Barron's face, Mrs.

Royall recorded, "is round and full, and his countenance open, benevolent, and pleasing. His air and manners are altogether affable and gentlemanly." She observed that a large ship of the line—the *Delaware*—was nearly completed at the yard, "but they are no longer curiosities to me."

Mrs. Royall was struck by the harbor and the apparent advantages Norfolk and Portsmouth possessed. Hampton Roads, she wrote in *The Black Book,* is

> one of the most spacious and safe harbors in the world; all the fleets that ever floated, might be anchored in them and the waters beyond. Protected as they are, they afford an asylum for the vessels of war, and for the merchant vessels, against both an enemy and the storms, leaving them in security, while they remain here to refit or refresh, and may always choose their own time to depart. Its central position, as it regards the whole coast, besides its being free from ice, and of easy access, may be accounted advantages rarely met with. . . .

Others had previously said very much the same thing and later Matthew Fontaine Maury, the celebrated "Pathfinder of the Seas," was to express the like opinion in his writings. Indeed, there was a certain illusion of progress in these years. The centenary of the Royal Charter was celebrated in 1836 and Norfolk became a city in 1845, with certain changes in its charter and legal status. But the fact is that between 1815 and 1861, between the two wars, the city of Norfolk stagnated. It failed to grow; it failed to prosper.

Obstinate statistics tell the truth. By the census of 1810 Norfolk's population was 9,193, but the city lost population by 1820 (8,478) and grew little in the decades thereafter—9,814 (1830), 10,920 (1840), 14,326 (1850), and 14,992 (1860). That is an average annual growth rate of less than 1 percent over a period of 50 years. Baltimore, by contrast, grew from 35,583 people in 1810 to 62,738 (1820), 102,054 (1840), and 212,418 (1860)—an increase of sixfold in the same span of time.

What happened to Norfolk? Why did it stand still?

The Chesapeake colonies were favored by geography in colonial times, when the economic staple was tobacco and almost every plantation had its own wharf. The access to water was almost essential then, and there were obvious reasons why Hampton and Norfolk and Portsmouth prospered. Following the Revolutionary War, the American colonies were in a position to profit from the political turmoil that engaged the European powers from the French Revolution to Napoleon's overthrow at Waterloo. For instance, it was American wheat which fed the troops of General Wellington when he was fighting the French in Spain. But the abnormal advantage enjoyed by the new nation was not to last when the British were free to return to the commercial policies of peacetime, which simply meant the monopolizing of their trade.

It is true that a first flush of prosperity came to Norfolk and to Virginia with the peace of 1815. Since trade had been largely stifled by the war, commercial energies were pent-up and waiting to be released. The merchants of Norfolk naturally thought they were entering upon a postwar recovery such as the city had known in 1790, and that lasted for a generation thereafter. But the burst of expansion and investment and optimism was to be blighted by the Panic of 1819, and Norfolk never really recovered.

There were a number of reasons. After 1815 the city failed to regain the once-prosperous West Indian trade it had enjoyed in earlier years. There were several explanations for this: British mercantile policies, the retaliatory tariff voted in Washington, the declining economic importance of the Caribbean islands, and the fact that the merchants of Norfolk were ill-equipped to compete in a changing economy. They were factors, middlemen, the agents of interests owned by others. Norfolk was a capacious port. It might offer "one of the most spacious and safe harbors in the world," in Mrs. Royall's words, but it was not a center of shipping. Banking and capital were inadequate, the hinterlands of North Carolina and eastern Virginia were largely undeveloped, and little was locally manufactured or produced to stimulate trade.

The Panic of 1819 was compounded by tobacco's exhaustion of the soil and by the migration of population to the west. In the area about Norfolk's waters, as Peter C. Stewart wrote, the average farmer:

> . . . lived near subsistence level and was neither contented nor self-sufficient. He was able to provide fish and some small game for his family. The farm always yielded corn and a few vegetables and the women managed to keep up with family clothing needs with homespun. But there were too few cattle to fill basic necessities for meat and milk. More

importantly, the majority of the farm population anxiously waited for a time of higher prices when they could discard their apparent economic independence and resume selling commercial goods.

The economy of the nation was changing, to the disadvantage of Norfolk. Where the exports from Virginia were greater than any other colony's on the eve of the Revolutionary War, Pennsylvania surpassed Virginia by 1791 and within a decade was joined by four other states. The trend was accelerated between 1815 and the coming of the Civil War.

The flow of immigrants and the growth of manufacturing in the northern states were to give the Union a decisive economic edge in that war. Cotton was becoming king in the states south of Virginia. Around 1825 cotton was planted widely in Virginia, but the fad was short-lived—victim of a combination of falling prices and unfavorable weather. Already cotton dominance had passed to the Deep South, the region facing the Gulf of Mexico and not the Atlantic seaboard. The boom in cotton nourished *The Flush Times of Alabama*

and Mississippi, as Joseph G. Baldwin's frontier sketches were titled, and by 1860 three out of every four bales of cotton in the nation were grown there. By 1860, too, cotton constituted more than half the total value of all American exports, and New Orleans, the capital of the cotton kingdom, exceeded even New York in its export trade.

Cotton's sway was felt in another way in Virginia. It came to employ the great majority of the slaves. In economic terms, there was a slave surplus in Virginia and a demand in the Deep South, so trade between the two was steady through the years. Estimates vary, but it seems safe to say that the average number of slaves sold "down the river" from Virginia was more than 10,000 per year in the four decades from 1820 to 1860. Although the profits served to tide many a slaveowner over the hard times in Virginia, the traffic was evidence of the economic shift to the Deep South.

The implications of the shift were described by the historian U.B. Phillips in his classic study *Life and Labor in the Old South:*

What London was to the colonial Tide-

View in the Harbor of Portsmouth *was made by J.O. Montalant in 1843. From Henry Howe,* Historical Collections of Virginia, *1845.*

water, Richmond became to the tobacco Piedmont in the nineteenth century, Charleston and Savannah to the eastern cotton belt, and New Orleans to her own great hinterland. A chain of minor markets arose not only at the lesser seaports but at the heads of steamboat navigation—Fayetteville, Columbia, Augusta, Macon, Columbus, Montgomery and at convenient points on the mighty Mississippi and its branches; and in supplement to these a miscellany of villages at county seats, mill sites, or merely where highways of some importance happened to cross. Finally when railroads began to change the channels of commerce, a few junction points gave origin to incipient highland cities, the chief of which was Atlanta.

Besides the cotton economy, factors that were to change the South were the growth of infant industries and the coming of the railroad. The developments were interrelated, and again Norfolk was to get the short end of the stick. What industry there was in Virginia—flour milling, ironworks, textiles, tobacco—was concentrated in the cities of the fall line. Distilling was about the only "industry" of any note in southeast Virginia.

The early railroads were not built to meet the needs of rural regions, but were developed by entrepreneurs to enlarge the trade of the city or port that they favored, much as one sinks a well. The capital and energies of the entrepreneurs in

Hampton Roads proved to be inadequate in the railroad struggle with Petersburg and Richmond. (The competition was sometimes physical; at one point a crew tore up the tracks of the Portsmouth and Roanoke Railroad in the fight between the cities of the fall line and Hampton Roads to extend rail service to the town of Weldon.) Although the Portsmouth and Roanoke Railroad was completed in 1837, it failed in 1845 because of mismanagement and, as Forrest recorded, "the hopes of those who had been most sanguine of its success, and of its inestimable advantages to Norfolk and Portsmouth, were blasted." By 1860 the cities of Hampton Roads did have rail service to the south and to the west, but it was rudimentary and soon to be interrupted by the war. Norfolk was not to be linked to the nation's rail system, in a commercially meaningful sense, until well after the Civil War.

Apart from the fight with its rivals upstate, another reason for the isolation of Norfolk was the exaggerated hopes Virginians attached to canals. The Dismal Swamp Canal did feed intracoastal shipping—and business in Norfolk—once it was opened to regular traffic at the end of 1828. But it was hardly a real rival to the Baltimore and Ohio Railway, just as Norfolk was hardly a real rival to Baltimore in the business world. Virginia was betting on the wrong horse, the one that pulled a towboat; the future lay with the iron horse, on its iron rails.

As Norfolk had been blockaded earlier by the British from the sea, so it was now to be

blockaded from the land by the powers-that-were in Petersburg and Richmond. Since the decisions shaping the system of transportation also determined the distribution of wealth in Virginia, the citizens of Norfolk and their neighbors were the losers in pride and pocketbook. "There is little doubt," Jean Gottmann judged, writing a century later, "that Virginia was governed from Richmond by circles who delighted in the maintenance of graceful living and who were often themselves people of great charm and culture, but who were generally unaware of the major driving forces shaping the world of that century." Frustrated repeatedly by Richmond, it is not so surprising that the local papers suggested that Norfolk ought to secede from Virginia and join North Carolina, "who would at least treat us with decent and common justice." North Carolinians, it might be noted, resented their commercial "enslavement" to Virginia and sought to improve the inlets of the Outer Banks and develop their own deep-water port.

While its pace may have slowed, life about Norfolk's waters was pleasant in the antebellum period. The development of truck farming in the 1840s helped to stimulate the coastal shipping that was the mainstay of the port. Boatbuilding continued on a modest scale and there was employment in marine services and the traditional work of the waterfront, as well as fishing and oystering to supplement the fare on local tables. Certainly those who lived in the "grand old establishments" enjoyed the good life, as William Lamb recollected in 1879 in *Norfolk Long Ago*, "before the light of other days had clean gone out on the old hearthstones." Here is his description of one of those establishments:

I recall one representative home, standing at a corner, with its thick walls, two stories and a half high. A broad wainscoted hall running through the building, a capacious parlor with its brass andirons and lion-legged fender on one side; a sunny sitting room and a big hospitable dining-room on

the other; the broad sideboard, as dissipated-looking as the tap room of an old time country tavern; no carpets but waxed hard-pine floors, with an occasional rug, and on the large one in the dining-room its constant companion, the house dog; no counterfeit chromos nor daubs, with Dutch gilt frames, disfigured the walls, but some masterpieces adorned the parlor, a pair of hunting scenes in water colors enlivened the dining-room, while in the hall, ancestors with pretty faces emerged out of indescribable dresses, with no waists to speak of, and intelligent and brave-looking gentlemen were narrowly escaping strangulation in villainous stocks. Up-stairs was redolent with rose-leaves in vinegar; the bed-rooms, with great high-post bedsteads, with curtains defying the changes of temperature without. The kitchen, a Dutch-roofed one-story brick house, with tremendous chimneys at either end, sufficiently far from the mansion to prevent the smell of cooking even with a favoring wind; and a large, square smoke-house, where the family bacon was cured, stood in the paved yard; then there was the stable for the horse and the inevitable cow, which an English poet said every lady in Norfolk kept somehow; the wood-shed, with its autumn wood-pile, reminding one of a steamboat landing on James river in the olden time. Then the flower garden flanking the residence, with the old-fashioned lilacs, snow-balls, wall-flowers and roses; and the big back garden for vegetables, with a stray sun-flower or two, and in it, enclosed by a forbidding wall, the family burial vault.

The development and growth of the Gosport Navy Yard, which by 1860 was the largest in the nation, served to offset the economic isolation of Hampton Roads from the rest of the state. The merchants of Norfolk and Portsmouth supplied the varied wants of the yard, and its activity is the basic reason why the population of Portsmouth

This 1845 woodcut depicting Norfolk's harbor appeared in Henry Howe's Historical Collections of Virginia. *Courtesy, Virginia State Library.*

roughly tripled in these years. It was "a considerable village" of about 3,000 only a short walk from the Navy Yard, when Mrs. Royall visited in 1827. By 1860 its population was nearly 9,500.

Andrew Sprowle's shipyard had been the biggest in the colonies when it was burned in 1779 and the property, which was declared forfeit in 1784, was first loaned to the United States by the Commonwealth of Virginia when the navy was revived in 1798, and then bought by the federal government three years later. (There was no navy from 1783 to 1798.) The ill-fated frigate *Chesapeake* was built at the Gosport Yard.

After the Navy several times urged the Congress to authorize the building of a drydock for the overhaul and repair of its warships, funds finally were voted in 1827 to build two facilities: one at Charlestown, near Boston, and the other at the Gosport Navy Yard. Colonel Loammi Baldwin, a civil engineer educated at Harvard, was appointed to superintend the construction of the drydocks, the first in the New World.

Drydock Number One, as the facility at Gosport was called after a second was commissioned at the same site in 1889, was the first to be put

into service. It started as a big hole in the ground—340 feet long, 100 feet wide, 40 feet deep. Pilings were driven and a foundation of brick, stone, and wood was fitted to receive the blocks of dressed granite that were ferried from a Massachusetts quarry. The work went slowly, but the drydock finally was ready to receive the ship of the line *Delaware* on June 17, 1833.

A considerable crowd gathered for the occasion, which had been announced several days earlier in the *Herald*. The actual docking, scheduled at 10 o'clock, was moved ahead to catch the favorable tide, and many missed that. All did get to see the drydock pumped and the *Delaware* steadied on its blocks, however, and the entire operation proved successful.

"A signal gun was fired, when the ship moved towards the dock, and a second upon her being safely embedded in it, which was followed by a national salute from the Navy Yard," the *Sailor's Magazine* reported. The account characterized the

drydock as a monument to its builders and designers. Indeed it is. Drydock Number One is still in use and at this writing is about to enter its 150th year.

There is a footnote to the *Delaware* story. The 74-gun ship was laid down at the Gosport Navy Yard in the summer of 1817 and launched in 1820, but was not ordered to be fitted for sea until 1827. After she was drydocked to be recoppered and repaired in 1833, she sailed as flagship of the Mediterranean squadron under Commodore Patterson.

She returned to Hampton Roads in 1836 and was docked for overhaul the next year. It is believed that the figurehead originally placed on the *Delaware*, a full-length, nine-foot statue of the Indian chief Tamanend, was replaced at this time by a bust of an Indian. Both works were executed by the Portsmouth wood-carver William Luke, according to the available evidence, and "the splendid and appropriate head of St. Tammany"

Ship-of-the-line Delaware *became the first vessel to enter Drydock Number One at the Gosport Navy Yard on June 17, 1833. The 340-foot-long dock was the first to be opened for the overhaul and repair of Navy warships. Courtesy, The Mariners' Museum.*

was mentioned in Luke's obituary when he died in 1839.

The *Delaware* was decommissioned in 1844 and burned at the Norfolk Navy Yard in 1861. When the wreck was raised after the war, the figurehead from the *Delaware* was found to be well preserved. It was presented to the U.S. Naval Academy and mounted on a pedestal there. The midshipmen passing the bust daily dubbed him "Tecumseh" and by the turn of the century the figurehead had passed securely into the Academy's, and the Navy's, traditions.

Life in Norfolk was shadowed from time to time by the threat of deadly epidemics. Its people had been scourged by yellow fever in 1795 and 1802, and there had been milder outbreaks in 1821 and 1826. But for nearly 30 years there had been no occurrence of the pestilence until the steamboat *Benjamin Franklin* put into port on June 7, 1855. The ship was bound from St. Thomas, where the fever was prevalent, to New York when she was compelled to come into Hampton Roads. She was unseaworthy and there was sickness on the vessel.

After being held in quarantine for 12 days, the *Benjamin Franklin* was permitted to proceed for repairs to Page and Allen's shipyard, which was adjacent to the Navy Yard. The captain denied, meantime, that two deaths on shipboard were caused by yellow fever. Nevertheless, the fever's first local victim was a laborer working aboard the ship, and the first 20 or 30 cases "occurred within a stone's throw of the vessel."

Although confined initially to the Gosport section, the infection quickly spread to neighboring

Portsmouth. In Norfolk the first cases were reported in the Barry's Row tenements. As the disease spread, panic spread too. Those who could fled the pestilence. The Reverend George D. Armstrong recorded visiting a fellow pastor in Portsmouth, who was one of the sick:

> It was the first time I had been there for several weeks, and I was most forcibly struck with the scene of desolation presented on every side. . . . The streets were literally deserted. In passing from the ferry-wharf to Mr. Handy's house, I had to go through fully half the length of the main street of Portsmouth; and yet in all that distance I met but one white person, and saw but one store open. As I passed the end of the market-house, looking down toward Gosport, in the part of the market usually crowded by the country-people, I saw but two market-carts. The negro drivers of these carts were sitting on the curb-stone beside them, and they, with their horses, looked as if wilted down by the heat; and I saw no one there present to buy their marketing.
>
> In returning, I took a somewhat circuitous route, going around by the courthouse, then taking my way through parts of the town which I had not seen in going. Everywhere the same deserted appearance met the eye. I noticed in one place a man knocking at the door of a house; and, instead of the door being opened, a woman appeared at an upper window and conversed with him from thence, as if afraid to come any nearer to him, lest she may take the infection. . . .

Norfolk soon took on the deserted look of

Norfolk's waterfront in the 1830s is depicted in this genre painting from the family of Aaron Milhado. In the foreground Aaron Milhado II is seated on the bottom of a boat overturned on the shore, shotgun in hand, while buying ducks. The painting, which was done from the Portsmouth side of the river, hangs in the Myers House. Courtesy, The Chrysler Museum.

Portsmouth. Barry's Row was burned on the night of August 9 in the hope of checking the fever, but the contagion spread wildly. Norfolk's streets were deserted and gloomy, Forrest reported, and the buildings closed and dark. "The dogs banded themselves together, howling dolefully, and prowled about silently, as if aware that something sad and unusual was going on and in search of their masters and of food." The harbor was shunned, the wharves were empty of shipping.

The fever raged and 400 Norfolk residents were buried in the first week of September. "The corpses accumulated so rapidly that coffins could not be supplied for them," Forrest wrote. "The hearses were driven rapidly out to the grave-yards with two, three, and four at a load, and the coffined dead were piled up on the ground awaiting the opening of the graves and pits, by the insufficient force at work with the spade, the hoe, and the shovel."

There were both fearful and generous responses to the news of the plague. The authorities in nearby Weldon, North Carolina, enacted a punitive quarantine. Those visiting Weldon within 15 days "after such person or persons shall have been in such infected cities" would be fined $100 for every day that they stayed in the town. If a slave, then the owner was to be fined $50, provided that he knew of the visit. If not, the slave was to be given "nine-and-thirty lashes on his or her bare back." The first of the good samaritans who came to nurse the sick was Miss Annie M. Andrews, "a young lady from Syracuse, N.Y., and formerly of Louisiana," and she was followed by dozens of doctors and nurses in September, when the fever was at its worst.

The pestilence passed with the frost of late October. We know now that the disease was transmitted by fever-laden mosquitoes; there was much theorizing at the time of "plague-flies" and prevailing winds, as well as divine judgments of the municipalities. There was a high mortality among the doctors, nurses, and pastors who tried to minister to the suffering. No fewer than 25 of the doctors who came from north and south to Norfolk and Portsmouth were to die there. Also among the dead in Norfolk was Mayor Woodis. The toll is estimated at some 2,000 persons. Of those who remained in town, one in three succumbed to the yellow fever.

The white-columned Naval Hospital, in the right background, was completed in 1830. The artist probably painted the picture from a spot at about the end of Freemason Street. This painting from the Aaron Milhado family hangs in the Myers House. Courtesy, The Chrysler Museum.

Entered according to Act of Congress, in the Year 1862, by Harper & Brothers, in the Clerk's Office of the District Court for the Southern District of New York.

The Mayor & Councils of Norfolk meeting the Federal forces under a flag of truce

The Council Tree

Hoisting the old flag on the Custom house

Entering the City of Norfolk

Burning of the Gosport Navy-Yard

CHAPTER FIVE

CIVIL WAR:
1861 - 1865

The United States was not only transformed into a modern nation between 1815 and 1860, it also became a divided one. Americans turned their energies westward with the coming of peace in 1815. Chicago was incorporated as a city in 1837 and joined by rail to New York by 1855. Texas was annexed in 1845. The California Gold Rush was launched in 1849 and the territory was admitted to the Union in the following year. The Anglo-American dispute over the Oregon Territory was peacefully settled in 1846 and Oregon became the thirty-third state in 1859. The Pony Express was established in 1860, inaugurating mail service by relay riders between St. Joseph, Missouri, and San Francisco. Americans had absorbed the continent by 1860, but had not digested it.

Yet the United States in 1860 was divided in two—free and slave, North and South. The sectional struggle had been growing for 30 years. It dated from Nat Turner's Rebellion in 1831, rekindling the fears of a slave uprising and effectively quashing any abolitionist sentiment in the South, and from the Nullification Controversy of 1832, foreshadowing the secession threat. John C. Calhoun of South Carolina emerged as the Cotton Kingdom's tribune in Washington, and in 1831 William Lloyd Garrison published the first number of his paper, *The Liberator*. Abolition was building into an irresistible force; the South was

becoming an immovable object on the question of slavery. Increasingly, the nation's politicians were preoccupied with evading the inevitable.

As life in Norfolk recovered from the pestilential summer of the yellow fever, the fevers of national strife were growing more and more virulent. The election of Democrat Franklin Pierce in 1852 had signaled the continuing disintegration of the Whigs, and a new Republican Party was rising to fill the vacuum. A second failsafe President, James Buchanan of Pennsylvania, was chosen in 1856—and there would not be another Democrat elected for a generation. "A house divided against itself cannot stand," Abraham Lincoln said in a famous speech in Springfield in 1858. "I believe this government cannot endure permanently half slave and half free." Senator William H. Seward, thought to be the likely nominee of the Republicans, warned of the "irrepressible conflict" in a speech in Rochester, New York. In 1859 came John Brown's raid at Harper's Ferry and a madman was elevated into martyrdom. By 1860 sectionalism had sundered the Democratic Party: The Democrats nominated Stephen Douglas, the faction of Southerners who withdrew named John Breckinridge of Kentucky, and the remnants of the Know-Nothings and the Whigs chose John Bell as their standard-bearer. Everywhere feelings ran high; there was a fistfight between a Bell elec-

Union forces occupied Norfolk on May 10, 1862, and Brigadier General Egbert L. Viele was appointed to govern the town. Theodore R. Davis depicted the events in these sketches published in Harper's Weekly.
Courtesy, Virginia State Library.

In 1860 Abraham Lincoln was elected President of the United States. Seven states in the Deep South had seceded by the time he was inaugurated, and the rest of the Confederate states followed after the firing on Fort Sumter. Lincoln personally supervised the taking of Norfolk in 1862. Photo by Alexander Gardner. Courtesy, New York Historical Society. From Cirker, Dictionary of American Portraits, Dover, 1967.

tor and one pledged to Breckinridge at a meeting in Norfolk. The election totals in the city were Bell 986, Breckinridge 438, Douglas 232, and none for Lincoln, the candidate of the Republicans. The candidates finished in the same order in Portsmouth, where Lincoln got four votes. But Lincoln was the winner when the nation's votes were counted up.

The election of Lincoln precipitated secession talk in Virginia, and action in South Carolina. On December 20 an ordinance of secession was enacted without a dissenting vote. By February 1, 1861, the other states of the "Cotton South"—Mississippi, Florida, Alabama, Georgia, Louisiana, and Texas—had voted to follow South Carolina out of the Union. The Confederacy chose Jefferson Davis of Mississippi as President and Alexander Stephens of Georgia as Vice President. On March 4 Lincoln was inaugurated as President in Washington. Both Davis and Lincoln were content to wait while their governments got organized. Meanwhile, eight other slave states—Delaware, Maryland, Virginia, North Carolina,

Tennessee, Kentucky, Missouri, and Arkansas—remained undecided. They feared Lincoln, feared secession, feared war. "I can anticipate no greater calamity for the country than a dissolution of the Union," Robert E. Lee had written to his son in early January from his post in the Southwest. It is safe to say that he spoke for the majority in the border states.

But events were moving at their own speed. When South Carolina seceded on December 20, Fort Sumter was still unfinished. On December 26 Major Robert Anderson, commanding the federal garrison, withdrew his forces from Fort Moultrie to the fortifications three miles out in the harbor, and less vulnerable. For four months there they waited, while the Confederacy was formed, and Buchanan dithered, and Lincoln was sworn in, and the cabinet deliberated the fate of Fort Sumter. On April 11, General P.G.T. Beauregard, commanding in Charleston, delivered an ultimatum to Major Anderson, who had been his instructor at West Point. Beauregard demanded the fort's surrender. Anderson refused. The affair was conducted with great punctilio. "Gentlemen, if you do not batter us to pieces, we shall be starved out in a few days," Anderson remarked when he delivered his reply. Another delay followed. Neither wanted to fire the first shot. In the early hours of the 12th Anderson agreed to surrender at noon on the 15th; he was informed that the Confederate batteries would begin to fire in an hour's time. The Southerners would not wait; they knew Northern relief ships were already at sea. At 4:30 in the morning the guns opened up. The honor of firing the first shot was claimed by Edmund Ruffin, aged sixty-seven, a true believer, the Dixie equivalent of John Brown. The bombardment continued during the day. Anderson, who could not hope to hold out, soon surrendered. Honor had been satisfied. And the fat was in the fire.

On April 15 Lincoln called for 75,000 volunteers "to cause the laws to be duly executed," and three days later offered command of the army he was raising to Robert E. Lee. On April 20 Lee resigned his commission in the United States Army. "Save in defence of my native State," he wrote to General Winfield Scott, "I never desire again to draw my sword." On April 22 he accepted appointment as "commander of the military and naval forces of Virginia."

The weeks of ambiguity and anxiety had been ended by the firing on Fort Sumter. The border states were forced to decide whether to fight with the North or the South. On April 17 the Virginia State Convention voted to secede, 88 to 55, and in the evening many of those from western

Virginia who wanted to stay with the Union met in a hotel in Richmond. That was the first step toward their secession from Virginia and the creation, made official in 1863, of the State of West Virginia. Virginia was admitted to the Confederacy on May 7 and the decision was made to move the capital from Montgomery, Alabama, to Richmond.

In their own time and way, North Carolina, Tennessee, and Arkansas went with Virginia. Kentucky and Missouri nominally voted to secede, but both were divided in sentiment and, in any event, were occupied by Northern forces without ever effectively playing a part in the war. Delaware and Maryland stayed with the Union, even though a week after the firing on Fort Sumter a Baltimore mob attacked a contingent of Massachusetts militia on its way to Washington.

Although few stopped to calculate such things, the advantage in the conflict lay overwhelmingly with the Union. "The South in 1861 had less than half as many people as the North, less than half the railroad mileage, less than one-third the bank capital, and less than one-tenth the manufacturing output," Emory M. Thomas wrote in *The Confederate Nation*. The North had a navy; the Confederacy did not. There is little point in rehashing the arguments of historians and partisans over who was right and who was wrong and who was to blame for the Civil War. Almost certainly the conflict was inevitable, in retrospect, and as to its causes one need not look beyond Mary Chesnut's diary: "We have hated each other so."

In February 1861, when delegates were elected to the State Convention, Norfolk and Portsmouth were strongly Unionist, but both cities were carried on the current of events toward war. The *Day Book*, hitherto sympathetic to the Union, was moved by the inauguration of President Lincoln to these words: "He proclaims to the South war! war!! war!!! He has exposed his cloven foot plainly and openly to the gaze of all, that they may be no longer deceived; and we must say that henceforth we can have but little patience with any Southern man who would pretend that there is yet hope." There was great excitement at the news of the firing on Fort Sumter, and on the day following a group of Norfolk's young men sailed to Craney Island and raised the Confederate flag over the old blockhouse there; it was lowered as soon as they left.

When Anne Royall had visited Commodore Barron at the Gosport Navy Yard in 1827, she had noted prophetically: "As a place to fit and

refit, it may do; but for a great naval arsenal, it seems to me rather too much exposed to a land attack." In the spring of 1861 the commandant of the Norfolk Navy Yard was Commodore Charles S. McCauley, 68, who had been instructed not to provoke trouble and who was fearful of the companies of State Militia drilling just outside the walls. Both Commodore McCauley and General W.B. Taliaferro, commanding the militia of Virginia, were aware of the great prize at stake. The steam frigate *Merrimack* was drydocked for repairs to her cranky engines and there were a number of old sailing warships at the Navy Yard, as well as invaluable stores—including more than a thousand cannon of every type. Secretary of the Navy Gideon Welles in Washington was worried over the yard. He dispatched Commodore Hiram Paulding on board the *Pawnee* as McCauley's replacement, with a detachment of marines from the Washington Navy Yard and orders to prevent the arms from falling into "the hands of the insurrectionists." If necessary, Paulding was to destroy the yard.

Mississippian Jefferson Davis was elected president of the Confederacy in 1861. He would be imprisoned at Fort Monroe at the end of the Civil War. Courtesy, National Archives, Brady Collection. From Cirker, Dictionary of American Portraits, Dover, 1967.

When the *Pawnee* reached the Navy Yard about eight o'clock on the night of April 20, Commodore McCauley had already ordered the scuttling of the *Merrimack* and the other vessels which were in no condition to go to sea. He thought that the militia were about to storm the yard. Paulding probably would have been able to defend it with his force of marines and sailors, but decided to destroy the yard. *Pawnee* fired a rocket as a signal, and the buildings and ships were put to the torch. The conflagration was compared to the "day of judgement" by a correspondent from the *New York Times* who was aboard the *Pawnee*, and the explosions and the inferno's roaring soon wakened the few citizens of Norfolk and Portsmouth who had not stayed up. The Union forces withdrew on the *Cumberland*, which had been on station at Hampton Roads, and *Pawnee* at daylight the following morning, and immediately the Southerners sought to save whatever they could in the yard. They found many of the buildings still standing and the dry-dock intact. Although most of the wooden warships, including the huge old *Pennsylvania*, were consumed by the flames, hundreds of cannon and invaluable naval stores were untouched. Almost immediately work was begun to repair the sloop-of-war *Germantown* and the *Merrimack*, whose engine and hull had been damaged only slightly.

At the approach of hostilities in 1861 Fort

Monroe was deemed by the Corps of Engineers to be "in excellent condition, needing minor repairs only." In mid-May Major General Benjamin Franklin Butler, an energetic politician-soldier from Massachusetts who was to earn a lurid reputation in the war, was appointed to command the Department of Virginia, with headquarters at Fort Monroe, and by the end of the month reinforcements swelled his total troops to more than 4,000. Camp Butler was established and earthworks erected from about Thirty-Second Street, as it is today, to Newport News Point. On June 10 there was "something approaching a battle," in Douglas Southall Freeman's phrase, at Big Bethel, halfway between Newport News and Yorktown. The federal forces were repulsed by Confederates commanded by Colonel John B. Magruder, a flamboyant leader known as "Prince John" to his troops. In the confused fighting the Unionists lost 76 men and the Confederate casualties were one killed and seven wounded, which encouraged the thinking that one Southerner was worth 10 Yankees.

Meanwhile, on the opposite shores of Hampton Roads, the defense of Norfolk and Portsmouth was undertaken by General Benjamin Huger of South Carolina, who had succeeded General Taliaferro when authority passed to the Confederacy from the Commonwealth of Virginia. There were engagements between the batteries at Sewells Point and the *Monticello*, and between the Portsmouth Rifles and the steamer *Harriet Lane* at Pig Point. Much was made of them at the time.

The encampments of the soldiery were bustling places, and the Episcopal ladies of Norfolk advertised in the local papers that they would be available at Christ Church "every morning from 9 to 12 o'clock, to receive any work, either making, washing, or mending clothing." Clashes broke out among the troops without any Yankees to fight, and in one "difficulty" on Main Street two members of the Norfolk regiment were shot and wounded. About a week later an Alabama lieutenant was killed by Claiborne Hughes of Norfolk, who was jailed for murder. The brawling soon was stopped by General Huger, who first imposed a curfew on all barrooms in Norfolk and Portsmouth and, the following February, closed down the drinking places and liquor stores.

The first big battle of the Civil War was fought in July at Manassas, or Bull Run, and ended in a victory for General Beauregard and the Confederates. The Union forces panicked and retreated, and elated Southerners thought the war was won. Naturally the news stirred excitement in Norfolk, as Burton recorded, "and even the 'petticoat-

During the Civil War, the Norfolk Navy Yard was sacked twice. It was burned by the Federal forces when it was abandoned to the Confederates in 1861, and again by the Confederates evacuating Norfolk and Portsmouth in 1862. This photograph of the destroyed yard was taken in 1864. Courtesy, Portsmouth Naval Shipyard Museum.

dodgers' (the stay-at-home young men) assumed an air of patriotism that made them bold and war-like." But Manassas was followed by inaction, North and South, and a period of passive testing and waiting.

At Fort Monroe General Butler was succeeded by Major General John E. Wool, and moved on the next spring to command the occupation of New Orleans. It was there that he earned the sobriquets of "Beast" and "Spoons" (from the story that he stole the silverware at the house where he was staying), and it was there that he issued the infamous General Order No. 28 on May 15, 1862:

> As the officers and soldiers of the United States have been subjected to repeated insults from the women (calling themselves ladies) of New Orleans, in return for the most scrupulous noninterference and courtesy on our part, it is ordered, that hereafter, when any female shall, by word, gesture, or movement, insult or show contempt for any officer or soldier of the United States, she shall be regarded and held liable to be treated as a woman of the town plying her avocation.

Besides evoking outrage in the South, the order brought a protest from the British Prime Minister on the floor of Parliament.

While the armies were readying for the battles to come, the Union was attempting to blockade the more than 3,500 miles of Confederate coastline. At first the Navy was inadequate to the task, and the blockade was run by some 800 ships in the first year. But it grew increasingly tighter throughout the war, and the chances of a blockade-runner's success shrank from nine out of ten in 1861 to two out of three by 1864, with consequences fatal to the hopes of a Southern victory.

In 1861 a Northern squadron under Flag Officer Silas Stringham, with Ben Butler commanding a force of 800 troops, took the Confederate forts at Hatteras Inlet and closed the door to Pamlico Sound. At the beginning of 1862 a bigger expedition was mounted threatening the back door to Norfolk. The object was Roanoke Island (where the English had landed in 1585) and the defenses guarding the approaches to the Dismal Swamp Canal and the Albemarle and Chesapeake Canal, just opened in 1859 and navigable by larger vessels. Roanoke Island lies like a cork in the neck of water which connects Albemarle and Pamlico sounds. The plan was to pull the cork, and it was done easily. After a day's fighting 2,675 Confederate soldiers surrendered to General Ambrose E. Burnside and most of the Confederate "mosquito fleet" of gunboats were sunk by Union warships. The blockade of the sounds was tightened and it became an open question whether the Confederates could hold Norfolk.

The battle of Roanoke Island "was a classic Confederate disaster," revealing the inadequacies of a system where authority was divided and ineffective. The *Day Book* recorded the city's "distress and gloom" at the loss of Roanoke Island,

Above left
Fort Monroe remained a stronghold of the Union throughout the Civil War. A balloon view of Fort Monroe and the mouth of Chesapeake Bay was published in Harper's Weekly *in the summer of 1861. Courtesy, Virginia State Library.*

Above
Fort Monroe looks much the same today as it did during the Civil War, when Federal troops under the command of General Butler and others used it as a base of operations. Courtesy, U.S. Naval Institute.

Right
Union General Benjamin F. "Beast" Butler commanded troops at Fort Monroe during the Civil War. Butler was disliked and distrusted not only by Southerners, but also by his fellow generals. From Ben Perley Poore, Perley's Reminiscences, Philadelphia, 1886. Courtesy, Virginia State Library.

Far right
Union General John Ellis Wool succeeded Benjamin Butler as commander of Fort Monroe. Although the ailing general was 78 years old, he directed the occupation of Norfolk on May 10, 1862, an expedition suggested and supervised by Abraham Lincoln. Engraved by J.C. Buttre from a photo by Matthew Brady. From Cirker, Dictionary of American Portraits, Dover, 1967.

and Norfolk and Portsmouth overflowed with refugees and rumors in the defeat's wake. On February 27, the day he received the power from the Confederate Congress, President Davis directed General Huger to place the two towns under martial law and to prepare "for the removal of that part of the population who could only embarrass the defense." Authorities designated the next day as a day of fasting and prayer, and suspended all business in Norfolk. On March 1 martial law was extended to Richmond.

Almost everywhere events now were to take a turn for the worse. The war in the west was going badly; Forts Henry and Donelson had fallen in February, and in April bloody Shiloh was followed by the capture of New Orleans. In mid-March General George McClellan started the transfer of the Army of the Potomac, by water, to the peninsula between the James and the York, to move on Richmond. McClellan moved slowly, as usual, and was checked in June.

There was also good news: the Confederate ironclad *Virginia*, formerly the *Merrimack* and generally known by that name (though the final "k" is lost in the popular spelling), had made a successful sortie into Hampton Roads on March 8 and, as we shall see, fought the *Monitor* on March 9. It now protected Norfolk's waters. And General "Stonewall" Jackson marched and countermarched in the Shenandoah Valley in the spring of 1862, disconcerting and diverting a force that greatly outnumbered his own.

But with one army at the back door and another debarking on the Peninsula, Norfolk and Portsmouth were vulnerable. The cities' fate was sealed at a daylong discussion in Richmond on April 14 involving President Davis, Secretary of War George Wythe Randolph, and Generals Lee, Joseph E. Johnston, James Longstreet, and G.W. Smith. Johnston and Smith wanted to abandon Norfolk and the lower Peninsula, combine the Confederate forces, and attack McClellan or invade the North. Randolph, who had once been a midshipman in the U.S. Navy, saw that the loss of Norfolk would mean the loss of the *Virginia*. Lee joined with his fellow Virginian. Davis and Longstreet took neither side. About one o'clock in the morning, the decision was made to hold Norfolk and Yorktown, with the command of the combined forces given to Joe Johnston—who was opposed to the strategy. He did not protest. As he explained later, he was convinced "that events on the Peninsula would soon compel the Confederate government to adopt my method" and by the end of the month he was ordering General Huger to prepare to withdraw.

The Confederate decision to evacuate Norfolk coincided with an initiative on the side of the Union, undertaken by no less a personage than the President. Lincoln had come down to Fort Monroe, together with Secretary of the Treasury Salmon P. Chase and Secretary of War Edwin M. Stanton, for a firsthand look at operations on the Peninsula. Amazed to find there were no plans to

80

capture Norfolk, now seeming so vulnerable, he stirred things up. General John E. Wool, the veteran of the War of 1812 who was commanding Fort Monroe, was willing. Not only that, though he was 78, and infirm physically, he wanted to command the expedition himself. With Lincoln personally supervising the work, Union forces were ferried over to Ocean View on the morning of Saturday, May 10. They met with no opposition. General Huger had quit the town and was retiring toward Petersburg, destroying the railroad on the way. The approaching troops were met by a delegation headed by Mayor W.W. Lamb, who informed Chase and Wool that they were prepared to surrender. The mayor, stalling to allow the Confederates time to try to wreck the Gosport Navy Yard, was carrying "a large bunch of rusty keys and a sheaf of documents which he insisted on reading, down to the final line, before making the final formal gesture of handing over the keys," in Shelby Foote's retelling of the story.

Now the control of Norfolk's waters was unquestioned. And with the abandonment of the Gosport Navy Yard, any hope of a Confederate Navy was abandoned too. Although the North's forces reoccupied the yard, they were mindful of its vulnerability and decided not to put it to use. Norfolk and Portsmouth were out of the war.

The cities would be occupied for the next three years. Brigadier General Egbert L. Viele was named to govern Norfolk and, as he later recalled, was left on the evening of May 10 "the solitary military occupant of the city hall, without a soldier within two miles, and with not even an aide-de-camp to assist me." Of course, the occupation was unpopular and the efforts to govern Norfolk and Portsmouth were resisted in small ways. The invaders were unwelcome; the rebels were to be suppressed. A constant source of ten-

sion was the Northerners' employment of blacks in and out of uniform. The bitterness exploded in an incident in the summer of 1863.

On the afternoon of June 17, Dr. David M. Wright, a Norfolk physician who had been one of the heroes in the time of the yellow fever, made a remark to Second Lieutenant Anson L. Sanborn, who was marching a detachment of the First U.S. Colored Volunteers along a Norfolk sidewalk. Sanborn turned upon Wright and told him he was under arrest, whereupon the doctor drew a pistol

Left
Crowds cheer the raising of the Stars and Stripes over the main street of Portsmouth after the cities of Norfolk and Portsmouth were surrendered to the Union. From a sketch by J.H. Schell. Engraving from Frank Leslie's Illustrated Newspaper, *June 21, 1862. Courtesy, Norfolk Public Library.*

Below
Federal troops are depicted embarking on May 10, 1862, to capture Norfolk. Their landing near Ocean View was unopposed and the city surrendered peacefully. Note the figure of Abraham Lincoln at bottom center. Watercolor by G. Kaiser. Courtesy, The Mariners' Museum.

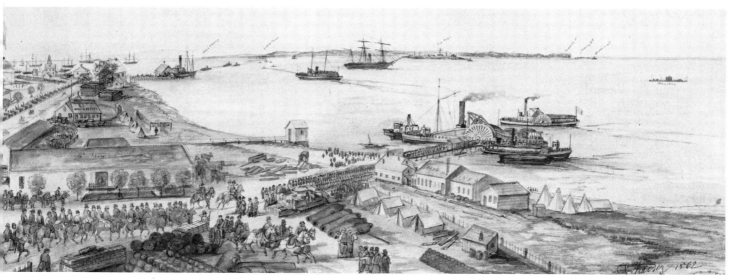

and shot Sanborn twice. He died, the doctor was found guilty of murder, and the sentence was affirmed by Lincoln on presidential review. Dr. Wright was hanged on October 23, 1863, a martyr to Norfolk and to the South.

In November "Beast" Butler returned to the command of the Department of Virginia and North Carolina, which included the governing of Norfolk and Portsmouth. Butler was disliked and distrusted by his fellow generals, who considered him incompetent in military matters, and since his days in New Orleans every loyal Southerner had despised him. At the same time he was an astute and popular politician. Dispatching the general to Fort Monroe kept him out of the field, if not necessarily out of politics. (Simon Cameron of Pennsylvania would make a special trip to Fort Monroe in 1864 to inform General Butler that Lincoln wanted him to run on the Republican ticket as his Vice President. Butler declined, for once outsmarting himself politically.) Early in 1865, once the election was over, Butler was relieved and returned to his home in Massachusetts. One reason why General Grant wanted him out of the way was to check the extensive smuggling of supplies to the Confederates from the Norfolk vicinity. Many suspect that Butler connived in that, though it is unproven. In any event, following the general's removal, Grant reported within a few weeks, "I have put a stop to supplies going out through Norfolk to Lee's army." By then, the war was almost over.

Certainly Norfolk thought Butler was a villain. Here is Burton's view, written in 1877, of the military occupation:

It was not until after the Federals took possession of Norfolk that the honest Southern men and the sneaking hypocrites in the city were truly known. It was not until then that Ben Butler's thieving propensities, and his impious and merciless acts as a military commander, brought him to the scornful notice of the honest and Christian people of the country. It was not until then that a "scallawag" was known in Virginia—known by the untiring energy he displayed in his efforts to humiliate, degrade and destroy the very people with whom he had lived for life, and among whom he had prospered—known by the bull dog tenacity with which he clung to the skirts and licked the boots of the Federal officers, ever whispering in their ears tales about honest men's loyalty to the South, and ever trying to sow the seeds of discord and trouble.

However, in his study of the military occupation of Norfolk and Portsmouth, Spencer Wilson suggests that Generals Viele, Wool, and John A. Dix, who succeeded Wool, were notable "for the consideration they showed for the welfare of the populace, rebellious and loyal alike. Their restraint reflected the prevailing war aim in Washington." Certainly Dix and Viele worked to alleviate the blockade's effects in Norfolk and Portsmouth, and General Viele was comfortable enough in Norfolk to bring his wife and son to live in the residence vacated by Dr. William Selden at the corner of Botetourt and Freemason streets on the waterfront. Furthermore, when he was transferred to Ohio in 1863, his family remained in Norfolk until the war was over.

For those who stayed throughout the war, the occupation was a period of privation. Hardship, hunger, and shortages were the common lot, and by the inexorable working of Greshams's Law one gold dollar was worth three "greenbacks" or 22 Confederate dollars by the spring of 1864. Business was bad to nonexistent and the conditions in Norfolk were described in a letter to the *Richmond Enquirer* as, "Take the oath of allegiance or starve."

Conditions were worse for the hundreds of refugee slaves who crowded first into Fort Monroe and later into Norfolk and Portsmouth. Often they met with prejudice and violence from the Northern soldiers. Some were impressed into military service and paid less than white soldiers. But other Northerners sought to help the black people, notably two Quaker sisters, Lucy and Sarah Chase, who came down from Worcester, Massachusetts. With extensive help from groups and individuals in the North, they managed to organize a program of relief that had clothed, fed, sheltered, and taught thousands by the end of the war.

When General Butler returned to the Department of Virginia and North Carolina, he employed black troops on duties in Norfolk and Portsmouth and generally sought to improve the lot of the liberated slaves. He established programs that were the prototype for the Freedmen's Bureau in the postwar Reconstruction, and dealt harshly with critics and dissenters among the local populace.

By the time Butler left in January of 1865, the cause of the Confederacy was doomed. On April 9 General Lee surrendered at Appomattox Courthouse and five days later President Lincoln was assassinated at Ford's Theater in Washington. Jefferson Davis was captured in Georgia on May 10 and the final holdout, General Kirby Smith, surrendered on May 26. More than 600,000 men had lost their lives in the war, and now the task was "to bind up the nation's wounds," in the late President's words.

The occupation of Norfolk and Portsmouth was a prologue to that task. Almost every element in the postwar program of Reconstruction, whether advocated "with malice toward none" or by the Radical Republicans who saw the Confederate states as "conquered provinces," was rehearsed in Norfolk and Portsmouth. And, as elsewhere in the South, the legacy of the occupation was to determine politics and race relations in the region for a century to come.

Facing page:
Top
United States troops destroyed the Norfolk Navy Yard to prevent arms and stores there from falling into "the hands of the insurrectionists." Courtesy, Virginia State Library.

Bottom
Robert E. Lee, the Confederacy's great hero, was asked to command the forces of the Union by President Lincoln in 1861. He was honored on his Norfolk visit in 1870. From Cirker, Dictionary of American Portraits, Dover, 1967.

Below
There were attempts to aid black refugees in the Norfolk vicinity. Teaching the Freedmen appeared in The South by J.T. Trowbridge in 1866. Courtesy, Norfolk Public Library, Sargeant Memorial Room.

THE *MONITOR* AND THE *MERRIMAC*

The American nation—North and South—was unready for war in the spring of 1861. If the Confederacy had no navy, the one that was left to the remaining United States was inadequate and scattered. Loyalties were uncertain. More than a hundred of the captains, commodores, and lieutenants had resigned, sympathetic to the South, and others were asking for foreign service as a matter of principle. Almost all of the effective ships were on foreign station. And one of the finest ships in the Navy, the steam frigate *Merrimack,* was lost at the Norfolk Navy Yard.

Lincoln's Secretary of the Navy, "Uncle Gideon" Welles, faced a formidable task. The Navy must be rebuilt and restructured in time of war. He did the job well. By early 1862 the Union would have more than 300 warships, and double the number by 1864. The blockade, ineffective at the start, would grow tighter with each month's passing and, by 1864, would be strangling the South.

If Welles' task was formidable, the Confederacy's was impossible. It had to build a navy from scratch. That would be the responsibility of a former Florida senator, Secretary of the Navy Stephen R. Mallory, who proved to be energetic and resourceful. But the efforts to buy a Confederate Navy in Europe or to build one in the South were doomed to fail. Finally, one story would be told time after time: A lone ship—the *Virginia,* the *Arkansas,* or the *Tennessee*—against an entire fleet.

The first was the *Virginia.* After the holocaust at the Norfolk Navy Yard the Confederates examined the frigate, found that the hull was sound, and thought that the engines might be repaired. Mallory okayed a scheme to turn the *Merrimack* into an impregnable iron monster ship that would be christened the C.S.S. *Virginia,* but generally known and spelled as the *Merrimac* today. The conversion commenced under the supervision of John M. Brooke, John L. Porter, and William P. Williamson, all former U.S. Navy officers. A kind of sloping shed was built on the deck to support an iron-over-oak outer shell—specifically, a sheath of oak planks, four inches thick, and a double layer of iron plates, rolled at Richmond's Tredegar Iron Works, each two inches thick. The carapace carried over the sides of the ship, like the eaves of a house, to protect the engines and the hull. The monster was armed with 10 big guns: seven-inch rifles in the fore and aft gunports, and batteries broadside consisting of a six-inch rifle and three nine-inch smoothbores. The final touch was a cast-iron ram two feet below the waterline.

There was no secret to the undertaking. The North needed no spies. In the fall of 1861 Henry Davis, a shoemaker who had been living in Norfolk for nearly a year, had left the town for the North. An account of what he had seen in Virginia appeared in the New York *Tribune* on November 2, 1861. Davis told of high prices and shortages, but reported that the town was well defended. "It is difficult to tell how many soldiers are at Norfolk, so many are about the town," the newspaper said. "The estimated number varied from 10,000 to 20,000." In accurate detail Davis described the work being done at the shipyard:

The Merrimac has been transformed into a great battering ram, with a steel nose, for running down vessels. All her internal works are completed, but her plating is only partially effected as yet. She is to be sheathed from the water line upward with iron plates one foot wide and two inches thick, the same way as her planks, and then again sheathed with simple plates over that, running up the same way as her ribs, the whole to be bolted through and through. They expect to get her finished by the 1st of January, but, from the scarcity of the plates and the slowness of the work, it will probably be nearer the 1st of June before she is ready for sea. When completed, she is to run down some dark rainy night to the Roads, and smash up and sink the fleet. Her engines are four feet below the water line, and her sides slope inward. She is to be covered overhead with a bomb-proof network of railroad iron. She is not to have any decks, except forward and aft for the big pivot guns, with galleries for her broadside armament. It is thought that she will be so hot inside, from want of ventilation, that very few persons are willing to ship in her. Her armament is to be of the heaviest and best rifled cannon known, and there is no doubt, if she has a chance, she will do an immense amount of damage to our fleet.

The North responded to the rumors which had begun reaching Washington in the summer of 1861. A board was convened to consider designs for ironclad warships. It approved three. The gunboat *Galena* was conventionally familiar. The huge *New Ironsides* was ponderous and powerful. But the design of the *Monitor* was radical. It was the idea of John Ericsson, a Swedish tinkerer—a

genius really—who had come to the United States in 1839. He was 58 years old when he gave the *Monitor*'s plans to the board of commissioners. They were skeptical. But Lincoln looked at a cardboard model at one session. "All I have to say is what the girl said when she put her foot into the stocking," the President remarked. "It strikes me there's something in it." Ericsson was awarded a no-confidence contract with a kind of money-back guarantee: if the design proved unworkable, the government must be repaid.

The keel of the *Monitor* was laid on October 25, 1861, and she was launched on January 30, 1862, not quite a hundred days later. The deck of the strange vessel was iron-over-wood and the only major superstructure was a turret, 9 feet high and 20 feet in diameter, eight inches thick, housing two 11-inch, muzzle-loading, smoothbore Dahlgren guns. Both the *Monitor* and the *Mer-*

rimac were exceedingly odd vessels. The first indeed looked like "a cheesebox on a raft," and the second was described as resembling "a barn with only its roof showing in the water" and "a terrapin with a chimney on its back."

But events were not moving at a terrapin's pace. By mid-February the *Merrimac* was in the water, with a crew of 300 volunteers mostly recruited from the Confederate soldiery. Her guns remained untested. She was about to have a historic tryout voyage.

At 11 o'clock on the morning of Saturday, March 8, the *Merrimac* left the Navy Yard and moved slowly down the Elizabeth River and into Hampton Roads. She was accompanied by the *Beaufort* and the *Raleigh*, armed steamers tagging along behind the ironclad like small boys; later three more would come down the James River to join in the day's sport. The commanding officer of

The ironclad Merrimac rams the USS Cumberland during the engagement on March 8. The hole created in the side of the Cumberland was big enough for "a horse and cart," and the wounded ship sank. From the Illustrated London News, *April 5, 1862. Courtesy, Virginia State Library.*

the *Merrimac* was Captain Franklin Buchanan, who in the 1840s has been the first superintendent of the U.S. Naval Academy and who had gone to Japan with Commodore Matthew Calbraith Perry in the 1850s. Ahead and waiting were five wooden Union warships. The sailing ships *Congress*, a frigate, and *Cumberland*, a newer sloop with big Dahlgren guns, were lying at the mouth of the James River. The sail-and-steam frigates *Minnesota* and *Roanoke* and the frigate *St. Lawrence* stood off Old Point Comfort.

The crew of the *Congress* had hung out their

wash and it was drying in the rigging when a lookout saw the *Merrimac*'s plume of smoke. He approached an officer and said, "I wish you would take the glass and have a look over there. I believe that thing is a-coming down at last." The action began at 2 o'clock in the afternoon. Although the *Congress* was nearer, the *Merrimac* plowed straight toward the *Cumberland,* the newer ship. Broadsides from both Union warships caromed off the shell of the turtle, while the guns of the *Merrimac* punished the wooden vessels. Soldiers on shore saw the *Merrimac* ram the *Cumberland,* opening a hole in the side of the sloop that was big enough for "a horse and cart," one of the *Cumberland*'s officers said. The ship sank at about half-past three with all colors flying. (Divers found the wreck in 1981.) The *Merrimac* then turned upon the *Congress* and forced her to surrender. Buchanan ceased firing when the frigate's flag was struck, but a Union battery on the shore didn't stop shooting at the two vessels. Buchanan was hit by a splinter and aboard the *Congress* his brother, a lieutenant who had stayed with the Union, was wounded. (He would die with the ship.) Enraged by the fire from the Yankees, the *Merrimac* now tormented the frigate with red-hot shot that started fires where they struck. The *Minnesota,* the *Roanoke,* and the *St. Lawrence* tried to enter the fight, but each grounded in the shoal waters. The *Merrimac* turned away from the *Congress,* doomed now, to deal with the *Minnesota,* but could not come within range of the stranded vessel. Enough. She could finish the job tomorrow.

The ironclad withdrew, with an assortment of

ents in her sides, 21 killed and wounded, and her ram broken off in the *Cumberland*'s side. The *Cumberland* had sunk, the *Congress* was a funeral pyre, the other ships would wait. The burning *Congress* "made a beautiful light—illuminating the heavens and the country for miles around," an eyewitness reported. "About midnight her magazine exploded with a tremendous noise. Her burning was witnessed by thousands of spectators from our harbor and shores who never saw a ship on fire."

The battle's outcome was telegraphed to Washington and caused a panic there. The Cabinet was in an uproar and, in the story told by Welles, the most upset was Secretary of War Stanton. He was convinced the monster was coming up the Potomac to Washington, and thought it "not unlikely we shall have a shell or cannon-ball from one of her guns in the White House before we leave the room."

Meanwhile, the blazing *Congress* had lighted the *Monitor*'s way on the evening of March 8 to a berth under the guns of Fort Monroe, where her officers were told of the day's events by one of the *Minnesota*'s officers. The *Monitor* was commanded by Lieutenant John L. Worden, who had been a Confederate prisoner at the start of the war. He had recruited the crew from the Navy's receiving ships in New York. On the evening of March 6 the *Monitor* had put to sea under the tow of a tug, and almost foundered in a storm on the trip to Virginia. Now the crew had little time to rest in getting her ready for Round Two.

On Sunday morning the *Merrimac* returned, under the command of Lieutenant Catesby ap Roger Jones now, to finish off the Yankees. The battle began early. The *Merrimac* opened fire on the *Minnesota* about eight-thirty and was surprised when an apparition emerged from the frigate's shadow. It was the *Monitor*. The duel was on.

The antagonists were evenly matched. The *Monitor* was more maneuverable, but could fire only at intervals of seven to eight minutes. The *Merrimac* was slow, but fired faster and outgunned her opponent. Iron versus iron on Sunday was different from iron versus wood on Saturday. Despite the noise and the smoke and the spectacle, the two ships were not hurting each other. After a time the guns of the *Merrimac* fell silent. "Why are you not firing, Mr. Eggleston?" Jones asked the gunnery officer. "Why, our powder is very precious, and after two hours' incessant firing I find I can do her about as much damage by snapping my thumb at her every two minutes and a half," he replied.

The bigger *Merrimac* sought to run down the

An engraving of the gun deck of the Merrimac, *as the artist fancied it, appeared in the pages of the* Illustrated Times *on May 31, 1862. The engraving inaccurately depicts the guns as Armstrong breech-loading rifles; there were no guns of this type on the* Merrimac. *Courtesy, U.S. Naval Historical Center.*

Monitor, with the notion of boarding the enemy ship in the best swashbuckling tradition. But the sluggish turtle could not catch the cheesebox. About noon the battle was broken off. Stalemate. The *Merrimac* retired unmolested. The *Monitor* had "saved" the Union. Each claimed victory. "As soon as the news reached Europe," judged Sir Winston Churchill, a famous Former Naval Person, "it was realised that all of the war-fleets were obsolete."

Or soon would be. The *Monitor* and the *Merrimac* really were obsolete themselves. Both were unseaworthy. The *Merrimac* drew 22 feet of water and was about as navigable as a fallen tree. She needed a half mile to turn in flat water. The engines of the old steam frigate were faulty to start with, and flooding had not helped them when she was sunk in '61. She was no threat to Washington. She was fit to fight in Hampton Roads, and only there. The *Monitor* was a bit faster and navigable in shallower waters, but with barely a foot of freeboard she was no less unseaworthy.

Neither survived the year. When the Confederates evacuated Norfolk, the homeless ironclad had nowhere to hide and nowhere to run. Since she drew too much water to retreat up the James to Richmond, the Confederates had to destroy the *Merrimac* themselves. "There was no dissenting opinion," in the language of the official report of Commodore Josiah Tatnall. "The ship was accordingly run ashore as near the main land as possible, and the crew landed. She was then fired, and after burning fiercely fore and aft for upward of an hour, blew up a little before five o'clock in the morning of the eleventh."

There was an encore of a kind when the Northern fleet, including the *Monitor* and the *Galena,* was repulsed by the batteries at Drewry's Bluff, below Richmond, with the crew of the *Merrimac* manning some of the Confederate guns. That was on May 15, four days later. On December 30, 1862, the *Monitor* was lost off Cape Hatteras in a storm. Her legacy was a line of later Monitors in the U.S. Navy—big-gunned, unseaworthy, and largely useless.

Above
*When the
Confederates
evacuated Norfolk,
they were forced to
destroy the
Merrimac
themselves.
According to the
official report of
Commodore Josiah
Tatnall, the ironclad*
*was grounded and
the crew landed.
"She was then fired,
and after burning
fiercely fore and aft
for upward of an
hour, blew up a little
before five o'clock in
the morning . . ."
Courtesy, The
Chrysler Museum.*

Facing page
*In 1874 James
Hamilton
(1819-1878)
painted the* Burning
of the Merrimac.
Night. *The oil
painting is in the
collection of The
Chrysler Museum.
Courtesy, The
Chrysler Museum.*

CHAPTER SIX

NORFOLK'S RECOVERY: 1865 - 1914

Two days after General Lee surrendered at Appomattox Court House, Abraham Lincoln delivered his last speech, by candlelight, from the balcony of the White House to an "immense throng." He read from a "carefully written paper" that dealt with the government of Louisiana and the problem of restoring the Southern states to the Union.

"We all agree," the President said, "that the seceded states are out of their proper practical relation with the Union; and that the sole object of the government, civil and military, in regard to those States is to again get them into that proper practical relationship. ... "

Three days later, on Good Friday, Lincoln was shot by John Wilkes Booth while watching a performance of *Our American Cousin* at Ford's Theater. Mortally wounded, the President was removed by soldiers to a boarding house on the other side of the street and died there at 7:22 the following morning in the bed in a room rented by William Clark. All across the country the murder of the President was made the subject of Easter Sunday sermons. Few were forgiving in spirit.

Had he lived, Lincoln would have been forced to contend with the harsh vengefulness voiced by Thaddeus Stevens when he described "the late rebel States" as "carcasses lying with the Union." It was up to Congress to determine the fate of the "conquered provinces," Stevens said, and mean-

while military rule was warranted. Let the rebels "eat the fruit of foul rebellion."

It was inevitable that without Lincoln the course of Reconstruction would be charted by Radical Republicans, such as Stevens and Charles Sumner of Massachusetts, who claimed to represent the popular will of the victors in the war. (Sumner had been brutally caned on the floor of the Senate by Preston Brooks of South Carolina in 1856 after he made a biting speech on slavery and Southerners.) Andrew Johnson, Lincoln's successor, sought to implement his predecessor's policies of reconciling the South to the Union. He recognized the "loyal" governments in Arkansas, Louisiana, Tennessee, and Virginia which Lincoln had set up. Congress refused to accept the action of the President and imposed a program of military rule over his veto. Led by Stevens and like-minded Radical Republicans such as former General Benjamin F. Butler, now sitting in the House of Representatives, the Radicals came within a single vote of impeaching Johnson and effectively paralyzed the President politically. In 1868 General Ulysses S. Grant was elected President on a platform that endorsed Radical Republicanism.

But it was a policy that was doomed to failure. For a time the Radical Republicans were able to impose their will by force upon the South and, also by force, to impose the political rule of "car-

Frank Leslie's Illustrated Newspaper *printed this engraving of Norfolk's market on August 25, 1866. The caption, which reflects the paternalistic white sentiment of the time, commented that "the sable race, who monopolize the great share of the business in Southern towns know how to praise their own wares, and at the same time to flatter an indifferent visitor into a prompt investment of any stray dimes he may happen to possess, while there is nothing you need they will not obtain for you or promise." Sketch by James E. Taylor. Courtesy, Norfolk Public Library.*

petbaggers" (those who came down from the North) and "scalawags" (Southerners who cooperated with them) to disfranchise the Southern whites and manipulate the votes of the emancipated slaves. But both black and white Southerners were victimized. "We have turned, or are about to turn, loose four million slaves without a hut to shelter them or a cent in their pockets," said Stevens in 1865. "The infernal laws of slavery have prevented them from acquiring an education, understanding the common laws of contract, or of managing the ordinary business of life. ... If we do not furnish them with homesteads, and hedge them around with protective laws; if we leave them to the legislation of their late masters, we had better left them in bondage. ..."

There were efforts to improve the lot of the ex-slaves through the agency of the Freedmen's Bureau and a variety of humanitarian and legislative resources. A number of schools were established for the former slaves; Hampton Institute is one of them. It remains one of the area's best colleges today. But in the eyes of the majority of Southerners, these efforts were politically tainted. For a brief, heady moment the blacks in the South were allowed a measure of political power; it would be denied to them in the "Solid South" systematically thereafter for years. The old system of legal slavery yielded to a new system of economic subservience and segregation, which the nation tacitly sanctioned.

By 1877, with the compromise which handed the disputed election of 1876 to Rutherford B. Hayes and withdrew the last of the occupying troops, Reconstruction was ended everywhere in the South. In human terms, the Emancipation Proclamation would not be redeemed until the coming of the civil rights revolution a century later. In economic terms, the entire region suffered—the South stayed underdeveloped.

Defeated, exhausted, hungry, there was nothing for the prostrate and ruined South to do except endure in the Reconstruction years—and remain "unreconstructed." Hear the voice of the Reverend Robert L. Dabney, a leading Presbyterian theologian, who had defended the institution of slavery before the war: "I do not forgive," he declared in 1870. "I try not to forgive. What! forgive those people, who have invaded our country, burned our cities, destroyed our homes, slain our young men, and spread desolation and ruin over our land! No, I do not forgive them."

It was not the Confederate soldier who was the most implacable. He wanted to get on with life and looked to the example set by General Lee, who accepted a college presidency and peacetime. It was the women. The Confederacy's daughters did not forgive the Yankees or forget what they had done. They kept the memories warm when they became the mothers and grandmothers of the "New South." The busy and businesslike North soon tired of the Civil War, except for a few ritual remembrances, and turned to other concerns. But there was hardly a crossroads in Dixie without its Confederate monument and the South was to remain separate and unequal, a disaffected region within the United States for generations. Not until the New Deal, the Second World War, and the legal and political upheaval summarized by the *Brown* decision, the sit-ins, the speeches of the Reverend Martin Luther King, Jr., and George C. Wallace, and the election of Jimmy Carter, the first real Southerner in the White House since Zachary Taylor, was the breach healed. It took a century to restore the South to Lincoln's "proper practical relation with the Union."

In November 1865 the Norfolk *Virginian* lamented, "The cost of living is now double that which prevailed five years ago, and bears peculiarly hard upon all classes." For instance, a bushel of corn had increased from 50 cents to 75 cents, a pound of butter from 18 cents to 55 or 65 cents, and a dozen eggs from seven cents to 35 or 40 cents. Except for the hard times, though, the citizens of Norfolk, living under military rule, had been untouched by actual fighting for three years. Many thousands of ex-slaves had taken refuge behind the Union lines in the Norfolk vicinity during the war. Now there was friction between blacks and whites. Ironically, some of the incidents involved the federal troops who were meant to be protecting the freedmen, but the Northern press luridly reported these as attacks on blacks by Norfolk whites. The incidents in the South were played up by the Radicals, who were confirmed in their control of the House and Senate in the elections of 1866. Governor Francis H. Pierpont, a native of what was now West Virginia, was succeeded by General John M. Schofield when Virginia was declared Military District Number One under the first Reconstruction Act.

However the period of Radical Reconstruction in Virginia was to be comparatively short-lived. With the election of Gilbert C. Walker as governor of Virginia in 1869, and of John B. Whitehead as mayor of Norfolk in 1870, the conservatives were politically reestablished. And in 1870 Virginia rejoined the Union.

Symbolically, the course of Reconstruction in the area around Norfolk's waters may be marked by three events: the imprisonment of Jefferson Davis at Fort Monroe in 1865, General Butler's return to Norfolk in 1867, and General Lee's Norfolk visit in 1870.

The Confederate President had left Richmond when the capital was evacuated by General Lee and was captured in Georgia on May 10, 1865, a month after Lee's surrender. It was erroneously, and gleefully, reported that he was taken while wearing his wife's clothing. Davis was escorted to Port Royal, and brought by steamer to Fort Monroe on May 22. There he was forcibly

The Norfolk Virginian *was born on a Tuesday morning, November 21, 1865, and cost five cents a day or eight dollars per year, payable in advance. There was no paper on Sunday until 1874. Courtesy, Landmark Communications.*

SEA BOARD
COTTON PRESS

Norfolk was a major cotton port in the postwar years. Cotton compresses, such as the Seaboard Cotton Compress, helped to enable foreign shipments from Norfolk's wharves. From Guide to Norfolk as a Business Centre, 1884. *Courtesy, Alderman Library, University of Virginia.*

shackled, to his own shame and the great outrage of Southerners when the action became known. The shackles were removed four days later, but Davis remained a prisoner for two years. He was indicted for treason, but because of his health and the legal questions raised he was never tried. On May 13, 1867, Davis was freed on bond of $100,000 (among the signers were Horace Greeley and Cornelius Vanderbilt) and received a hero's welcome when he came out of the courtroom in Richmond. On the 14th he arrived in Norfolk on board the steamer *Niagara*, "bound for Canada, to join his family there," as Burton recorded. "A large number of citizens paid their

respects to the unfortunate but dearly loved ex-president of the lost Confederacy."

Butler returned to Norfolk in the fall of 1867 (he was interested in a scheme to drain the Dismal Swamp) and an Irish hackman named Adams became a local hero by refusing the general a ride. A fable telling of all the city's silver being taken to hiding places "as a wise precaution against our '*distinguished visitor*'" was printed in the *Virginian* of November 19. Butler left town that day. And when he was defeated for renomination for the House in 1868, the paper was overjoyed that "the Yankees of his district spit upon a bully, a liar, a coward and a spoon finder."

General Lee was accorded the kind of welcome in the spring of 1870 that had been given to General Lafayette on the occasion of his visit. Crowds in Norfolk and Portsmouth received him with rebel yells, and "many of his old soldiers came to shake his hand and to gaze once more—and for the last time—on his calm countenance," in biographer Douglas Southall Freeman's words. General Lee was sorry that many Norfolk residents were leaving the city to seek work; "Virginia needs her young men," he said. He died in October of that same year.

As General Lee's remark suggested, the city's economic recovery was slow-starting. Although two carloads of cotton had made their way from Georgia to Norfolk by rail as early as 1866, the city's development as a cotton port was tied to the cotton crop's recovery and the consolidation and growth of the railroad system. It would be nearly 20 years before cotton production in the Confederate states returned to the level of 1860, and it was not until the 1880s that the city finally was linked by a mature rail system to the west.

Nevertheless, Norfolk was again becoming an important port by the 1870s, as it had been in colonial days and in the infancy of the American republic. Cotton was the first staple of its revived seaborne trade. Because of its inadequate rail system, the city had not been a cotton port in the prewar years. In 1858, it had received only 6,174 bales of cotton, but the figure topped 100,000 by 1869 and exceeded 400,000 by 1874. The Norfolk and Portsmouth Cotton Exchange was estab-

lished in July of that year, and by then Norfolk was second only to New Orleans in the number of bales of cotton handled. In a special edition in 1879 the *Virginian* was able to boast not only of cotton exports, but of the grocery, lumber, and peanut trade too. The facts and figures "must silence the croaker and satisfy the most incredulous that our city has at last entered upon an era of permanent prosperity," the newspaper proclaimed. "From all parts of the country trade is setting in this direction."

On March 17, 1883, there occurred what may be the most significant economic event in the history of Norfolk's waters: the first carload of coal rolled into town over the Norfolk and Western tracks, and was greeted by an artillery salute and a display of flags. The carload was consigned to Mayor William W. Lamb, who also happened to be a coal merchant. The shipment, said the mayor, was "the precursor of a trade which is destined to make our port the most important coaling station on the Atlantic coast." So it would. Here it might be noted that a new record for coal loading over the N&W piers was set on February 8, 1982, when 166,060 tons of coal were poured into waiting vessels. The "transloading" for the previous week was 1.03 million tons, also a record, and impressive proof of Mayor Lamb's prophecy a century earlier.

It is necessary now to backtrack and describe the development of the railway system that was to transform the cities of Hampton Roads in the latter part of the 19th century. Its inadequate railroads had stunted Norfolk's growth before the Civil War and the city had no rail service whatsoever at the end of the war. In addition, its infant railroads—the Seaboard and Roanoke to the south, the Norfolk and Petersburg to the west—had been casualties of the conflict. The bridges

Above left
General William Mahone became a political power in Virginia after the Civil War. He consolidated several railroads into the Atlantic, Mississippi & Ohio and became its president. Engraving from Harper's Weekly. Courtesy, Virginia State Library.

Above
Norfolk had become a big cotton port by the mid-1870s, second only to New Orleans. Some of the thousands of bales of cotton could be seen stacked up along the docks at the waterfront. Courtesy, Norfolk Redevelopment and Housing Authority. (NRHA)

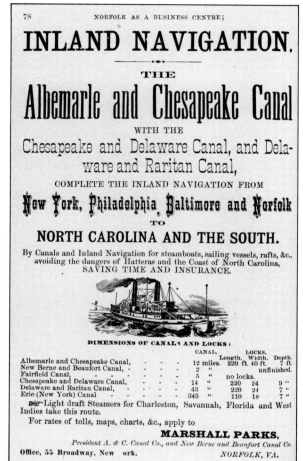

had been burned, the tracks torn up. It would take months to restore service and it would be inadequate even then.

The man who was to change that was the engineer who had built the Norfolk and Petersburg in the 1850s, and who was to become one of the chief figures in the postwar politics of Virginia. He was General William Mahone. The son of a tavern keeper, "Billy" Mahone was a graduate of Virginia Military Institute who had distinguished himself at the battle of the Crater, near Petersburg, in 1864. At the end of the war he resumed the direction of the Norfolk and

Petersburg and had it running by 1866. His eyes then turned west. In 1867, with the help of Governor Pierpont, Mahone pushed through the General Assembly a bill for the consolidation of the Norfolk and Petersburg; the Southside Railroad, which ran from Petersburg to Lynchburg; and the Virginia and Tennessee Railway, linking Lynchburg to Bristol on the Tennessee border. The consolidated company would be called the Atlantic, Mississippi and Ohio and would be required to extend its line westward within five years.

Mahone was elected president of the A.M.&O. with a salary of $25,000, as much as the President of the United States received. (The initials stood for "All Mine and Otelia's," said the wags; Mahone's wife was named Otelia.) The charter of the company lapsed when it was unable to buy up all the railroad stocks and bonds held by the state, and it was necessary to get the General Assembly's approval a second time. This led to what was later termed "the most terrific railroad fight ever known in the history of Virginia," which Mahone won. The bill's passage in 1870, not long after Virginia had rejoined the Union, was the occasion of celebration in Norfolk, which would at last have rail ties to the markets of the west.

But the A.M.&O. was overextended and undercapitalized, and was forced into receivership in 1876. It was bought by interests in Philadelphia and reorganized as the Norfolk and Western Railroad Company. (It became the Norfolk and Western *Railway* after another reorganization in 1895.) If Mahone was the man with the energy and political savvy to put the railroad together, Frederick J. Kimball was the one who made it profitable. He was elected its president in 1883, inheriting a line that was little more than 408 miles of single track from Norfolk to Bristol. When it was next reorganized, with Kimball keeping the presidency, it was an integrated system of more than 1,500 miles and carrying 14 times its earlier traffic.

"If an institution is, as Emerson wrote, the

lengthened shadow of one man, the great Norfolk and Western system is an embodiment of the dominating personality of Frederick J. Kimball," Joseph T. Lambie observed in his history of the railroad.

As Mayor Lamb prophesied, the Norfolk and Western was to have a great impact on life in Norfolk. It built a new railroad station with an 80-foot clock tower in 1882 and a larger station and warehouses at the foot of Main Street in the 1890s. It bought nearly two miles of waterfront and began regular shipments from the Lamberts Point piers in 1885, expanding facilities and building new piers to handle the increasing tonnage from year to year.

If Norfolk was energized by one railroad, the city of Newport News was called into being by a second. This was the Chesapeake and Ohio, a moribund road transformed by Collis P. Huntington, who extended the line to the seaboard and made it profitable.

Huntington was born in Connecticut in 1821, and abandoned his business in Oneonta, New York, to join in the California Gold Rush in 1849. A decade later he was a partner in a hardware store in Sacramento with Mark Hopkins; together with two other merchants, Charles Crocker and Leland Stanford, they organized the Central Pacific Railroad. When the Golden Spike was driven at Promontory Point to join the tracks of the Central Pacific and the Union Pacific on May 10, 1869, the dream of a transcontinental railroad was realized. It was a moment that caught the imagination of the nation. "There is more poetry in the rush of a single railroad train across the continent," exulted poet Joaquin Miller, "than in all the gory story of burning Troy."

What Huntington now visualized was one railroad tying the Atlantic Ocean to the Pacific, which meant carrying the C. & O. eastward to the water. After assuming control of the railroad, the group headed by Huntington had extended its tracks to the Ohio River, opening the coalfields of West Virginia—and giving his name to the city founded in 1871 as the railroad's western terminus, Huntington, West Virginia. The C. & O.'s eastern terminus was Richmond and the question was where to locate the railroad's tidewater terminal. Several sites were suitable: Norfolk, the point of land on the Peninsula still generally known as Newport's News, Yorktown, West Point, and the mouth of the Piankatank River. Norfolk sought to attract the C. & O. and the city government pondered purchasing a wharf front and giving it to the railroad. As late as 1880 the *Virginian* was arguing the advantages of Norfolk and a businessman's committee was established to appeal directly to the leadership of the railroad.

But the decision was made to locate the C. & O. terminus at Newport's News, which was farmland still showing evidences of Camp Butler's earthworks. The line would be shorter, and therefore cheaper to construct, and moreover there was no competing railroad on the Peninsula route. On March 4, 1880, the General Assembly authorized the Chesapeake and Ohio Railway to construct a railroad from Richmond to a terminus at Newport's News, and to acquire property there. Huntington, the C. & O.'s president, specified the advantages of the site in the annual report in

September:

This is a point so designed and adapted by nature that it will require comparatively little at the hands of man to fit it for our purposes. The roadstead, well known to all maritime circles, is large enough to float the ocean commerce of the world; it is easily approached in all winds and weather without pilot or tow; it is never troubled by ice and there is enough depth of water to float any ship that sails the seas; and at the same time it is so sheltered that vessels can lie there in perfect safety at all times of the year.

In October 1880 the Old Dominion Land Company was chartered for the development of Newport News. Lots were laid out, and construction soon started. Temporary tracks were extended from Lee Hall to Yorktown to accommodate the centennial of Cornwallis' surrender, and the first passenger train left Newport News for the Centennial Celebration grounds at Yorktown on October 19, 1881. Regular service from Newport News to Richmond and the west began in 1882. The Hotel Warwick, an impressive structure that was to dominate the town for years, welcomed its first guests on April 11, 1883. Later in the month the first Newport News newspaper was published, *The Wedge.*

To complement his railroad and the deep-water terminal that he was building for it, Huntington needed a shipyard too. The Chesapeake Dry Dock and Construction Company was incorporated in 1886 and renamed the Newport News Shipbuilding and Dry Dock Company in 1890. "It was my original intention to start a shipyard plant in the best location in the world, and I have succeeded in my purpose," Huntington later said. "It is right at the gateway to the sea. There is never any ice in winter, and it is never so cold but you can hammer metal out of doors."

The first drydock was opened in 1889 with the docking of the monitor *Puritan* and shortly thereafter the company decided to build ships as well as repair them. The first was the tug *Dorothy*, Hull No. 1, delivered in 1891—and built at a loss. The infant shipyard was awarded a contract for three gunboats in 1892, the first of many U.S. Navy vessels which would be built by the Yard. The *Nashville, Helena,* and *Wilmington* were completed in 1897, also at a loss. In fact, the company lost money on most of the work it undertook in the early years. "There is something that is fearfully wrong; in fact, so wrong that I am afraid to take any more work until we have

reached a point where we can get as much to build a ship as it costs to build it," Huntington wrote. Had it not been sustained by his private resources, the shipyard surely would have soon gone out of business. After Huntington's death, in 1900, the company's directors, dealing with his heirs, authorized $5 million in bonds and $6 million in preferred stock to settle the claims of the estate. The Huntington family controlled the company until 1940, when it was reorganized as a corporation traded on the New York Stock Exchange. Newport News Shipbuilding became a division of Tenneco in 1968.

The diverse enterprises of Collis P. Huntington had built a city and put thousands of people to work. The C. & O. carried coal and general merchandise over its tracks to the Newport News piers and terminals, where the cargo could be loaded on oceangoing vessels. Employment at the Newport News Shipbuilding and Dry Dock Company climbed from the hundreds into the thousands. By early 1898 there were more than 3,300 workers on the payroll of the Yard. An apprentice at that time received a starting salary of three dollars per week. Houses were built on the Old Dominion Land Company's lots. Churches followed. Casino Park was developed for guests at the Hotel Warwick, and enjoyed by the local residents too. The Huntington interests donated land for a courthouse and Newport News became the seat of Warwick County in 1888. The Newport News Light and Water Company was organized in 1889 and horsecars soon were replaced by an electric trolley that linked Hampton, Newport News, the shipyard, and the Chesapeake and Ohio terminal. In 1896 the city of Newport News was incorporated by the General Assembly, acknowledging that the company town had come of age.

The story of the third of the coal-carrying railroads is equally remarkable. The Virginian Railway was conceived and constructed by one man, relying upon his own convictions, credit, and resources. The man was Henry Huttleston Rogers, who was one of John D. Rockefeller's ablest lieutenants in the Standard Oil trust. Rogers saw the actual and potential profits in the coal trade at the turn of the century and determined to build an entirely new railroad from the coalfields to Norfolk's waters. Because he had been successful in the ruthless wars of Wall Street, he was able to finance on his own the building of the $40-million railroad.

The corporate parents of the Virginian Railway

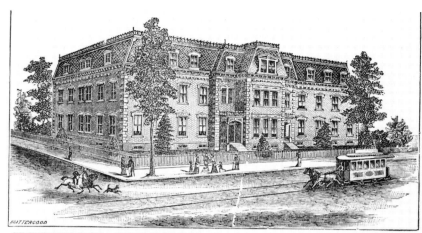

were the Deepwater Railway Company, incorporated in West Virginia in 1898, and the Tidewater Railway Company, established in 1904 in Virginia. The railroad was built from Deepwater, West Virginia, to the coal piers that were operated at Sewells Point by a subsidiary of the Virginian, as the consolidated company was called after 1907. The distance was 442 miles and the engineers were instructed to design a direct and efficient line linking the two terminals. They made the most of the advantages gravity offered in bringing coal downhill from the mountains of West Virginia. The new railroad went into operation on July 1, 1909, six weeks after the death of Rogers. It moved nearly a million tons in 1910, more than four million in 1913, and over six million in 1916.

With the development of the railroads to bring the earth's riches to Norfolk's waters, Hampton Roads became the greatest coal port in the world. Millions of tons were dumped from hopper to hold at Lamberts Point and Sewells Point on the Norfolk side of the water (the Virginian was merged into the Norfolk and Western in the early 1960s) and at the Chesapeake and Ohio terminals, and carried by colliers and coastal steamers to fuel the globe. Coal was king, and remains so today. Although there have been ups and downs in the trade, the great ships of the 1980s are carrying a far greater tonnage than was

ever dreamed by Collis P. Huntington or Henry H. Rogers.

The network of railroads was completed by the turn of the century, excepting the Virginian. The Elizabeth City and Norfolk began operating in 1881, was extended to Edenton the next year, and became the Norfolk and Southern. The New York, Philadelphia and Norfolk—familiarly known as the "Nyp 'n N"—ran its track to Cape Charles on the Eastern Shore and thence by car float to Norfolk, and by 1884 offered the best passenger service, by boat and train, to New York. The old Seaboard and Roanoke, which

Above
Norfolk College for Young Ladies advertised facilities such as steam radiators in 1884. The building still stands at the corner of College Place and Granby Street. Courtesy, Alderman Library, University of Virginia.

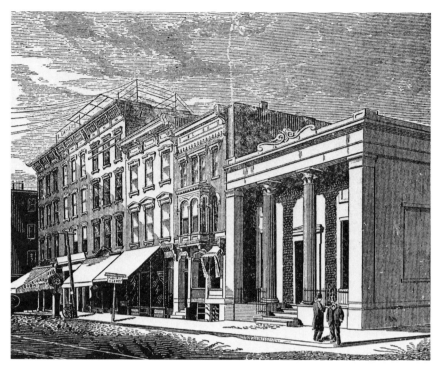

Main Street, looking west (top) and east (above) from Bank Street, was lined with a variety of businesses. From Guide to Norfolk as a Business Centre, *1884. Courtesy, Alderman Library, University of Virginia.*

traced its ancestry to the Portsmouth and Roanoke in the 1830s, became a component of the Seaboard Air Line Railroad, which had its headquarters in Portsmouth for years.

General Lee was welcomed at the Seaboard station when he came to visit in 1870; the people of Portsmouth set their watches by the 6:10 Seaboard train that "traverses the entire breadth of the city," George Nowitzky wrote in 1888; the "new" passenger station of the Seaboard, which

also housed the offices of the railroad, was built in 1894 and given to the city of Portsmouth when the railroad removed to Richmond in 1958.

By 1890 a line from Pinner's Point to Tarboro tied the area to the Atlantic Coast Line system, and in 1895 linked up with the Southern Railway over the same trackage. That was a stopgap for the Southern until it could lease the Atlantic and Danville's tracks in 1899; the latter had gone into receivership and was reorganized in the 1890s. Local rail service was established between Norfolk and Ocean View in 1879 and between Norfolk and Virginia Beach in 1883. The development of the resort dates from the opening of the 18-mile Norfolk and Virginia Beach Railroad, offering passengers a ride of 40 minutes "passing through an interesting and varied country" and terminating at the Princess Anne Hotel, owned and operated by the railroad.

With the passing of Reconstruction and the development of rail travel, those who lived by Norfolk's waters were able to enjoy most of the pleasures typical of the time. Not only were there baseball games and boat races for the sporting, as well as political rallies, public speaking, and other amateur theatricals, but the country's leading thespians included Norfolk as a regular stop on their tours. Edwin Booth appeared as Iago in Norfolk in 1872, Joseph Jefferson played Rip Van Winkle "for the first time in this city" in 1873, and Mrs. Scott Siddons, "the Queen of Tragedy," came to town in 1875.

But the big event socially was the visit of the Russian warships *Svetlana* and *Bogatyr* in 1877, carrying the Grand Dukes Alexis and Constantine and assorted noble retainers. There was considerable excitement among the ladies over the royal visitors. "There was no empty show, false pride, cold formality or stiff haughtiness about any of the Grand Dukes' officers; they were all courteous, pleasant, genteel and sociable, and were at once invited into the best of Norfolk society," Burton wrote in describing the two-month visit. The Norfolk German Club gave a complimentary German, or dance, for the Russian visitors. There was another ball honoring them at the Navy Yard ("the scene was lovely beyond description") and the Russians reciprocated with a reception aboard the *Svetlana.*

This was the age of the great hotels. Old Point Comfort continued to be a popular spa. Ladies brought their daughters to be wooed by the Coast Artillery officers at Fort Monroe. The famous Hygeia Hotel, a favorite prewar resort, was demolished in 1862 for military reasons, but a new one was built on a considerably larger scale. The Hygeia Hotel of 1880 was a frame, gingerbreaded structure with "ample capacity for 600 guests." A decade later it was flanked by the bigger, brick Chamberlin Hotel. (The Hygeia was torn down in 1902; the Chamberlin burned to the ground in 1920. The current hotel of that name opened in 1928.) "Bathing" was becoming popular at both Ocean View and Virginia Beach and the ample "cottages" were crowded in the summer. Ocean View, which had once been a distant resort, was annexed to Norfolk in 1923.

Apart from polite society, there was another and lustier Norfolk. As it had in the past, the city offered the kinds of pleasures sailors are accustomed to find on shore. This was the Norfolk described in 1900 by *Town Topics*, a scandal sheet that was published in New York, as "the wickedest city in the country." Saloons thrived and the city's liquor sellers were a force in its politics. Gambling was widespread. "Prostitution was taking on the aspects of an important industry," as Lenoir Chambers noted in his history of Norfolk's newspapers. "It spread throughout much of the older town and acquired a reputation that attracted business from far beyond Norfolk." This would be a familiar refrain in the press through two world wars.

Norfolk had always been a sailor's town. It was only intermittently a Navy town. That was because there were periods when the Navy was in disrepair physically and disrepute politically. There was no Navy between 1783 and 1798, and an obsolete one prior to the Civil War. By 1880 the American Navy again had sunk to uselessness. As always, there were a few outstanding officers,

Sailors land at Old Point Comfort, a popular spa, during the International Columbian Naval Rendezvous in 1893. The Chamberlain Hotel, on the left, burned down in 1920, and the Hygeia Hotel, on the right, was torn down in 1902. Courtesy, Portsmouth Naval Shipyard Museum.

Right
Located on the beach at Old Point Comfort, the Hygeia Hotel, built in 1880, boasted luxurious features such as 15,000 square feet of glass-encased verandas and a spacious ballroom. The quarter-mile-long hotel was torn down in 1902. From M.B. Hillyard, The New South, 1887.

Facing page:
Top
Built in 1902, the schooner Thomas W. Lawson had seven masts whose names in nautical terminology were foremast, mainmast, mizzenmast, spankermast, jiggermast, drivermast, and pushermast. But the crew preferred a simpler system and called the masts Monday, Tuesday, Wednesday, etc. Courtesy, The Mariners' Museum.

Bottom
Joseph L. Jones depicted a naval review at Hampton Roads in this lithograph dedicated to the Honorable R.W. Thompson, Secretary of the Navy under President Rutherford B. Hayes. The naval vessels shown are (from the left) the Marion, Tallapoosa, Constitution, Kearsarge, Saratoga, Powhatan, Portsmouth, and Minnesota. Courtesy, U.S. Naval Historical Center.

but the service was stagnated by its own seniority system and starved by Congress for funds.

One story suffices. The *Wampanoag* was a cruiser designed by the engineer Benjamin Franklin Isherwood, a genius of steam who was ahead of his time. She was a hybrid—a sailing ship with four funnels, an ugly duckling ordered in 1863 but not completed until 1869. In her trials the *Wampanoag* proved to be the fastest ship in the world. Then the admirals got her. Cut down the number of her boilers to improve her speed under sail, a board decreed. After all, coal was expensive. In any event, the fastest ship in the world was never again to put to sea. She rotted and went to waste, and so did the rest of the Navy vessels left after the Civil War.

The new Navy was born on March 3, 1883, when Congress voted the money to build four steel warships. These were the cruisers *Atlanta*, *Boston*, and *Chicago* and the dispatch boat *Dolphin*. All of them proved to be quirky. But the Navy's revitalization had begun. The Naval War College was opened in 1885 in the former poorhouse in Newport, Rhode Island. One of the teachers was Alfred Thayer Mahan, who published his study *The Influence of Sea Power Upon History* in 1890. And more new ships were built for the new Navy. One was the *Maine,* really an armored cruiser, fated to be remembered as the "battleship" *Maine.*

On the evening of February 15, 1898, just after the bugler had sounded taps, the *Maine* was blown up in Havana harbor. Two hundred and sixty-six officers and men were killed; fewer than a hundred of the crew survived. The cause of the explosion remains unsolved. Admiral Hyman Rickover has speculated that an accidental fire detonated ammunition, but Americans blamed Spain. Jingoism was rampant. The two nations

were at war within weeks.

The Spanish-American War was a mismatch. The American Navy outgunned Spanish squadrons in Cuba and the Philippines, winning hugely popular victories. The conflict was "a splendid little war," Teddy Roosevelt said. And so it was. It propelled Roosevelt to the White House, where he was to be a champion of the Navy. It appeared to prove Mahan's theories. And its implications in Norfolk's waters were far-reaching.

The captured cruiser *Reina Mercedes* was brought to the Navy Yard as a prize and put into service under the American flag. A number of Spanish seamen were treated at the Portsmouth Naval Hospital, including Admiral Cervera, who was accorded the courtesies of his rank. There was a great patriotic stir that translated into appropriations to build the fleet "Manifest Destiny" required of the United States. It was a busy time for the Navy Yard and for the Newport News Shipbuilding and Dry Dock Company, which built a number of the Navy's new warships.

The United States was beginning to flex its muscles to the world. As a result of the Spanish-American War, the Americans acquired the Philippine Islands and Wake Island, a dot in the Pacific that would become famous in the Second World War. There were other developments as American self-confidence grew. The United States annexed Hawaii as a territory. The Samoan Islands were partitioned among Britain, Germany, and the United States. American troops were sent to China to join in suppressing the Boxer Rebellion in 1900. Cuba gained its independence and American troops there were withdrawn in 1902. Americans intervened in the Panamanian revolt and undertook to complete the construction of the Panama Canal begun by the French (the canal would be opened to traffic in 1914). "I ook the Canal Zone," President Roosevelt said. The statement was both typical and true.

The United States acted as peacemaker in the Russo-Japanese War in 1905, and his mediation won President Roosevelt the Nobel Peace Prize the next year. Japan and the United States were becoming the great Pacific powers—rivals—and it was primarily to impress the Japanese that the "Great White Fleet" was sent on its cruise round the world in 1907.

Appropriately, the armada assembled in Hampton Roads—seven of the 16 battleships had been built by the burgeoning Newport News Shipyard. Liberty parties of sailors said their farewell to girls in the local ports, while a ball was given the officers at the Chamberlin Hotel. At 9:45 on the morning of December 16, 1907—the day was warmish and windy—anchors were hoisted and the fleet passed in review, single file. The harbor was filled with small craft, and crowds had gathered on the shore to watch. Shipboard bands played "The Girl I Left Behind Me" and Admiral Robley D. Evans, "Fighting Bob" to the fleet, stood to attention as the *Connecticut* passed the presidential yacht *Mayflower*, where Teddy Roosevelt was proudly watching.

The cruise was a triumph. The Great White Fleet went down one coast of South America and up the other to San Francisco, crossed to Japan, and returned by way of the Suez Canal and Mediterranean, steaming 46,000 miles. Everywhere it received an impressive diplomatic welcome. The battleships symbolized the new status of the United States as a great naval power. The nation had followed the fleet's progress in the newspapers. Americans felt proud of "Fighting Bob" Evans and his ships.

There was a reprise of the earlier scene when the fleet returned to Hampton Roads on February 22, 1909, a year and sixty days later. The morning was raw. Again boats filled the harbor, and again the *Mayflower* and the President were waiting. At mid-morning the first smoke smudged the horizon and it was almost eleven o'clock when the *Connecticut* signaled a 21-gun salute. This time the bands played "There's No Place Like Home." The moment must have been satisfying to Teddy

Roosevelt, who was about to leave the White House.

Actually, the Great White Fleet was obsolete when it sailed. Britain's *Dreadnought,* launched in 1906, mounted 10 big guns; the 16 ships of the Great White Fleet had two forward and two aft, as did the battleships of the day in every fleet. As had the *Monitor* and the *Merrimac,* the *Dreadnought* revolutionized shipbuilding. Americans entered the race willingly. We could build "dreadnoughts" too—*Michigan* and *South Carolina* in 1909, *Delaware* and *North Dakota* in 1910, *Utah* and *Florida* in 1911, *Arkansas* and *Wyoming* in 1912, *New York* and *Texas* in 1914, seven in the First World War, five more in the 1920s. Beyond the ships themselves, the Navy now was somehow special in the eyes of the public. "American mothers don't want their boys to be soldiers, so nothing really big can be done at present about expanding the Army," President Franklin D. Roosevelt said in 1940. "But the Navy is another matter; American mothers don't seem to mind their boys becoming sailors."

In 1910 another event had happened in Hampton Roads that was to revolutionize shipbuilding. The first flight of Orville and Wilbur Wright at Kitty Hawk, North Carolina, in 1903 had set men to thinking that the flying machine

might have military uses. Captain Washington Irving Chambers, an engineer, was converted to the idea of flying machines when he was assigned to handle the mail the Navy was receiving on the subject. He arranged an experiment, using contributed funds and a civilian pilot. Eugene Ely volunteered to fly his Curtiss-Hudson plane off a makeshift platform that was built on the deck of the cruiser *Birmingham.* Wilbur Wright was asked first; he refused.

By November 14, 1910, everything was ready. The inclined platform was just 83 feet long and 22 feet wide, and the distance from the deck's edge to the plane's wheels was 57 feet. The *Birmingham* lay at the mouth of the James River. Ely was supposed to take off while the ship was steaming into the wind. But he did not like the overcast sky and did not want to wait. The 50-horsepower engine was revved up and the biplane rolled off the platform ... dropped from sight, momentarily touched the water, gained flying speed, and climbed into the lowering sky. Five minutes later Ely landed near a row of cottages on the shore. The risky, tricky experiment had succeeded.

Ely was to make more history the next year. On January 18, 1911, he landed his plane on a platform on the stern of the cruiser *Pennsylvania*

while she lay at anchor in the harbor of San Francisco Bay. An hour later, he took off and landed safely on the shore. He had proved that the aircraft carrier could be practical. The dreadnoughts were doomed, though that would not be proved for another 30 years. Ely's reward was a letter of thanks from the Secretary of the Navy. He was killed in a crash later that year. Congress was moved to vote the first funds for naval aviation. The collier *Jupiter* would be converted to the *Langley*, the first American aircraft carrier, nicknamed "the Old Covered Wagon." The work would be done at the Norfolk Navy Yard from 1919 to 1922.

By the turn of the century the commercial possibilities in the great harbor of Hampton Roads, possibilities which had long been recognized by so many visitors, were beginning to be realized. According to the census of 1900, the population of the city of Norfolk proper was 46,624, and it was estimated that 100,000 people lived within a radius of four miles of the courthouse. There were nearly 20,000 people in booming Newport News and almost as many in Portsmouth. The Norfolk County population was 50,780 and Princess Anne County's was 11,192. Annexation would become a big issue as the century waxed.

By 1900 Norfolk already was the largest coaling station in the world, a leading cotton and lum-

ber port, and the largest peanut market in the United States. More than 2,000 men worked at the Norfolk Navy Yard, which was located in Portsmouth, to the bafflement of outsiders. The Newport News Shipyard was bigger and busier, employing more than 5,000. Because of it Newport News ranked second in the state as a manufacturing town. The area around Norfolk's

bage, spinach, peas, beans, radish, lettuce, turnips, beets, onions, melons, potatoes, tomatoes, eggplants, celery, asparagus, strawberries, and numerous similar crops, while many thousands of acres within this circle are devoted to the growing of crops of corn, rye, oats, hay, peanuts, and sweet potatoes and other staple annual crops. The aggregate sales of the truck crops grown in this circle amount to from $3 million to $4 million annually . . .

It is not surprising, then, that the wave of national pride and patriotism that was abroad in the country set off a response locally or that it focused upon the celebration at a site in Tidewater Virginia of the 300th anniversary of the Jamestown settlement. "A great exposition of some kind should be held," argued the *Dispatch* as early as 1901. "Norfolk is undoubtedly the proper place . . . and every historical, business, and sentimental reason can be adduced in favor of the celebration taking place here rather than in Richmond. . . ."

A company was formed in 1902, with General Fitzhugh Lee as its president, and the decision was made to hold the Jamestown Exposition along a mile of rural waterfront. The Sewells Point tract that was bought by the company faced Hampton Roads and was accessible to all of Tidewater Virginia. But problems plagued the Exposition from the start. The General Assembly at first refused to vote any money. The $1 million in capital stock that the charter required by January

waters was a center of truck farming, too. According to a handbook issued by the Commissioner of Agriculture in Richmond in 1893, within a 10-mile radius of Norfolk:

> more than forty thousand acres are entirely devoted to truck crops such as kale, cab-

1, 1904 was not subscribed until the last minute. Fitzhugh Lee died in 1905 and was succeeded by Henry St. George Tucker. The Exposition was planned as a small city and all amenities and services had to be supplied—landscaping, streets and sidewalks, the piers on the waterfront, electricity, lights, the newfangled telephones, water.

The Exposition was an early world's fair. Its amusement area, known as "the War Path," was a carnival of history and thrills. There were representations of the battle of Gettysburg and the fight between the *Monitor* and the *Merrimac*; the echoes of gunfire mingled with the midway's music and the pitchmen's spiels. You could enjoy the Temple of Mirth and ride the miniature railroad or the "Shoot the Chutes." A number of states and territories erected buildings along broad boulevards. Many of the colonial-style mansions have been preserved and now are used as elegant officers' quarters. Pennsylvania's pavilion was a replica of Independence Hall, and also survives today as an architectural monument

to the Jamestown Exposition.

But on April 26, 1907, much still was unfinished when President Roosevelt opened the Exposition. The government piers that would be united by an arch to form an artificial basin supposed to be the showpiece of the fair were not completed. Everywhere there was mess and mud—and embarrassment and explanations. Criticism in the press was widespread. But there was a huge turnout on Virginia Day, with a great parade. The naval review was a success. When the construction was completed by mid-September, the Jamestown Exposition offered a marvelous spectacle. Nevertheless, attendance was disappointing and fewer than half of the nearly three million persons who passed through the Exposition's gates by the time it closed down in November represented *paid* attendance. Whatever its artistic success, the Jamestown Exposition was a financial failure. The company entered receivership within a week. But the Exposition site was there, waiting. Within a few years it would be turned into the greatest naval base in the world.

When I Return
To The
U·S·A·
And You.
March Song
Myrtle Mae McCay
U.S. NAVY
ELCOME
ETURN

CHAPTER SEVEN

TWO WORLD WARS:
1914 - 1945

There is a tablet on the wall above a street corner in Sarajevo, in modern Yugoslavia. It marks the spot where Archduke Franz Ferdinand, the boorish heir to the Hapsburg throne, was assassinated by the boy Gavrilo Princip on the feast of St. Vitus, June 28, 1914. Princip was a Serb. With the backing of the German Kaiser, the Austro-Hungarian Empire presented Serbia with an ultimatum. They went to war. The Czar came to the help of Serbia and on August 1 Germany declared war on Russia. England and France honored their treaties with Russia and the whole of Europe was convulsed within a week.

There were almost 100 million people in the United States in the summer of 1914, and few gave much thought to anything that had happened in Sarajevo. Those who concerned themselves with foreign affairs at all looked to Mexico and our own troubles there; American Marines had seized Vera Cruz in the spring.

The political catchword was "progressive." It was applied to both President Woodrow Wilson and to Teddy Roosevelt, whose candidacy on the Bull Moose ticket in 1912 divided the Republicans and made possible Wilson's winning. Amendments to the Constitution in 1913 had sanctioned the federal income tax and the direct election of United States senators. The suffragettes still were the butt of hundreds of jokes, but their cause was steadily gaining ground.

So was the cause of Prohibition. "During the last six months I have attended forty-seven banquets," Elbert Hubbard reported in the winter of 1913-1914. "Sixteen were dry. Eighteen were semi-arid; these have started with a cocktail and stopped there. The rest, thirteen, were the old-fashioned kind beginning with cocktails, running into wine, and often there were beer and whiskey." The nation was entering happily into the age of the automobile. At the beginning of 1914 Henry Ford had made his historic pronouncement that he would pay his workers a minimum wage of five dollars for an eight-hour day. There were more than a half-million Model Ts on the country's horse-and-buggy roads. The age of advertising was changing the habits of the marketplace. Corsets were shrinking. Cigarette sales were on the upswing. Americans were flocking into the nickelodeons to watch Charlie Chaplin and Douglas Fairbanks and Mary Pickford and a popular serial, *The Perils of Pauline*. Baseball fans were following the Federal League, which would last just two years, as well as familiar heroes like Ty Cobb, who was on his way to his eighth straight batting title, and Walter Johnson, who would win 28 games in the 1914 season. Americans hailed Jack Johnson, laughed at Mr. Dooley, learned the dance steps of Vernon Castle, listened to Enrico Caruso on the gramophone, sang the songs of Irving Berlin, and were

Sheet music of "When I Return to the U.S.A. and You," a popular song during the First World War, papers a Norfolk store window. From the Harry C. Mann Collection of Photographs. Courtesy, Virginia State Library.

saved from their sins by the Reverend Billy Sunday. And on the day Franz Ferdinand was killed in Sarajevo, advertisements invited North Dakotans to see "Buffalo Bill in person" at a Wild West show on the Fourth of July.

The Balkans were far from Norfolk's waters—and the distance from Buffalo Bill in North Dakota to Franz Ferdinand in Sarajevo is unimaginable. Americans were unconcerned when Europe went to war. The events were headlined in the newspapers but it was not our war. "We must be impartial in thought as well as in action," proclaimed President Wilson. "The United States must be neutral in fact as well as in name." Certainly that was the overwhelmingly popular sentiment in the United States and as late as 1916 the political slogan "He kept us out of war" was a factor in the President's reelection.

The conflict had already come home to Norfolk's waters. In March 1915 the *Prinz Eitel Friedrich,* a German liner that had prowled the Pacific as a raider, slipped into Hampton Roads with 80 passengers and 247 seamen from the ships she had sunk. In April another merchant raider, the *Kron Prinz Wilhelm,* sought sanctuary. The German ships, named for two of the Kaiser's sons, were interned at the Norfolk Navy Yard and taken into service when the United States entered the war. Meanwhile, the homesick sailors spent their time in building a German village with materials scrounged from the Navy Yard, and it became a popular spot to visit.

On May 7, 1915, the Germans torpedoed the Cunard liner *Lusitania* off Ireland with a great loss of life. One of the Americans lost was Albert L. Hopkins, president of the Newport News Shipbuilding and Dry Dock Company. Together with the accounts of the atrocities of "the Huns" in Europe—which were mostly untrue—the *Lusitania's* sinking served to turn American thinking on the war. On January 31, 1916, the *Appam,* a captured British ship with a German prize crew, dropped anchor off Newport News. She too was interned, and litigation over the ship ultimately went to the Supreme Court. In the summer of 1916 the German merchant submarine *Deutschland* passed through the Virginia Capes and up Chesapeake Bay to Baltimore, carrying cargo and mail and making a big publicity splash.

Although the United States was officially neutral, the British controlled the high seas. American trade with the Central Powers plummeted from nearly $170 million in 1914 to $1 million in 1916, while trade with the Allies increased from not quite $825 million to $3 billion. Exports from Norfolk and Newport News rose sharply. Coal was the chief export and, after 1917, men and horses by the thousands and all the goods of war were shipped out of Hampton Roads.

In Europe the armies and navies had reached a stalemate by 1917. The butchery in France was fruitless and terrible. At sea, the Battle of Jutland in 1916 had proved a standoff. Neither side was winning the war. Exhaustion now was the policy, and stubbornness the strategy. The last soldier in the trenches would be the winner. And so the Germans gambled on resuming unrestricted submarine warfare. After the *Lusitania* and a blizzard of diplomatic notes from Washington, the Germans had instructed their U-boats not to sink passenger vessels without warning. On January 31, 1917, Ambassador von Bernstorff delivered a new note in Washington: "All sea traffic will be stopped with every available weapon and without further notice."

Almost certainly the decision was going to push the United States into the war. The Germans knew it. But they hoped that the British could be starved into submission and the war won while the Americans were still getting ready. The gamble nearly succeeded. In February the U-boats sank 500,000 tons of shipping, in March more than 600,000, in April nearly 900,000. (In April one out of every four ships that departed English ports was sent to the bottom.) The answer was the convoy system, which Prime Minister Lloyd George ordered over the Admiralty's adamant opposition. Convoys would not work, the admirals said. They were wrong. Fewer than one percent of convoyed ships were sunk. England would not be brought to its knees by U-boats.

As expected, in April 1917 the United States entered the war and, all told, more than two million American troops were sent "over there." The American Expeditionary Force hardly won the war. American battle casualties in France were 48,909 dead and 230,074 wounded. More men died from influenza in the A.E.F. than were killed in the war. (That was true worldwide. In India the flu killed 16 million people.) But when the Armistice came on November 11, 1918, the Americans were the only fresh fighting men—and there appeared to be an endless and swelling torrent of Yanks.

For most of the four million soldiers who were drafted or volunteered, and for the half-million men and some 11,000 "yeomanettes" in the Navy, the First World War was an exhilarating time. But most returned to the farm, or the small town, after they had seen "Paree." The effect on the nation was transitory.

The cities of Hampton Roads, however, were an exception to the rule. They were transformed

Fire fighters had to battle the bitter cold as well as the flames on New Year's Day, 1918, when the Monticello Hotel burned in downtown Norfolk. From the Harry C. Mann Collection of Photographs. Courtesy, Virginia State Library.

by the First World War. Norfolk, Newport News, and Portsmouth turned into boom towns, with all the problems and shortages and stresses that are implied in those two words. The payroll at Newport News Shipbuilding and Dry Dock Company swelled from 7,600 in mid-1917 to more than 12,500 in late 1919. Employment at the Navy Yard in Portsmouth topped 11,000. The Norfolk Shipbuilding and Dry Dock Company increased its work force from 40 in 1916 to 700 in 1918. The new population of war workers needed housing. Cradock in Portsmouth and Hilton Village in Warwick County were born as emergency housing projects.

"Within the space of a few months Norfolk has sprung into the dimensions of a great city," the *Virginian-Pilot* wrote in early 1918. "The population has increased by leaps and bounds, transportation lines are overtaxed with shipments by land and water. ... Business of all kinds has expanded beyond facilities to handle it. Public utilities are inadequate to the business imposed on them." A corollary, inevitably, was discontent and grumbling among the civilian and military newcomers who found themselves in a strange town in wartime. Norfolk would have to struggle with its "bad" reputation through two world wars.

Above
Brigadier General Billy Mitchell proved that bombers could sink battleships in a series of tests in 1921. Here the German dreadnought Ostfriesland, which was turned over to the United States at the end of the First World War, is shown sinking about 75 miles off the mouth of the Chesapeake Bay. Courtesy, U.S. Naval Institute.

Adding to the boom-town problems and the strains of war was the abnormal weather. The harbor was frozen solid for a time in the severe winter of 1917-1918 and the bitter cold was an extra problem for the transients of war. The conditions were dramatized—fire and ice—when the Monticello Hotel in downtown Norfolk burned on January 1, 1918. NORFOLK SWEPT BY GREATEST FIRE IN ITS HISTORY, screamed the *Virginian-Pilot* in its biggest headline type.

Meanwhile, the waters around Norfolk were filled with ships—battleships camouflaged in painted zig zags; colliers carrying fuel to heat the homes of the Eastern Seaboard; the armada of supply ships and transports that took 288,000 troops to France from Hampton Roads, together with everything they needed over there.

But the daily drama in the harbor was less significant than what was happening on shore. The character of Hampton Roads was transformed in 1917-1918 and this time the change would not

be transitory. What would become the greatest naval base in the United States was created on the former site of the Jamestown Exposition, which was bought by the government in 1917. The Army constructed its own modern terminals at Sewells Point, and by 1919 had spent $30 million there. A drydock to accommodate the biggest of battleships was built at the Navy Yard in Portsmouth, and there was a considerable expansion of the facilities of the Naval Hospital. An air base was built at Langley Field on the Peninsula. An artillery range was established at Mulberry Island in the James River and Camp Eustis was constructed nearby; some 20,000 passed through the training center there.

After the boys came home and normalcy returned, the bustle and expansion of the war years yielded to a peacetime somnolence. But the changes in the destiny, the economy, and the geography of Hampton Roads were permanent. The blueprints for the growth that was to come to Norfolk's waters in the Second World War were drawn in the years from 1917 to 1919.

"Prohibition makes you want to cry into your beer," archy the cockroach, the creation of humorist Don Marquis, philosophized, "and denies you the beer to cry into." The issue was critical to the nation's politics from the late 19th century until Repeal was voted.

It certainly dominated the politics of Virginia, where James Cannon, Jr., a Methodist preacher, took the lead in the activities of the Anti-Saloon League. He would become Bishop Cannon—"the Dry Messiah"—and for a time the most powerful politician in the state. As early as 1908 legislation was passed to ban liquor sales in the state, except in "cities, towns of over 500 population, summer resorts, and areas contiguous to cities where there was police protection." Nevertheless, the *Landmark* reported in 1909 that dealers daily shipped from 10 to 12 carloads of liquor from Norfolk into the dry sections of North Carolina and Virginia. In 1914 Secretary of the Navy Josephus Daniels banned alcohol on Navy ships, and in the same year Virginia voted to adopt Prohibition statewide, 94,251 to 63,886, with Norfolk and Richmond voting wet. It went into effect November 1, 1916. The law, which came to be known as the "Quart-a-Month Act," permitted the purchase of a quart of whiskey, a gallon of wine, or three gallons of beer monthly from out-of-state suppliers, but banned their production or sale in Virginia. When the Eighteenth Amendment was proposed at the end of 1917, Virginia was the second state in the Union to ratify it, conforming the law of the nation to the practice of the state. Inevitably, it meant that rum-running would be one of the activities pursued in Norfolk's waters until the law proved unworkable.

From 1914 to 1919 the cost of living in Norfolk went up 107 percent, according to Department of Labor statistics that were published in the local papers in 1920, to the accompaniment of comments reminiscent of those printed in the Reconstruction years. Following the national pattern, there was a downturn in the local economy in the early twenties. The war-born boom ended for real estate speculators. Employment at the Newport News and Portsmouth shipyards sank to between 2,000 and 2,500, and the Washington naval treaties of 1922 stopped construction on capital ships. (The *Constellation* and the *Iowa*, being built in Newport News, and the *North Carolina*, being built in Portsmouth, were scrapped under the treaties.) But commerce continued to flourish and there was a gratifying increase in imports, though the export of coal, cotton, and tobacco continued to be the mainstay of the Hampton Roads trade. Conditions were very bad in Newport News. Renovation of the former troop transport *Leviathan* at a calculated loss saved the shipyard.

City government improved markedly. The city manager system was adopted by Portsmouth in 1916, Norfolk in 1918, and Newport News in 1920. Annexation added to Norfolk's and Portsmouth's population. Municipal services were improved to keep pace with the area's growth in the war. Locally and nationally the economy improved. The Cavalier Hotel was built at Virginia

Facing page, top
On October 12, 1918, an F-5 seaplane taxies into the wind on the waters of Hampton Roads. From the National Archives.

Below
Tents were used as hangars at the Naval Air Station in 1917. Buildings from the Jamestown Exposition of 1907 can be seen to the right, and beyond, the coal pier. Courtesy, U.S. Naval Institute.

Above
Norfolk and vicinity are shown in this 1921 bird's-eye view. Note the railroad station (bottom right) and the expanse of farmland at the top. Courtesy, Library of Congress.

Beach, and became an immediate landmark. The James River Bridge, then the longest in the world, was opened in 1928. Times were good.

In 1925 Harry Flood Byrd gained the governor's seat and instituted what was considered a progressive program in the state at the time. He also assumed the leadership of the Democratic organization in Virginia, and would be its acknowledged master for 40 years, resigning his seat in the U. S. Senate in 1965 so that his son, Harry F. Byrd, Jr., might be appointed in his stead. The "Byrd machine" was to run the state until the civil rights revolution and the revival of the Republicans in Virginia, and its conservative political truths appear to be marching on today.

Calvin Coolidge choose not to run for reelec-

tion in 1928 and the Republicans turned to Herbert Hoover, who won in a landslide. The Democrat, Governor Alfred C. Smith of New York, was a Catholic, a "wet," and contaminated by Tammany Hall, thus triply unacceptable to many Southerners. Hoover captured Virginia and carried Norfolk and Portsmouth. In his final message on the State of the Union, at the end of 1928, President Coolidge told the American people that they might "regard the present with satisfaction and anticipate the future with optimism." So it seemed. Business was thriving. Automobile production would peak at 5.36 million in 1929. As many as a million Americans were speculating in the stock market, and it appeared that a lot of them were "getting rich quick." By September 1929 the amount of loans to those who were buying on margin—speculating with borrowed money—reached $8.5 billion, or approximately half the national debt in those thrifty times. Then the bottom fell out of the market in October 1929.

Whether the Crash caused the Depression or vice versa is a chicken-and-egg question for economists to ponder. But the collapse of the economy followed the collapse of the market. "The economy is fundamentally sound," Hoover reiterated, but by 1932 manufacturing had slumped to half the level of 1929.

Steel production fell from 40.6 million tons

in 1930 to 13.6 million in 1932. In the same period retail trade shrank from $8.1 billion to $4.1 billion. More than 80,000 businesses closed their doors. A total of 5,504 banks failed from 1930 to the bank moratorium decreed by President Roosevelt in early 1933. Farm income in 1932 was less than half of what it had been in 1930—and the farmer had not shared in the boom times of the twenties. Average family income shrank from $2,300 in 1929 to less than $1,600 in 1932. The most painful statistic was unemployment: it exceeded 4 million in 1930, 8 million in 1931, and 12 million in 1932, when one in five of the normal work force was out of a job. More than 100,000 American workers applied for jobs in the Soviet Union; there were none to be had at home.

The election of Franklin D. Roosevelt was a foregone conclusion in 1932, and he was inaugurated on March 4, 1933, saying: "The only thing we have to fear is fear itself." The New Deal was launched in Washington and, in Robert Bendiner's words, the gloomy depression of Herbert Hoover was replaced by the exhilarating depression of Franklin D. Roosevelt. As late as 1940 there were still more than seven million unemployed. The American economy suffered throughout the thirties, a decade equated with hard times, and did not really recover until the coming of the Second World War.

In Norfolk there was an early hint of trouble when the Guaranty Title and Trust Company closed in the summer of 1929. After the crash in October the *Virginian-Pilot* still was guardedly

optimistic. "The country has passed through a disturbing experience, and, everything considered, has kept its head remarkably well," the paper said at the turn of the year. "The prevailing view is one of confidence tempered with caution."

The optimism was unfounded. The Seaboard Air Line Railroad went into receivership in 1930, to be followed by the Norfolk Southern in 1932. Farmers suffered from drought and falling prices. The big hotels, those citadels of good times, went under. At the beginning of 1932 citizens owed the

City of Norfolk upwards of $4 million in delinquent real estate taxes. Belt-tightening was the general response. On January 13, 1932, Governor John Garland Pollard recommended a 10 percent reduction in the salaries of all state workers and cut his own pay. City employees in Norfolk took a 10 percent cut in 1932 and for most the reduction reached twice that or more by the next spring. There was a 10 percent pay cut and a shortening of the workweek at the Newport News shipyard in 1932, and another 10 percent slash the following year.

But the Navy still was spending about $20 million a year in the Norfolk vicinity, and the Newport News shipyard won a contract in 1930 for the USS *Ranger*, the first ship to be built from scratch as an aircraft carrier, and another contract, in 1933, to build the carriers *Yorktown* and *Enterprise*. (The *Langley*, the experimental first flattop, was a converted collier; the *Lexington* and *Saratoga* were built on battle cruiser hulls.) The *Ranger* was completed in 1934, the *Yorktown* in 1937, and the *Enterprise* in 1938. As the disarmament that the democracies had introduced in the twenties yielded to the reluctant rearmament of the thirties, the area benefited economically from the Navy's program of shipbuilding. The carrier *Hornet* was launched at Newport News in 1940, and would be followed by eight *Essex*-class carriers in the war years. The battleship *Indiana* was built in Newport News, and the *Alabama* in Portsmouth.

The thirties were a decade of depression world-

wide. They were also a time when people sensed the inevitability of another global war as aggressors moved against their weakened victims. The Japanese invaded Manchuria in 1931, and then marched into China. The League of Nations proved to be an empty shell when Mussolini sent troops into Ethiopia in 1935. The Spanish Civil War, which began in 1936 and ended in March 1939, served as a dress rehearsal for the Second World War. Hitler moved into the demilitarized Rhineland in 1936, repudiated the Treaty of Versailles in 1937, and swallowed Austria and Czechoslovakia in 1938. His invasion of Poland on September 1, 1939, started the Second World War. It would last six years and take the lives of more than 50 million persons, some of whom would die in Hiroshima and Nagasaki when the atomic bomb ended the war.

Americans would remember 1939 nostalgically. It was the year when the New York Yankees' Lou Gehrig was benched by his fatal illness while his team swept toward their fourth straight world's championship. The New York World's Fair, symbolized by the Trylon and Perisphere, gave us a look at the future. Orson Welles' radio broadcast of a fictional Martian invasion spooked thousands. John Steinbeck's *The Grapes of Wrath* was praised widely. Broadway cheered Tallulah Bankhead in *The Little Foxes*, Katharine Hepburn in *The Philadelphia Story* and Ethel Merman in *Du Barry Was a Lady*. *Helzapoppin* and *The Man Who Came to Dinner* also had long runs on the stage. *Gone With the Wind* and *The Wizard of Oz* were among the hit movies, and Shirley Temple, who was getting older at 10, still was Number One at the box office. The King and Queen of England visited the White House.

When Britain declared war on Germany, there was no question where American sympathies were. "This nation will remain a neutral nation," President Roosevelt said in September, "but I cannot ask that every American remain neutral in thought as well."

Americans would be debating the issues of isolationism and preparedness for the next two years and, as late as the summer of 1941, the House of Representatives was barely willing to extend the draft. It won by the narrowest of votes, 203 to 202. But Roosevelt, who in 1940 would become the first President to be elected to a third term, was resolute in the White House. After the collapse of France, Roosevelt, the graduation speaker at the University of Virginia, was contemptuous of Italy's intervention at the last minute. "The hand that held the dagger has struck it into the back of its neighbor," the Presi-

Fire swept the Norfolk waterfront on June 7, 1931. The blaze, reportedly started by a blast on an oil barge, spread rapidly over seven business blocks east of Commercial Place and south of Main Street and raged for five hours. Sixty business establishments were damaged or destroyed, and losses were estimated at two million dollars. From the National Archives.

dent said. There would be no neutrality now. "Let us not hesitate. The whole of our sympathies lie with those nations which are giving their life blood in combat."

General George C. Marshall had been appointed as the Army's chief of staff in 1939. Politics-as-usual was put aside. Frank Knox was named Secretary of the Navy and Henry L. Stimson, Secretary of War. Both were prominent Republicans. Big Bill Knudsen, the president of General Motors, and Edward R. Stettinius, Jr., the chairman of U. S. Steel, were recruited to direct the drive for preparedness. The bases-for-destroyers deal was made in September 1940, when the Battle of Britain was starting. In November the voters ratified Roosevelt's view of the war. "We must be the great arsenal of democracy," the President proclaimed in the first week of January. Congress enacted the Lend-Lease Bill by mid-March, and in the summer of 1941 Churchill and Roosevelt met in Newfoundland waters on warships and signed the Atlantic Charter. By the fall of that year the U.S. Navy was already fighting an undeclared war against German U-boats in Atlantic waters. The destroyer *Kearny* was torpedoed and then the old four-piper *Reuben James* was sunk.

As it had in the First World War, the conflict in Europe invaded Norfolk's waters before the United States officially went to war. The part that the city was to play was recognized when President Roosevelt, who had just been nominated for a third term, chose to come to Norfolk on an inspection tour on July 29, 1940. He visited the Navy Yard, where a thousand workers were being added each month, and then was driven to the Naval Base, created when he was Assistant Secretary of the Navy in 1917. It bustled with construction since more than 1,000 acres of land had been condemned in June to expand the Naval Air Station. "A year from now we are going to be a lot safer," Roosevelt said.

The people of Norfolk championed the British cause wholeheartedly. "Bundles for Britain" was popular volunteer work, and in 1941 Norfolk residents were given the opportunity to extend Southern hospitality to the men of the Royal Navy. The aircraft carrier *Illustrious* came into port on May 12, 1941, four months after she had been badly bombed in the Mediterranean, patched up, and sent around the Cape of Good Hope to be repaired at the Navy Yard under the Lend-Lease program. Friendships were made in the six months the *Illustrious* stayed, while the carrier's flight deck was extended and the after-deck largely rebuilt. Five days after Pearl Harbor, the *Illustrious* and the *Formidable*, another Brit-

ish carrier repaired in Norfolk, sailed with American aircraft to be delivered to the United Kingdom.

By 1940 boom conditions and defense dollars were fueling a repeat of the World War I story in and around Norfolk. The area was crowded with newcomers and the inevitable housing shortage would not be relieved by the construction of thousands of emergency dwelling units in the war years. The cost of living was rising rapidly. People grumbled over shortages and inadequate services. "A restaurant, no matter how bad its food, how ill kept its tables, how dilettante or hectic its service, how shoddy its walls and floors and front, can do a land-office business here at the moment, and will for the duration, simply because there is always a line of defense workers, soldiers, sailors waiting for a table," a customer lamented in the

In 1921 at the Norfolk Navy Yard, the collier Jupiter *was transformed into the first aircraft carrier in the U.S. Navy, the* Langley *(CV-1). The* Langley *was commissioned in 1922 and sunk by Japanese planes while serving as a seaplane tender in 1942. From the National Archives. Courtesy, Portsmouth Naval Shipyard Museum.*

Virginian-Pilot in September 1941. (Note the reference to "the duration" when the United States was not yet in the war.) And, of course, the old tensions surfaced. Norfolk complained about the sailors; the sailors complained about Norfolk.

Whether they had eaten Sunday dinner at home or in an ill-kept restaurant, most in Norfolk still were digesting the midday meal when they heard the news of the attack on Pearl Harbor on December 7, 1941. The city manager ordered the arrest of all alien Japanese as soon as he heard the news, and an extra edition of the *Virginian-Pilot* was on the streets by six o'clock. But in many respects the city had already been at war for two years. Soon it would come to terms with blackouts and civil defense and rationing and spy scares, and people would be explaining every problem with the ritual refrain, "Don't you know there's a war on?"

Anybody could see that. Civilians found that the sentries at the gates to the military bases were a lot stricter. Bananas disappeared. (In April 1942 a federal inspector could find just 14 in all of Norfolk.) Somebody stole the city tire adminis-

trator's spare tire. In 1943 the city council enacted an ordinance that made it a misdemeanor to throw away a tin can. Small boys were fascinated by the searchlights installed in the dunes of Virginia Beach, and further intrigued when landing craft practiced in the surf there. (Since the skippers were beginners, the landing craft constantly got stuck.) It was difficult to escape the fact that there was a war on.

And a real war. In the first months of 1942 a comparative handful of German U-boats (there were never more than a dozen operating at one time) prowled the coastal waters of the United States with complete inpunity, sinking ships wherever they found them. A favorite hunting ground was off Cape Hatteras, and the heavily laden tanker was the favorite victim. One U-boat commander named Mohr radioed to Admiral Doenitz in Germany:

The new-moon night is black as ink.
Off Hatteras the tankers sink
While sadly Roosevelt counts the score—
Some fifty thousand tons—by Mohr.

On the last night in March the U-574 shelled and sank a tugboat and three barges off Cape Charles; there were two survivors. A tanker was sunk off Cape Henry the same night while picking up a pilot. It was mid-April before the first German submarine was destroyed in American coastal waters or the bright lights that had silhouetted the ships against the night sky were effectively doused. What the men of the U-boats called "the American shooting season" was finally brought to an end when a coastal convoy system and air patrols were set up. By that time, it had ceased to be big news when the oil-soaked survivors of another ship were brought into Norfolk.

The most dramatic incident occurred on June 15, 1942, in plain sight of thousands who were splashing in the surf or sunning themselves at Virginia Beach. Two vessels were outbound offshore, routinely, when the crowd heard a distant, dull explosion, followed by a second, and soon witnessed a busy counterattack on the supposed U-boat. Aircraft, a blimp, and Coast Guard and Navy patrol vessels sped to the scene. Actually, the ships had hit mines (ours, not theirs) and had not been torpedoed. But the episode fueled rumors and eyewitnesses were certain they had seen the ships sunk by a submarine, and even seen the sinking of the sub too. And, indeed, the incident has gone into history that way: "Burning tankers were not infrequently sighted from fashionable Florida resorts," Samuel Eliot Morison wrote in *The Two-Ocean War*, "and on June 15 two large American freighters were torpedoed by a U-boat within full view of thousands of pleasure-seekers at Virginia Beach."

There was another event in 1942 that brought the war home to Norfolk. Hampton Boulevard was closed to civilians one October Sunday while an endless parade of jeeps, trucks, and military vehicles went by, bound for a destination secret to all but a few. Something big was up. It was the invasion of North Africa, and this was the mounting of Task Force A.

The Western Task Force, which was to land at three points on the Atlantic coast of French Morocco, above and below Casablanca (the movie that later made the city familiar to Americans was filmed on Warner's back lot in the same year), was mounted and staged in Norfolk's waters. The convoy cleared Hampton Roads at dawn on October 24. It carried 33,737 fighting men, under the command of Major General George S. Patton, Jr., and 2,846 vehicles aboard 28 cargo ships and transports. Also aboard were a miscellany of war correspondents, diplomats, interpreters, and Navy personnel who would be the crews of the landing craft. The escort forces were commanded by Rear Admiral H. K. Hewitt.

The Navy succeeded in steering the convoy past the German U-boats undetected. It arrived at the offshore rendezvous without the loss of a man or ship, though the U-boats were able to score several kills among the fleet following the landings on the morning of November 8. Operation Torch, as the assault was called, was a success. One reason was the logistical planning that had led to the loading of the combat vehicles, ammunition, gasoline, rations, and supplies so that they might be off-loaded in the order they would be wanted. The invasion of North Africa, and particularly the part played by Task Force A, was one

of the most notable operations of the war. It schooled those who directed the later landings in the Mediterranean, the Pacific, and the cross-channel epic of June 6, 1944.

In 1942 at the battle of Midway, in the deserts of North Africa, during the siege of Stalingrad, the tide turned in the war. Meanwhile, the United States was retooling its industry for war. Americans built more than 85,000 tanks, nearly 300,000 airplanes, almost three million machine guns, and more than eight million tons of ships for the U.S. Navy and 55 million tons of merchant shipping—and did so while 15 million men and women went into uniform. The arsenal of democracy overflowed. Americans armed and equipped not only our own fighting men, but also British, Chinese, Dutch, French, Poles, Russians—whoever was fighting on our side.

The Hampton Roads Port of Embarkation was activated on June 15, 1942. As in World War I, its headquarters was located in the Newport News

125

Post Office. Throughout the war it was under the command of Brigadier General John R. Kilpatrick, who had run Madison Square Garden in peacetime. In a little over three years, nearly a million troops and more than 12 million tons of cargo were dispatched overseas on more than 3,000 ships. The port ranked third in total tonnage, after New York and San Francisco. On September 16, 1942, the first prisoners of war to reach Norfolk arrived, guarded by Polish soldiers, aboard the *Mauretania*. After the African campaign, where much of the Afrika Korps surrendered in Tunisia, the flow of POWs was steady. All told, the figure was 134,293 by V-J Day. As early as the end of 1943, combat veterans were coming home through Norfolk. But the large-scale movement started with the wounded, who were brought by hospital ships, and after V-E Day the flood of GIs headed for home topped 625,000.

To accommodate all the cargo, to house and train the men, to feed and fuel the ships, to load them with supplies and troops, to treat the wounded, to do everything that needed to be done, and done in a hurry, it was necessary to expand the bases built for the First World War and to build new ones. Existing facilities were modernized. The army base was renovated and

restored to service. Above Newport News some 1,700 acres of piney woods were turned into Camp Patrick Henry, a staging area where troops waited anywhere from a few days to two weeks to board convoys going overseas and, later in the war, where they returned to hot showers, steak dinners, and the chance to call home. By January 31, 1946, a total of 1,412,107 men and women had passed through the gates at Patrick Henry.

On the Norfolk side of the water, a gunnery school was established in the dunes at Dam Neck. Richard Eberhart later would write a poem about antiaircraft guns at night, and the flowers formed in the night sky by the tracers:

They do not know the dream-like vision ascending / In me, one mile away: they had not thought of that.

An air station was built in the fields near Oceana. The farm whose account books had once preoccupied Littleton Waller Tazewell was transformed into the amphibious base at Little Creek, where boys from Chicago or the cornfields of Iowa were trained to handle landing craft in all their awkward variety.

The cities of Hampton Roads were overcrowded, overtaken, overwhelmed in the war

Left
Brigadier General John R. Kilpatrick commanded the Hampton Roads Port of Embarkation during the Second World War. He had run Madison Square Garden before the port was activated on June 15, 1942. Courtesy, U.S. Army Transportation Museum, Fort Eustis.

Below
Warships docked at the Norfolk Naval Base piers in 1944 included the battleship Missouri, *and the battle cruiser* Alaska *(CB-1). From the National Archives.*

years. The normal population of Newport News was roughly 35,000 and soon there were that many people working in the shipyard alone. Portsmouth, too, was saturated with war workers. By early 1943 employment at the Navy Yard was nearly 43,000—and expansion had more than doubled the facility's physical size.

Norfolk was overpopulated, but hardly overlooked. It was criticized in *Collier's* magazine in 1942 and labeled "Our Worst War Town" in the *American Mercury* in 1943. Bedrooms rented in shifts. Within 90 days of the establishment of the Norfolk Housing Authority in 1940, the ground had been broken for the first "defense housing" project of 500 units and the first families moved into Merrimack Park in the spring of 1941. By the fall of 1943 more than 14,000 dwellings had been built in Norfolk and more than 10,000 in Portsmouth. Some would be temporary and others remain as reminders of the war years. Still the housing supply never seemed to catch up to the demands of servicemen and war workers.

The shortage of living space was only one of many; there were also shortages of coffee, fuel oil, gasoline, liquor, meat, and sugar. As everywhere else on the home front, the citizens of Norfolk patriotically supported the war. They contributed to blood drives, paper drives, scrap metal drives. A civilian defense effort waxed at the beginning of the war and waned when we began to sense victory. Elias Codd, a delicatessen owner, personally sold some three million dollars worth of war bonds. Norfolk's people were working hard, many were making a lot of money, and most went home at night tired but satisfied.

There was another city that was home to the sailors and strangers. "By tacit agreement," as Marvin W. Schlegel wrote in *Conscripted City: The Story of Norfolk in World War II*:

the sailors had been allotted East Main Street from the ferry landings to the Union Station. It was a street fitted out with everything a sailor could possibly ask for—except peace and relaxation. It was lined with glaring neon lights and blaring juke boxes. It held the dingy Gaiety, where sailors could get a close-up revelation of feminine charms. There were penny arcades with peep shows and shooting galleries and stands where an accurate baseball thrower could knock a girl out of bed. There were tattoo parlors and flophouses. Everywhere there were barrooms. There was plenty of wine, women, and song to be had for the right price.

This was the sailor-on-liberty's turf. It was policed by the Shore Patrol, which kept an eye on the sailors, and by Norfolk's Vice Squad, which kept an eye on the girls. Beyond East Main Street there were a number of after-hours clubs in Norfolk and Princess Anne counties, offering vice and occasional violence. A large part of Norfolk County was declared out of bounds to Navy personnel in 1943 after a brawl ended in the killing of a sailor. The club owners, gamblers, and prostitutes preyed upon the sailors, who were often willing victims, and the atmosphere attracted civilian drifters and juveniles who got into trouble too. "Allotment Annies," the girls who married servicemen who were about to go overseas, plied their trade. One was Elvira Tayloe, a 17-year-old

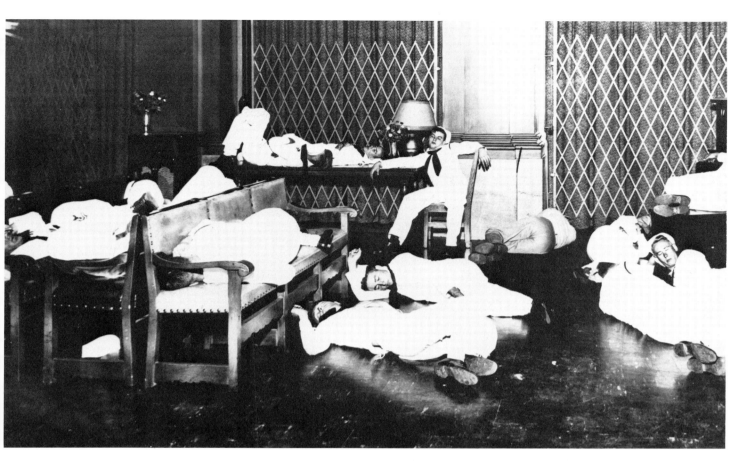

hostess in Norfolk who had married six servicemen and was looking for Number Seven when the authorities got her: two of her husbands met in an English pub and found that they both were carrying pictures of the same wife.

On the morning of June 6, 1944, sirens sounded to wake Norfolk to the news of D-Day on the radio. The death of President Roosevelt in the spring of 1945 shocked the nation, but it was followed shortly by the rejoicing of V-E Day, May 8. By June shiploads of soldiers were coming home from the European Theater to Norfolk's waters. In August came the news that atomic bombs had dropped on Hiroshima and Nagasaki, and then that the Japanese had surrendered. August 14 was another celebration, V-J Day.

But the Pacific war was not Norfolk's war, and already thoughts were turning to the city's postwar problems. On the morning after V-J Day one sailor suggested a solution in the pages of the *Virginian-Pilot*. "My postwar plan for Norfolk," he wrote, "is as follows: Bring all the ships of the Navy to Norfolk as soon as possible after peace has been declared and anchor them out in the bay. ... After the ships have been provisioned and their magazines filled to capacity, I suggest these ships shell Norfolk and all its money-hungry citizens off the face of the earth."

Above
At 4:22 in the morning, there weren't any beds for the sailors who were forced to sleep on the floor of the Navy YMCA. During World War II Norfolk suffered a severe housing shortage. (NRHA)

Left
A couple jitterbugs at a dance held for the crew of the USS Kasaan Bay (CVE-69) in 1944. From the National Archives.

129

CHAPTER EIGHT

POST WAR AND MID 20TH CENTURY: 1945-1982

When the boys came home in 1945, one in every 10 Virginians was living near Norfolk's waters. The figure is one in five today. That may be the best index to what has happened to the region since the Second World War.

In 1946, two ancient boats of the Old Bay Line remained in service and one Norfolk and Washington packet still was running to the capital city. The best of the Bay boats had been handed over to the British in 1942, and one subsequently wound up in the Mediterranean as the *Exodus* in 1947. You could ride passenger trains too. You took the boat over to the Eastern Shore to catch the Pennsylvania train to Philadelphia and New York. Norfolk passengers rode the C & O Railway's transfer steamer *Virginia* to Newport News to catch the westbound trains to Richmond and beyond. (The *Virginia* was a familiar sight in local waters for fifty years, affectionately known as "Smokey Joe" and not scrapped until 1951.) Of course, the automobile was getting to be the usual way of going places, but you still took the ferry from Norfolk to Portsmouth, or to Newport News, or to the Eastern Shore. Not until the Fifties and Sixties would the bridges and tunnels be built that would end the region's geographic isolation from the rest of the state—an isolation sometimes translated into cultural, economic, or political separation.

In 1946 there were no shopping centers; they would come with the flight to the suburbs in the postwar years. "Downtown" meant Granby Street in Norfolk, or High Street in Portsmouth, or Washington Avenue in Newport News. And if Carolina ladies liked to come to Norfolk to shop, the ladies of Norfolk often went to Richmond to buy things, as you left Norfolk to attend college or to go to a good museum or to see a show. In 1946 the entire nation was experiencing peacetime as a problem, albeit a happy problem. The catchword was "reconversion." One of Bill Mauldin's cartoons, drawn when he came home from overseas, showed a landlady saying to a veteran, "You soldiers just don't understand our problems." Housing was a major one. So were jobs, shortages, strikes—stimulating a desire generally to blame somebody for what went wrong. The discontent led to the election in 1946 of the first Republican Congress since the days of Herbert Hoover, soon to be stigmatized by President Truman as the "do-nothing" Eightieth Congress. It fed the growing meanness in politics that Joe McCarthy would exploit in the early Fifties.

Norfolk's problems had been garishly spotlighted in the war years. Now it was necessary to do something about them. In the cities of Newport News and Portsmouth, the big worry was the inevitable peacetime retrenchment of the shipyards. But there was to be no repeat of the extended slump of the Twenties. Employment fell to

Virginia National Bank towers over the Norfolk skyline, as downtown buildings silently watch a passing sailboat at sunrise. Courtesy, City of Norfolk.

an average of 7,200 at the Newport News Shipbuilding and Drydock Company in 1950 and to just over 9,000 in the Portsmouth naval shipyard that year, and then turned up with the Korean War. It would be sustained by the defense spending of the next 30 years.

Elsewhere on the fringes of Hampton Roads life in 1946 remained rural, segregated, and very much what it had been before the war. The passionate struggle to level the walls of "separate but equal" was still to be waged. Ahead too were the consolidations, first on the Peninsula and then to avert annexation around Norfolk and Portsmouth, that would bring into being, by the mid-Seventies, the seven cities circling Norfolk's waters. Change was coming to each of them, and Norfolk's would be the most startling transformation.

The business leadership in Norfolk had already started to exert its influence in the public sphere in a coherent, coordinated fashion in the Thirties. One of its first undertakings was a slum clearance commission organized in 1935, and another was the revival of the Community Fund in 1939. The leading personalities were Charles L. Kaufman, a lawyer who may have had more to do with determining Norfolk's direction over a longer period of time than anybody in the city's history, and Oscar F. Smith, a colorful personality who died in 1950.

Although its beginnings can be traced to the Thirties and the war years, the making of the new Norfolk really started in 1946. It began with the city council election of 1946, which brought into

city hall the kind of "businessman's government" that was to run things thereafter. Colonel Charles B. Borland, who had been the city manager of Norfolk since 1938, had resigned at the end of 1945 in a spat with the city council. He was given a testimonial, and a group of civic leaders, including Charles Kaufman and Oscar Smith, resolved to run their own ticket. They chose Richard D. Cooke, a lawyer; Pretlow Darden, an automobile dealer; and John Twohy II, who ran a sand and gravel business, as the candidates of the "People's Ticket." All were new to politics, promising "businesslike government, free from political influences" and pledging not to seek a second term.

The campaign was heated. Borland and the city's newspapers supported the Cooke-Darden-Twohy ticket. The June turnout of 17,000 voters (this was poll-tax Virginia, where few voted) was the highest in the history of Norfolk, topping the Roosevelt-Willkie vote in 1940 and the Roosevelt-Dewey vote in 1944. The "People's Ticket" won by nearly two to one over the Organization's slate.

Since the city council had only five members then, the newcomers were in control of city hall. Cooke was chosen as mayor in September and served two years, followed by Darden for the next two. In 1950 the business elements made peace with the politicians (Clerk of Courts W.L. Prieur, Jr., was the Byrd machine's Norfolk satrap) and acted on Darden's suggestion that they "get together behind three good men." The result was the "Harmony Ticket" of 1950, which brought W. Fred Duckworth into city hall.

Norfolk had traded a Chevrolet for a Ford

Darden operated the Colonial Chevrolet dealership, Duckworth ran Cavalier Ford) and would get good mileage out of Mayor Duckworth, who held the job for 12 years. He had a bulldozer directness that was well suited to the task of urban renewal, and his successor as mayor was another forceful businessman-in-politics, Roy B. Martin, Jr., who filled the post for an additional dozen years.

After an interlude of two years and another election that was fought over the firing of a second city manager, Vincent J. Thomas was elected mayor of Norfolk in 1976. From Cooke's election in 1946 to Mayor Thomas', the continuity of city government in Norfolk was extraordinary; the city's physical and spiritual transformation was made possible by the politics of progress-plus-stability.

The first significant step that the Cooke-Darden-Twohy team took in 1946 was to bring C.A. Harrell to Norfolk from Schenectady, New York, as city manager. Symbolically, Harrell's first act was to put the city's street cleaners into uniform. The big cleanup was getting started, a sweep that would not be limited to the city's streets.

In 1946 the bottle clubs, numbers, and prostitution still were wide open. The city's police, who had been overworked and underpaid in the war years, inevitably were subject to temptation. One afternoon in 1948 Captain C.J. Staylor assembled a dozen policemen at the ball park to raid two well-known joints on Church Street. No member of the vice squad was involved, and both the chief of police and the city's director of public safety were out of town. As he later testified, Staylor was not expecting to find what turned up—a list of Norfolk policemen who presumably were being paid for protection.

There was a scandal, and a grand jury recommended that the department be reorganized. The chief of police resigned and was replaced by Amor LeRoy Sims, a cocky disciplinarian who had been a brigadier general in the Marine Corps. Staylor would ultimately become chief of police, and then would be elected to the city council when he retired. Chief Sims, who brought his swagger stick to his new post, saw to a crackdown within the city limits of Norfolk.

But the after-hours clubs continued to flourish in both Norfolk and Princess Anne counties, and gambling was open and public in the resort of Virginia Beach until it was "exposed" in the pages of the *Virginian-Pilot*. It made a classic story in the *Front Page* tradition, with pictures snapped by a camera concealed in a cigarette package. There was another grand jury and an inconclusive investigation; the cleanup of the coun-

ties would be a corollary of the consolidation creating the cities of Virginia Beach and Chesapeake.

By 1950, there had been a police shake-up in Norfolk, with the result that the American Social Hygiene Association could say that the city "is as free from prostitution as any community of its size in the country." (By contrast, in 1947 it had reported that Norfolk's VD rate was the highest in the nation.) Although the police reform was the most spectacular undertaken while Harrell was running City Hall, it was hardly the only one. The city manager saw through to completion the construction of a new municipal airport (to be replaced by a bigger one in the Seventies) and a $13-million improvement of the water system. Buses replaced trolleys. There was a new building code, a new city code, a new zoning ordinance, and a minimum housing code. The Norfolk Department of Parks and Recreation and the Norfolk Port Authority were set up. Hampton Boulevard and Granby Street were widened under a new highway plan. The first Portsmouth tunnel was undertaken, and Norfolk's program of slum clearance and redevelopment was launched.

Mayor Roy B. Martin, Jr., a businessman-in-politics, was the chief personality in Norfolk politics in the 1960s. He succeeded W. Fred Duckworth as mayor and served in that post for 12 years. Courtesy, City of Norfolk.

Both Mayor Duckworth and City Manager Harrell were strong-willed and city hall was not big enough for both of them. Harrell left Norfolk to become the city manager of San Antonio in 1952. Duckworth would be the city's dominant personality throughout the Fifties, the decade of demolition in downtown Norfolk, and was mayor when the city's public schools were closed by Massive Resistance. That was to be his political undoing. Roy Martin, who cast a symbolic vote to keep the public schools open in the crisis of Massive Resistance, would be the chief personality in Norfolk politics in the Sixties, when the city's rebuilding really started.

The agency for the city's dramatic renewal was the Norfolk Redevelopment and Housing Authority (NRHA). It began as the Norfolk Housing Authority, created in 1940 in response to the emergency housing needs of the time. The five members of a citizens' commission the city council had named to conduct a "fact-finding" slum survey were appointed as the commissioners of the Norfolk Housing Authority. One of the five was Charles Kaufman, who was the authority's first vice chairman and became its chairman in 1942. He was to keep the job until 1969. Lawrence M. Cox served as the authority's director from 1941 to 1969. The continuity of direction is evidence in itself of the body's role in Norfolk's renewal.

Nathan Straus, who as administrator of the

U.S. Housing Authority had inspected the slum sections in more than 100 cities, had described Norfolk's this way: "I have traveled all over these United States, from one end to the other, and I have seen all kinds of slums, but this is positively the worst thing I have ever seen."

They were certainly among the nation's worst by the end of the war. The attack on the slums was begun in 1946 with the passage of the Virginia Redevelopment Law. The Norfolk Housing Authority changed its name to the Norfolk Redevelopment and Housing Authority that year. The importance of the legislation, which was initiated in Norfolk, was that it allowed the authority to acquire and clear land for resale to private investors as well as for public uses. Private partnership in redevelopment would be a key to the program's success.

"After five years as one of the nation's largest operators of war housing," the Norfolk Housing Authority reported in May 1946 that it was ready

to assume the role for which it was created: builder and operator of low-rent housing for low-income families.

This will mean the removal of hundreds and, we hope, eventually thousands of slum dwellings. When the wrecking crews begin their work, we believe the overwhelming majority of our people will exclaim with us: "This is it!"

The city was ahead of the nation. Anticipating the passage of the U.S. Housing Act, the city

council voted the money in 1948 to make a preparatory study. Norfolk was ready when President Truman signed the law the next year. The first cities to qualify under the act's allocations for public housing were Norfolk and Galveston, Texas. With the approval by Washington of the plans for Redevelopment Project No. 1, Norfolk was the first in the nation to execute a loan and grant under the Housing Act of 1949.

On December 11, 1951, the wrecking crews finally went to work. Bulldozers demolished a dwelling at 755 Smith Street to begin the clearance of 123 acres of downtown land for Redevelopment Project No. 1. (The site is part of Young Terrace today.) The tumbledown house on Smith Street would be the first of more than 10,000 units of substandard housing, to borrow the language of the law,

that would be razed. What was the city's "last slum" in many senses and certainly in the sense of the statement by Nathan Straus when the effort was getting started—was being cleared for the Church Street Huntersville II redevelopment project, with some 500 new units rebuilt by 1985 to replace the 1,200 old ones—and alleviate the overcrowding that caused the deterioration in the first place.

The story of Norfolk's renewal continues, though the emphasis has shifted through the years. The focus was on emergency housing during the war years, when the NRHA operated nearly 2,000 housing units in Merrimack Park, Oakleaf Park, Liberty Park and Roberts Park. The emphasis under the US Housing Act of 1949 was slum clearance and public housing projects; the Authority also operated more than 3,000 rental units which were built in the 50s.

Many an ecdysiast performed on the stage of the Gaiety Theater through the years, and the dancers bumped and ground to the tune of "Auld Lang Syne" at its last midnight show. The naked (what else?) stage of the burlesque house takes its final bow to the bulldozer in the early 1960s. (NRHA)

Both nationally and in Norfolk, the focus of urban renewal shifted in the '60s and '70s to community development and neighborhood conservation projects. That was reflected in the apartments for the elderly and the handicapped opened between 1918 and 1980 and in home-ownership and rent subsidy programs, together comprising nearly 1,000 more units. All told, the Norfolk Redevelopment and Housing Authority was landlord to approximately 25,000 low-income residents by the early '80s and had maintenance responsibilities to awe the average householder, such as cutting 30 miles of hedge per year.

The '60s also saw the beginnings of the most

East Main Street's sailors' strip wasn't much to look at during the daytime in the 1950s, but it became brightly lit at night. (NRHA)

ambitious piece of the NRHA plan, committing the city to a $26 million program to modernize 147 acres in downtown Norfolk. The infamous honky-tonks and tattoo parlors of East Main Street, the run-down buildings on crowded streets between Main and Brambleton, all met the bulldozer, and were replaced by widened boulevards, modern skyscrapers to anchor a downtown financial center, a new central library and a brand new Civic Center complex for Norfolk City offices, courts and Public Safety.

Commercial improvements that followed on the newly-available land downtown included the Golden Triangle Hotel (1960, now the Norfolk Radisson), the Rennert Building and parking garage (now on the site of MacArthur Center), and the Norfolk Cultural and Convention Center (including SCOPE and Chrysler Hall). The downtown renaissance would continue into the '80s and '90s.

Another dimension was the half-dozen neighborhood, conservation projects (Ghent, Berkley, Colonial Place/Riverview, Park Place, Downtown West, Lafayette-Winona) protecting some 3,000 structures on nearly 1,000 acres of property. Nearly-$16 million was granted or loaned at low interest to owners for rehabilitation so that the neighborhoods might be stabilized and upgraded. Finally, there was the conventionally financed housing that was built by developers on land that they bought from the NRHA in the East Ghent and Freemason Harbour redevelopment tracts, the Rosemont, Brambleton and Berkley areas, as well as the "fill-in" housing on lots here and there within the conservation neighborhoods. In sum, there were more new units added, in all phases of redevelopment, than old ones subtracted.

While the housing statistics give a good idea of redevelopment's scope, they are only part of the story. More than $400 million was invested in Norfolk's renewal by 1981. The figure included public and private spending. It brought a remarkable transformation. In downtown Norfolk the honky-tonks of East Main Street and the old slums are gone, replaced by the Civic Center and the Kim Library, Chrysler Hall and Scope, the bank buildings, the Federal Building, Granby Mall, Omni International Hotel, and an entire grid of highways and streets unimagined when it all began in the Forties. What used to be "Atlantic City" is home now to high-rise apartment buildings beside the Hague and a medical complex including Sentara, Norfolk General Hospital, Kings Daughters Hospital, Eastern Virginia Medical School, Medical Tower, Mental Health Center, Public Health Center, and Tidewater Rehabilitation Institute.

The Norfolk Division of the College of William and Mary, which was established in an old public school in 1930, and the Norfolk Division of Virginia State College, which began with classes in the Hunton Branch YMCA in 1935, grew into today's urban universities, Old Dominion and Norfolk State. The

Left
Johnny Reb, the Confederate soldier on the pedestal, is surrounded by bank buildings in downtown Norfolk today. (NRHA)

Below left
Developer James W. Rouse played an important part in changing the United States lifestyle with the suburban shopping center and the covered mall. In Baltimore, Boston, and Norfolk, he applied his persuasive talents and vision to bringing back the downtown water-front. Photo by R.L. Dunston. Courtesy, Landmark Communications.

temporary wartime housing at Broad Creek Village was demolished to make way for the Norfolk Industrial Park; the NRHA sold the 468 acres of land there to the City of Norfolk for $165,000, which later resold roughly three-quarters of the tract to nearly 100 business concerns for more than $5 million, total. The examples can be multiplied. And the best was yet to be on the Norfolk waterfront. On December 1, 1981 a cannon fired and, in the harbor, tugs tooted to celebrate the ground-breaking for the marketplace planned by developer James W. Rouse at Waterside.

Caveat everybody. Boosterism is endemic to the United States. Any city has its success stories. Americans seem to specialize in turning frogs into princes, or claiming to do so and Norfolk is not unique.

Which does not make the change in Norfolk any less real, or any less remarkable. And it is equally remarkable to the local resident who remembers the city market and the "railbus" to Virginia Beach as it is to the visitor who last saw the city as a sailor in wartime and now returns to a convention at the Sheraton, unbelieving.

When and where the making of the new Norfolk started is less significant today than where it

137

is going. The accomplishments are not solely the doing of any agency or individual, and are certainly not to be credited only to the Norfolk Redevelopment and Housing Authority. Although it was central to the process and its actions are conveniently symbolic, the NRHA is an agency of the city government in partnership with Washington. The idea of urban renewal and its legal resources are only tools to be used.

But the decision was made in Norfolk in 1946 to put them to use, and few municipalities have been so skillful in their application, so steadfast in their will, and so thoroughgoing in the transformation that they have worked.

At the close of World War II, Americans had turned eagerly to the tasks of peace, rebuilding their personal lives disrupted or postponed by the global struggle. Despite the enunciation of the Truman Doctrine and the launching of the Marshall Plan in 1947; despite the Berlin blockade in 1948; despite the formation of the North Atlantic Treaty Organization in the spring of 1949, President Truman's announcement on September 23 that "within recent weeks an atomic explosion occurred in the USSR," and the collapse of Chiang Kai-shek's regime in China at

the end of 1949, the nation was totally unprepared to go to war when the North Koreans struck on June 25, 1950.

Along the 38th Parallel in Korea it was dawn on Sunday the 25th, but it still was Saturday the 24th in Washington. It was early evening when the government initially reacted to the reports, and getting on toward midnight when Secretary of State Dean Acheson first telephoned Truman, who had flown to his home in Independence, Missouri, for the weekend, and next requested Secretary General Trygve Lie to call an emergency session of the United Nations Security Council for Sunday.

Both the United Nations and the United States were being tested, and by the end of that week the UN had voted to endorse forceful intervention "to repel the armed attack and to restore international peace and security," and General Douglas MacArthur had been ordered to use American forces to help in South Korea.

The first phase of the war was a disastrous retreat; the second was a breakout from the perimeter at Pusan timed to coincide with the Inchon landings and a northward sweep toward the Yalu River at the Chinese border by the forces of the United Nations under MacArthur's command; the third was the Chinese intervention and another frantic retreat. In 1951 President Truman recalled General MacArthur, which caused a political uproar, and armistice talks began in the summer of 1951. They dragged on until the truce in 1953.

History's judgment is that the general was insubordinate and the President was right in sacking him, though anybody looking at the cartoons on the walls of the MacArthur Memorial in Norfolk would be likely to conclude just the opposite. Although Americans had initially rallied to Truman in 1950, the country soon soured on the unpopular and unsatisfactory war.

That experience would be repeated in the Vietnam War, where by 1967 the American forces had passed the peak strength they had reached in Korea and rose to 543,400 by the spring of 1969. The Cambodian incursion in 1970 provoked protests in the United States that dwarfed the 1951 outcry over MacArthur. The last American troops were withdrawn from Vietnam in 1973 and the last American civilians were evacuated with the fall of Saigon in 1975. Korea was a stalemate; Vietnam was a modern Thirty Years' War. Everybody lost and Hanoi picked up the pieces.

Both conflicts had their impact on the communities around Norfolk's waters. Families lost loved ones, had husbands and sons wounded, or learned they were prisoners of war. The careers of

thousands of men in uniform were affected by the war, as were the lives of their dependents living near Norfolk's waters. Ships and squadrons were transferred. As elsewhere, the conflict stirred political passions in Virginia. Few were untouched by Korea and Vietnam.

But the impact was to confirm the course of events set by the two world wars. There was not much money for the military in peacetime; that had been the pattern of the past. Congress desired to revert to the tradition and cut defense spending to $13 billion in 1950. The army was down to half the size that It had been on the day of Pearl Harbor. Events quickly showed that we were woefully unprepared. The emergency in Korea was the beginning of the postwar rearmament of the United States. Defense spending through the 1980s stayed up, with beneficial consequences to the economy of a Navy town.

The buildup of the Navy, which began in 1950, translated into a payroll that exceeded a billion dollars a year in 1980 for the bases in Norfolk's waters and the communities serving them. Taken together with the boom in coal exports and containerized cargo shipment, it meant the port was thriving. So were the shipyards.

Newport News Shipbuilding was the biggest employer in the state, with roughly 25,000

workers, and its backlog of work was $3.2 billion at the end of 1980. The chilly Halloween of 1981 saw a gathering of notables at the shipyard when the keel was laid for the Navy's newest nuclear supercarrier, the *Theodore Roosevelt;* following that the nuclear submarine *Norfolk,* the third warship to bear the city's name, was launched by Jane Weinberger, the wife of then Secretary of Defense. The doubleheader—the *Norfolk* and the *Theodore Roosevelt*—tempts one to start talking of the Great White Fleet.

For most of the Navy's supercarriers, the battleship's equivalent in the Eighties, were built in Newport News—the *Midway* in 1945, the *Coral Sea,* the *Forrestal,* the *Ranger,* the *America,* the *John F. Kennedy.* So was the first of the nuclearpowered aircraft carriers, the *Enterprise,* delivered in 1961. She was followed by the *Nimitz,* the *Eisenhower,* and the *Carl Vinson.* Newport News is among the only shipyards with the capacity to construct the nuclear supercarriers of today, and it is also a lead yard in building nuclear submarines. The first to be delivered to the Navy by the yard also bore a famous name, symbolically tempting. She was the *Robert E. Lee,* launched late in 1959.

The Norfolk Naval Shipyard in Portsmouth is not only the oldest and largest of the government's naval yards, but has earned the reputation as the best of them too. Of the 27 ships worked on in fiscal 1980, the 12,000-man work force was able to deliver eight early, and 18 on time; only one ran over schedule. Against the delays encountered in other yards, that is an exceptional record.

This reputation is shared by the Norfolk Shipbuilding and Drydock Company, shortened to Norshipco nowadays, the largest private sector ship repair yard on the east coast, and the largest nonnuclear repair facility in the nation. Founded in 1915, Norshipco was acquired by United States Marine Repair, Inc. in 1998. A principal reason for Norshipco's growth has been the floating drydock known as Titan, which is big enough to accommodate the bulk carriers of today or the dowager *SS United States.* The structure became an instant landmark, if that is the word to apply to a floating drydock, and helps to define the harbor Norfolk and Portsmouth share, shaping the trapezoid that is formed by the big crane in the Naval Shipyard, the drydock, the downtown Norfolk skyline, and the bulk of the Naval Hospital, 17 stories tall.

Although they may not compare in size with the three big shipyards, there are more than 30 other yards in Hampton Roads, dedicated to everything from specialized repair work to building small craft. One of the oldest is Colonna's Shipyard, founded in 1875 by Charles J. Colonna, and today the oldest family-owned yard in the nation. Others were less lucky—Jonathan Corporation, founded in 1974, went out of business in 1995, and its former facilities on Front Street await a new tenant. That shipbuilding and repair work continue to be factors in the local economy would be bound to please William Byrd, Matthew Fontaine Maury, and everybody else who looked upon the great harbor of Hampton Roads and saw the future there.

Building and repairing ships for the U.S. Navy is one reason for the shipyards' success in Virginia, when the industry is one of the nation's

sickest. There is another and equally familiar factor in the health of Hampton Roads, and it is the coal trade.

Historically, Hampton Roads has shipped about three-fourths of the total tonnage of coal exported from the United States. That is because it offers shippers the deepest, ice-free harbor on the East Coast. The benefits to the economy of the region are tremendous. At the end of 1980 it was calculated that every ton of coal exported from Norfolk's waters was worth $18.42 to Virginia. The figure included $12.86 that it cost to coal companies to get the ton of coal to dockside, $3.78 to fuel and service the vessel which was to carry the coal, and $1.55 to load it on the vessel.

Multiply that by the 50 million tons of coal exported from Hampton Roads in 1980 and you had lots of coal dollars. As oil prices went higher and higher worldwide, the demand for coal rose sharply, too. The experts predicted that coal exports from Hampton Roads would be 100 million tons annually, within a few years, if the coal piers could handle the volume.

The expansion of facilities is a big "if" and

bound to be an expensive one too. Coal shipments accounted for 80 percent of the port's tonnage in 1980. From mid-1980 to the coal strike of 1981, there were more than 100 colliers waiting to get to the coal piers on the average day, and the check-erboard of ships moored in Norfolk's waters was reminiscent of the convoys of the war years. It cost about $15,000 a day to keep the huge ships waiting, sometimes up to 60 days or even longer, adding about $15 to the price of a ton of coal overseas. American ports scrambled to compete for coal exports and there were plans on paper to expand the capacity fivefold nationwide.

From the age of sail to the age of the loco-motive and the steamboat, from the first settlers to the great growth that was brought by two world wars, there was a constant to life by Norfolk's waters-the ferries from shore to shore. Another constant was complaints about the ferries. For instance, Isaac Weld, who crossed from Hampton to Norfolk in 1796, wrote:

> From this town there is a regular ferry to Norfolk, across Hampton Roads, 18 miles over. I was forced to leave my horses here behind me for several days, as all the flats belonging to the place had been sent up a creek some miles for staves, &c. and they had no other method of getting horses into the ferry boats, which were too large to come close into shore, excepting by carrying them out in these flats, and them making them leap on board. It is a most irksome piece of business to cross the ferries in Virginia; there is not one in six where the boats are good and well manned, and it is necessary to employ great circumspection in order to guard against accidents, which are but too common. As I passed along I heard of numberless recent instances of horses being drowned, killed, and having legs broken, by getting in and out of the boats.

Certainly conditions improved in time, but even in the 20th century it sometimes was "a most irksome piece of business to cross the ferries" and only the romantic would want to mourn the passing of the service.

The first to go was the oldest-and it died hard. The earliest ferry from Norfolk to Portsmouth was simply a slave in a skiff, but there was a continuous service for some three centuries. The downtown tunnel between Norfolk and Portsmouth was opened on May 23, 1952, but even then the ferries kept on running for three more years.

The midtown tunnel was opened a decade later, on September 6, 1962, and a third tunnel would open for traffic in 1986. The new tube is just south of the downtown tunnel and was built in nine phases. The cost of the project was estimated at $350 million total. The old tunnel was designed to handle some 25,000 vehicles a day, and the average daily traffic it accommodated in 1980 was roughly 40,000 vehicles. More than 25,000 vehicles use the midtown tunnel on the average day. The Elizabeth River Tunnel Commission was dissolved in 1973 and the facilities are now operated under the Virginia Department of Transportation.

The bridge-tunnel that connects Norfolk to Hampton and the Peninsula was first opened to traffic as a tollway on November 1, 1957. The second tube went into operation on June 3,

1976, at which time the tolls were lifted. (The tolls on the James River Bridge and the Coleman Bridge at Yorktown, which had been linked to the revenues of the Hampton Roads tunnel, were eliminated at the same time.) The peak traffic through the Hampton Roads tunnel was about 65,000 vehicles per day on a summer weekend in the 1980s.

The most spectacular of the postwar system of tunnels was opened on April 15, 1964. The Chesapeake Bay Bridge-Tunnel is one of the engineering wonders of the world. It is 23 miles from one toll plaza, on the southwestern tip of the Eastern Shore, to the other, on the Chesapeake Beach section of Virginia Beach. It crosses 17.6

Top
Ferry New York *docked at Colonna's Shipyard in 1949. After long service she was converted for use as a barge, when the ferries stopped running in 1955. Courtesy, Colonna's Shipyard.*
Above
Commuters travel homeward in the evening along Waterfront Drive. Courtesy, City of Norfolk.

miles of open water, which in places is as deep as 70 feet, and it tunnels under two of the busiest shipping channels in the world—the Thimble Shoals Channel, leading to the anchorage of Hampton Roads, and the Baltimore Channel, used by vessels bound for Baltimore and the Bay's upper waters. More than a million tons of rock were used to create the four man-made islands at either end of the two tunnels, which were fabricated of sections about the size of a 10-story building, towed from Texas to Tidewater by tugs. Most of the crossing is on low-level trestles that were built 30 feet above mean low water, and there are bridges over the North Channel and Fisherman Inlet.

It took three years and six months to build the Chesapeake Bay Bridge-Tunnel, at a cost of seven lives lost and $200 million. Since its opening in 1964 the Bay Bridge-Tunnel has been closed on occasion by accidents or storms, and its revenues have fallen far short of the bondholders' hopes. But it is a marvel nonetheless, and the most direct route from Norfolk to the north.

The Monitor-Merrimac Bridge-Tunnel opened in 1992, would complete the loop of interstate highways in the Hampton Roads.

The antecedents of the civil rights revolution of the Fifties and Sixties are to be found in documents like the 1947 report of the President's Commission on Civil Rights. Jackie Robinson broke baseball's color line with the Brooklyn Dodgers in the same year. Certainly the change in the nation's thinking was related to the experiences of millions of men in uniform in the Second World War. But the beginning of what would become a consuming legal and political struggle was the U.S. Supreme Court's decision, in *Brown* v. *Board of Education of Topeka* (1954), that segregation in the public schools was unconstitutional. The language of the opinion now seems to be unexceptional: "In these days, it is doubtful that any child may reasonably be expected to succeed in life if he is denied the opportunity of an education. Such an opportunity, where the state has undertaken to provide it, is a right which must be made available to all on equal terms."

The first reaction to the ruling in Virginia was a moderate one. "There will be no defiance of the Supreme Court decision as far as I am concerned," State School Superintendent Dowell J. Howard said. "We are trying to teach school children the law of the land, and will abide by it." Paul Schweitzer, the chairman of the Norfolk School Board, made a similar statement in the summer of 1955; "We intend, without mental reservation, to uphold and abide by the laws of the land."

The initial political response in the state was the "Gray Plan," which was designed to minimize the number of black pupils admitted to previously all-white schools by a pupil-placement system and to cushion desegregation by establishing a program of tuition grants for students attending private schools. The answer to *Brown* would not be defiance, but tokenism.

That was before Senator Harry F. Byrd, Sr., listened to those who were opposed to any desegregation of any public school anywhere in Virginia. Byrd was urged by the segregationists in Virginia and by his Senate colleagues from the Deep South to hold the line. He passed the word. There would be a change of course—and a new policy of "massive resistance" statewide.

A battery of laws was passed by the General Assembly to block desegregation, including one requiring the closing of any school under a court order to integrate. There also would be a cutoff of all state funds to the school. The General Assembly passed the laws in special session at the end of the summer of 1956. The crunch came in the fall of 1958.

Three high schools and three junior high schools were closed in Norfolk under the mandate of Massive Resistance. Some 10,000 students were locked out of Norfolk's schools; they became "The Lost Class of 1959," celebrated in the pages of *Life* magazine and chronicled on CBS by Edward R. Murrow. It was a bitter fall and there was many an angry, noisy meeting in Norfolk. The city council and Mayor Duckworth sided with the segregationists, who had organized under the impressive-sounding title of Defenders of State Sovereignty and Individual Liberties ("Defenders," for short).

The fight for the schools was led by the School Board and Chairman Schweitzer, Superintendent of Schools J.J. Brewbaker, the public school teachers (who boycotted the private schools the segregationists started), and the citizens and parents who formed the Norfolk Committee for the Public Schools. Lenoir Chambers, the gentlemanly North Carolinian who was editor of *The Virginian-Pilot,* was a clear, strong voice. Incredible as it may seem today, the *Pilot* was the only major newspaper in the state to say that closing the public schools was wrong.

Massive Resistance was brought down by a legal one-two punch on January 19, 1959. In carefully coordinated decisions the State Supreme Court held that the laws violated the state constitution, and a special three-judge federal court ruled that the state laws violated the United States Constitution. The business estab-

Mermaids on Parade decorated Norfolk in the summer of 2000. Area artists donated their work and businessmen adopted the sculptures with the proceeds going to support the arts. One imaginative mermaid at Townpoint Park has a painting of the Norfolk skyline on her body. Photo by David B. Hollingsworth.

A likeness of General Douglas MacArthur greets visitors to The MacArthur Memorial, where the general and Mrs. MacArthur are buried. Exhibits trace the history of the general through the wars he fought and the post-peace he engineered in Japan, including his showdown with President Truman during the Korean War. John Whitehead photo. Courtesy, Norfolk Convention and Visitors Bureau.

The Chrysler Museum of Art is home to over 30,000 art objects covering 5,000 years of civilization. Photo by Scott Wolff. Courtesy, Chrysler Museum of Art.

The annual Azalea Festival, which honors the nations of the North Atlantic Treaty Organization culminates in the crowning of the queen. Courtesy, Norfolk Convention and Visitors Bureau.

MacArthur Center, a new 1 million square foot, three-level urban marketplace in downtown has proven to be a catalyst for downtown redevelopment. With 150 stores, a 600-seat food court, upscale restaurants, and an 18-screen cinema complex, the center has drawn shoppers from as far away as Virginia Beach and Richmond to downtown Norfolk. Courtesy, MacArthur Center.

Bottom right
The building of Fortune 500 company Norfolk Southern on Main Street appears transparent. Photo by John Whithead. Courtesy, Norfolk Convention and Visitors Bureau.

Below
The Jones Institute of Reproductive Medicine on the campus of Eastern Virginia Medical School pioneered in-vitro fertilization in the United States. Courtesy, EVMS.

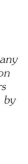

Above

Portsmouth, an historic seaport town on the Elizabeth River in Southeastern Virginia is located at the Zero Mile Marker on the Intracoastal Waterway. The city's 85 miles of navigable channels is a haven for boaters. Courtesy, Portsmouth Convention & Visitors Bureau.

Sailors manning the ship during commissioning ceremonies for the USS Harry S. Truman. Photo by Mark P. Mitchell. Courtesy, The Virginian-Pilot.

158

A variety of ways to tour the harbor in Norfolk include luxury yacht, sailboat, and riverboat. Courtesy, Norfolk Convention and Visitors Bureau.

Tall ships regularly make port visits to Norfolk during the annual Harborfest celebration each summer. Courtesy, Norfolk Convention and Visitors Bureau.

*After years of effort,
the MacArthur Center
Mall finally opened in
March 1999. Photo by
Nhat Meyer. Courtesy,
The Virginian-Pilot.*

CHAPTER NINE

THE HEART
OF HAMPTON ROADS

PORTSMOUTH, SUFFOLK, CHESAPEAKE,
NEWPORT NEWS, HAMPTON, VIRGINIA BEACH
AND NORFOLK

Oh what a diverse company we have in these seven cities by the sea!

A white egret rising, trailing its long legs in the air, head doubled back on its neck, the very signature of nature herself...At hint of trouble abroad, the great fleet moving out to meet it...Roadside markets with golden loupes, blushing peaches, sunfiery tomatoes to be bought or picked in summer fields...gray brown row on row aglow with puffs of blossoming white cotton...Harbor Park's riverside diamond where Mets in the making play ball...a tossing tumult of applause at a symphony orchestra's last sweet-strain of Mozart...sandpipers, running, hem-stitching the lacy edge of a wave advancing over golden sand as brown-limbed children rush to meet it...cypress trees, draped in Spanish moss, gray-bearded veterans up to their knees in dark lagoons, reflecting...tigers burning bright in lush zoo greenery...a passing cruiseship as the jumbled skyline turns orange in the sun's slant rays, coming to lights and nightlife.

They're all here and more, waiting for you.

PORTSMOUTH

One of the world's most arresting sights is that of a ship parked at the end of a tree-lined street. If the ship, a large one, is moored broadside to the street, that's all the more alluring. The sight is enhanced if the houses lining both sides are of an old vintage and limbs of the trees on both sides of the street nearly meet overhead.

You look down a leafy tunnel of time. It speaks of the pleasure of being secure at home even as it conveys the ship's lure to leave for the unknown.

Portsmouth offers many such views because the Norfolk Naval Shipyard is next door to downtown as is Norshipco, a fine private yard. Marine businesses line the Elizabeth River and its offshoots.

That Portsmouth's naval shipyard bears Norfolk's name is a source of regret, but a move to change it to honor Portsmouth always runs the risk that it would then be confused with the Portsmouth, NH shipyard which, by the way, is in Kittery, Maine.

When an aircraft carrier at the Norfolk Naval Station needs repairs it makes a majestic passage down the Elizabeth River and then up its Southern Branch to the shipyard in Portsmouth.

When the job is done, the carrier reembarks and moves back down the Southern Branch, which suddenly seems shrunken to the size of a creek.

Office workers in Portsmouth, looking out windows, gape at the gray bulk of the slowly passing carrier, its massive central island towering 24 stories. First floor workers rush out to watch the great moving wall glide by.

The carrier eases into the Elizabeth River's main stream, and, turning, seems to take Norfolk's skyline onto the broad back of its flight deck as it starts for home at the Norfolk Naval Station aided by a tough little red tug.

A Scot, Andrew Sprowle, founded the Yard in 1762. It survived being burned by the British in

Above
Portsmouth offers twilight walking tours of Olde Towne, called Lantern Tours, which are led by knowledgeable guides dressed in period attire. Visitors get a taste of the legends and folklore of Olde Towne but also learn about the district's unique architectural styles, which include Colonial, Federal, Greek Revival, Georgian and Victorian. Courtesy, Portsmouth Convention & Visitors Bureau.

Right
The Elizabeth River Ferry is a pedestrian ferry crossing the Elizabeth River between Portsmouth and Norfolk taking visitors to and from The Waterside, Norfolk. Courtesy, Portsmouth Convention & Visitors Bureau.

Bottom
The Commodore Theatre in Portsmouth is a luxuriously restored 1945 Art Deco-style motion picture theater with upholstered seating and crystal chandeliers that shows first-run movies while serving light dinners. The theater also offers traditional-style seating in an upstairs balcony area. Photo by Renee Wayland. Courtesy, Portsmouth Convention & Visitors Bureau.

1779, the U.S. Navy in 1861, and the Confederate Navy in 1862. It is here to stay, the oldest, biggest and, as many awards attest, the best of eight U.S. Naval Yards.

It built Dry-dock Number One, the oldest in the nation, of large blocks of granite in stepped tiers. It looks to be a steep amphitheater quarried out of the ground, a place for a giant to lie down. It built the first battleship commissioned by the Navy (USS Texas). After Billy Mitchell's bombers sank a captured German battleship in the Chesapeake Bay, the Navy ordered the building of a ship to launch airplanes in 1921.

Norfolk Naval Shipyard converted the collier USS *Jupiter* into a flattop with a 500-foot flight deck, 65 feet wide that was christened the *Langley* in honor of aviation pioneer Samuel Langley. It sank in the Battle of Java Sea in 1943, but it had proved itself, and its thunderous successors helped turn the tide against Japan.

The Yard is the world's largest for repairing, overhauling and modernizing warships. The major factor in its superiority is a work force that functions as a family in doing the best possible job on every ship.

Portsmouth is in resurgence, having recovered from the drain that shopping malls imposed on core cities. In the early 1980s, Portsmouth beautified downtown High Street, put in brick sidewalks, a median strip, and trees. Then, one by one the old favorites, now faded, empty buildings began to come

to life, transmogrified.

The downtown's heart on High Street has been restored.

The department store Famous, featuring hat sales that drew swarms of shoppers from North Carolina and the Peninsula, became the Tidewater Community College Visual Art Center offering classes in everything from computer graphics to puttering around with pottery. Anybody feeling an artistic impulse would do well to look around or sign up.

The Leggetts building was reborn as a top-flight, three-story Children's Museum in which the fathers often have to be dragged away from a giant layout of model trains.

The old Woolworth Building is reopening as Roger Brown's Sports Bar and Restaurant. The Virginia Sports Hall of Fame is being re-housed in a $9 million building with an array of relics, movies, and computerized interactive games. Hotel Dinwiddie has been restored to its old glory. The Commodore Theater has been re-rigged to serve meals along with films.

Plans are underway for a Performing Arts Center seating 7,000 on the waterfront. Nearby, a developer is building a mega-yacht facility and marina. The Renaissance Hotel has a high tech conference center.

Across town the Navy's Regional Medical Center greeted the year 2000 with a definitive hospital built at a cost of $390 million. The original 1835 Naval Hospital, the first in the nation, has been redone to house the Medical Center's administrative offices and library.

With all the city's giant strides, Portsmouth remains neighborly. Olde Town is undisturbed and the natives still call their city "Porchmuth." It's easier to say that way.

SUFFOLK

Plunked down amid a metropolis of a million people are 109,000 acres of Dismal Swamp, inhabited by more than 300 black bears and 200 species of migratory birds. It is an Eden shared by Suffolk and Chesapeake.

Such a mixed population would seem to pose multiple problems for Lloyd Culp, its manager at Swamp headquarters in Suffolk.

But the main concerns are when the swamp's denizens cross paths with human species that come calling. Most time, the animals flee.

As 2000 dawned, Culp's concern was the disruption of wildlife by the widening of Route 17 to ease increasing motor traffic between Suffolk and Portsmouth.

For years, bears have crossed Route 17 at a certain point—which was there long before 17—to visit friends along the Southwest River in Chesapeake. That's been helpful in reducing inbreeding among bears in Old Dismal.

Culp requested that the Virginia Department of Transportation include a bridge for bears to run under and culverts for their safe passage in its plans. After all, the bears were here first.

Suffolk has more than 8,000 acres of lakes and miles of river shoreline with some freshwater and salt-water fishing. Courtesy, City of Suffolk.

The Great Dismal Swamp National Wildlife Refuge was established to restore and protect a unique ecosystem on 109,000 acres. Courtesy, City of Suffolk.

Dismal has lured exotic humankind, as well. Poet Robert Frost, despondent over a rejection by a woman or a publisher, walked a railroad track by the swamp but went back without going into it. A pity he let the path go untaken. He might have left us a poem.

Long ago, when this author asked Old Dismal Swamp guide Sam Whitson how visitors got lost so readily in there, he replied, "You can't walk in a straight line because you have to follow thin areas to get around the undergrowth. So, you constantly lose your sense of direction. You don't even believe your own compass. You have to pick out a landmark far ahead, and then you have to walk a half mile one way and a half mile back to get around a spot you couldn't cross."

"A person finds just what he's looking for in Old Dismal," he said. "I carry parties up there on the lake, and they look around and say, 'Is this all there is?' and I say, 'Yes.' I turn round and get 'em back just as quick as I can. Still, I've taken others who can't get enough of it. For an inexpensive fare I've spent most of the day with them."

Why do we need wilderness, aside from the need to breathe? "We enjoy it as God intended the world to be. I don't think he ever planned a city," Whitson said. "That is a man-made institution. And the cities are spreading. All my great-grandchildren and your grandchildren will know of nature is what they read.

"It's tragic. I wish the state would buy one or two thousand acres around Lake Drummond. Even the bears are near extinct. And, the Army Engineers should buy 10,000 or so acres to safeguard the Dismal canal that feeds into the Intracoastal Waterways at Great Bridge," he concluded. "And then they should leave the swamp alone. Just cut a few trails, maybe, so nature lovers won't get lost—as often."

It looked then, in 1968, that Dismal Swamp was doomed. But, it didn't happen, thanks to gifts of swampland by Union Camp Corporation and Weyerhaeuser Co. The U.S. Department of the Interior rounded out the holdings to more than 100,000 acres. The U.S. Fish and Wildlife Services continues to add to the acreage.

So that people won't get lost there is a 400-foot boardwalk through a representative area of the swamp. A four-and-a-half mile hike or bike trail leads to mysterious Lake Drummond. Its sandy bottom shows no metal to hint at a meteor explosion. Indians say a firebird crashed and created the lake that is higher than the land around it. Some scientists say a deep-peat fire hollowed it out, but others find an irregularity in compasses in that area.

There is much bewitching in Suffolk today, including fine restaurants. In its downtown renovations, Suffolk moved forward by looking back, restoring the train depot with its witch's hat and its Victorian interior of rich, deep-hued woodwork.

Model railroad buffs created an elaborate layout of a town, scenic railway, and trains. Alumni are aiding in transforming old Suffolk High School into a cultural arts center.

An annual event in Suffolk is the Peanut Festival through which one may wander bemused at all kinds of entertainment and, meanwhile, help oneself without charge to handfuls of peanuts from burlap bags.

A peddler of roasted peanuts in Pennsylvania, Amadeo Obici visited Suffolk to learn more about the peanut, and stayed. In 1913 he borrowed $25,000 to buy a small brick factory. That was the start of the vast Planters Peanuts. His wife dreamed of a hospital in Suffolk. After her death in 1936 he provided funds for building Louise Obici Memorial Hospital and a nursing school and a $20 million endowment to run it. In the year 2000 Suffolk began constructing a new state-of-the-art hospital, perpetuating their memory.

In 1975, Norfolk's former city manager, G. Robert House Jr., had brought his expertise to Suffolk. During six formative years, he improved the city's basic services.

In 1976, the city bought 1,172 acres with 11 lakes that had been created by the Lone Star Mining Co. in the 1920s. It created first-rate recreational facilities. To assure Suffolk a water supply, House and his assistant and successor, John L. Rowe Jr., obtained 18 federal grants to fund nearly 90 percent of a $16.8 million water treatment plant installed at the Lone Star Lakes.

Later, while serving as city manager of Portsmouth, House died in a plane crash. In a heartfelt tribute to House, Suffolk Mayor George H. Barnett and the city council referred to him as a "water pioneer" throughout Hampton Roads.

In managing four cities in Hampton Roads and training assistants, House also left a rich legacy to carry on his progressive outlook.

Suffolk's cultural centerpiece is Riddick's Folly, built in 1837 and so nicknamed because people deemed owner Mills Riddick extravagant to want a 21-room, four story house. But his wife bore 14 children. Riddick's Folly sheltered his family for more than a century and now is still serving the large community family of Suffolk. Courtesy, City of Suffolk.

CHESAPEAKE

Patriots in the City of Chesapeake have banded together to burnish the reputation of the Battle of Great Bridge. Although ignored by history books, it was the first pitched battle of the American Revolution and merits as much attention as Concord or Bunker Hill.

In commemorating the battle with a museum, these history-minded citizens, headed by Mayor William E. Ward, will give to Chesapeake something it needs.

Rich in land and already a lure for businesses, Chesapeake lacks a prime tourist attraction of the type that enriches the culture of the cities of Hampton Roads and their municipal coffers. That battle, the Battle of Great Bridge, has the dramatic story to do it.

Before the battle, George Washington was worried that if Lord Dunmore were not defeated, the Royal Governor would gather forces like a snowball, divide the Colonies, and doom the Revolution.

"It was the most important battle in the first year of the war," said the late Judge Charles B. Cross, Jr. who wrote eight books about the city he helped to shape.

At sunrise on Dec. 9, 1775, coming from the direction of Norfolk, the British began attacking to the south, six abreast along an earthen causeway across 360 yards of marsh and open water of the Southern Branch of the Elizabeth River.

The patriots, 600 strong, waited behind breastworks at Great Bridge. The British had a regiment of the 14th Grenadiers and a couple of loyalist regiments raised in the area, and what Lord Dunmore called his Ethiopian Corps of slaves who had been promised freedom.

When the massed British troops were well within range, the colonists fired volleys into their ranks. There was no place to hide. Some 70 British died. One American was wounded.

"It was amazing," said Judge Cross. "It was really a suicide attack. No military man in his right mind would have ordered it, but Dunmore was neither a military man nor in his right mind. He had

let the patriots drive him crazy, I guess."

One American hero was Billy Flora, a free black from Portsmouth. At night he guarded stores on an island midway in the marsh. In the darkness before the dawn, when the British attacked, Flora stayed long enough to fire as many as eight times. "That takes a good while with a muzzle loader," Judge Cross said.

After the fight at Great Bridge, the British withdrew to Norfolk and two days later went aboard ships. They were confined there and couldn't regain a foothold in Virginia until 1779.

Their absence enabled Virginia to use the Chesapeake Bay as the main artery in supplying Washington for five years.

Two other persons of interest, Thomas Marshall and his 19-year-old son, John, were at the battle. John Marshall stayed with Washington most of the way and emerged as a captain. "I went in the army a Virginian and became an American," he said. After the war, he stuck with Washington as a Federalist, as did most of the Founders who were with him during the war, opposing Thomas Jefferson's reliance on states' rights. That period of John Marshall's education began at Great Bridge.

The Great Dismal Swamp National Wildlife Refuge is home to hundreds of species of birds, insects and other wildlife. Pictured is the beautiful and majestic Lake Drummond. Courtesy, City of Chesapeake.

Re-enactors relive the short, but decisive battle of the American Revolutionary War (Dec. 9, 1775) which took place in Great Bridge, not far from where the Chesapeake City Hall sits today. The Battle of Great Bridge event is held each December in Chesapeake City Park. Courtesy, City of Chesapeake.

As you drive south now, along Battlefield Boulevard nearing Great Bridge, you cross a small, barely noticeable bridge just short of a metal historic marker. Looking to the left, you catch a glimpse of the marsh, free of urban clutter, looking with its green reeds and marsh grass and blue winding waterways much as it was when Billy Flora fired his musket at invading Redcoats.

Today's patriots have formed a foundation to raise funds for constructing a visitors center in which to display artifacts and a documentary film on the Battle and two still functioning historic waterways, the Chesapeake and Albermarle Canal and the Dismal Swamp Canal.

The founders hope that Great Bridge will be the first leg in a Revolutionary Trail leading to Williamsburg, Yorktown and beyond.

Directing the project will be president, Chesapeake's Mayor, Dr. William E. Ward; vice president, Joe M. Law, president of the Norfolk County Historical Society; and executive secretary, Timothy Kerr, provost of the Chesapeake Campus of Tidewater Community College.

The excursion of private citizens into an historical venture is vital because municipal government has to cope with an increase in Chesapeake's population in the last decade in Chesapeake's population. That demands the concentration of funds to meet the needs of schools, roads, and water, as Mayor Ward has noted.

That has also required $300 million for new schools and more than $70 million for construction of a desalinization plant on the Northwest River. Blessed with vast acreage, Chesapeake has required developers to set aside open space in subdivisions.

"With space, good schools and a high quality of life," Mayor Ward observed, "Chesapeake has led the cities of Hampton Roads in attracting multi-national businesses. The largest number of Japanese companies within Virginia have chosen Chesapeake. When a company moves, it wants a good safe community and good schools."

Given the emphasis on the basics, how did he reconcile his part in promoting the Battle of Great Bridge?

"As a private citizen," the Mayor said.

And there are an unusually large number of them in civic-minded Chesapeake.

Rarely can a metropolitan area boast of having bottled milk delivered to its doorsteps. Hampton Roads has two. Yoders Dairy is in Norfolk and Bergeys Dairy Farm in Chesapeake also manufactures a famed extra-rich ice cream.

These are rich legacies from the Mennonites who moved into Virginia Beach and Chesapeake during the Depression to take advantage of the sprawling acreage in the then rural area.

A favorite haunt is the 105-acre Northwest River Park and each year Chesapeake hosts a Jubilee, a birthday party for the young city that draws people from throughout Hampton Roads. In fact, there are enough barbecues and oyster roasts, and shrimp fests going on from early spring to early fall that a body could exist simply by attending one consecutive moveable feast after another.

NEWPORT NEWS

"Newport News Shipyard is Newport News," people say, summing up its contribution to the city's economy.

Assurance that the Yard and the city will continue to do well came on March 8, 1999, with the groundbreaking for an aircraft-carrier design center.

"The center is going to bring lasting economic opportunity to working men and women in Newport News," said Gov. Jim Gilmore, "and it will ensure that Newport News continues to build the very best aircraft carriers the world has ever seen."

Its name is the Virginia Advanced Shipbuilding and Carrier Integration Center and it aims to increase the carriers' capabilities and reduce the cost of constructing them. A carrier cost at least $45 billion.

The Virginia General Assembly allocated $58 million to build the center and $45 million for its operation and for training workers. It will involve Virginia colleges and universities in research and will incorporate other state shipyards in the training and other programs. It opens in mid-2001.

In a green park next to the shipyard, which stretches two miles along the James River, the center is adjacent to the Victory Arch through which soldiers passed on their way to serve in two World Wars.

The sleek center, a low flat structure, is designed with a glass-walled office tower that will reflect carriers docked nearby. It will look as if it belongs in their company.

Just as trains knit together and energized the nation early in the 19th century, the technology developed in building new ships, and the ships themselves, are helping to transform the globe in the 21st century and pull countries closer.

The launching of any vessel at Newport News Shipbuilding is memorable. When Barbara Bush swung the bottle of champagne to christen the attack sub Houston in 1981, the bottle didn't break. Vice President Bush stepped forward to advise her. She waved him away, swung again, and sent champagne skyward. In 1967, 30,000 spectators, the most in history, watched the launching of the carrier John F. Kennedy. Attention was so focused on Jacqueline, Caroline, and John, Jr. that there was an air of intense intimacy throughout the ceremony. Photo by William Abourjilie. Courtesy The Virginian-Pilot.

Building a ship is an obviously huge and exciting job. Thus, when the job is complete, and the ship is christened, there is an air of lively celebration and near awe. One of the most memorable of these fetes occurred on September 7, 1967, when the *John F. Kennedy* was commemorated.

An hour before the ceremonies, the pace quickened among those streaming to the shipyard. Inside the Yard, the ship's bow reared in a great V above the platform, a gray cope against the blue sky.

Numerous Kennedys appeared in the guest section, including Jacqueline, regal as usual. But the crowd's eyes were on the children. Caroline bore the steady inspection with a slight, brave smile, as poised as if she had been painted by Reynolds in her white and azure dress, set off by her dark golden hair, caught at the back, briefly with a white bow.

But, John! First, he looked up, way up—at the huge, overhanging bow of the ship—and pursed his lips, his own head barely higher than the railing on the speaker's stand. As the proceeding continued, he doubled his fists and brushed his ribbed knuckles together, an interesting sensation, apparently, because he continued until he drew a long, wondering look from his sister.

He was impervious to the stares of the crowd, as his father had been on many a platform, his own man in the midst of a public spectacle. Nothing, one sensed, and hoped, would ever quench that individuality.

The faces of both children became intent when the shipyard official mentioned "the beloved President" whose name the carrier would bear.

And the crowd's emotions tightened during the predictably long prayer of Cardinal Richard Cushing, when he mentioned the dazzling Caroline, and John, a typical American boy with the potential to equal his father's example.

The three were escorted to the sponsor's bridge, high against the bow of the great ship. John backed to the rail, hooked his arms around it, and slid now one way and now the other, excitedly, as his sister swung once and failed to break the bottle of champagne, and then, with great vigor, swung again. Champagne splattered like swirling snowflakes.

Mrs. Kennedy put her gloved hands to her mouth, girlishly forgetful for just a moment, and a wide, delighted grin crossed the face of Caroline and went to the heart of the crowd, because at that moment she looked like nobody but her father.

The crowd roared at the second successful swat, and a middle-aged welder, his voice hoarse with emotion, shouted above all: "Atta girl! Atta, babe!" as if she were his.

The crowd was so stunned, so numb, that the next event, the moving of the great ship, its stirring to life, surprised them, as if a huge headland had begun to slide into the sea, slowly.

And as the ship left the shore, the sun shone with extra strength, the overhanging shadow from the bow eased away and left the mother and the two children watching in the light as the *John F. Kennedy* was put to sea.

The shipyard's progress would please Collis P. Huntington, a railroad magnate who selected Newport News, a tiny hamlet at the end of the 20-mile Peninsula, as a terminus for his coal-carrying Chesapeake & Ohio Railroad.

Among a host of scientific ventures is CEBAF, the continuous electron beam accelerator facility. It examines subatomic quarks through a 44-billion volt accelerator that fires an electron beam to split the nucleus of an atom.

Newport News is also bent on preserving its cultural heritage. The city purchased Endview, a 300-acre plantation. It restored another mansion, Lee Hall.

The carrier Harry S. Truman *as it left Newport News Shipbuilding in 1998 and pulled into the Norfolk Naval Air Station. It is the Navy's newest. Photo by Beth Bergman Nakamura. Courtesy,* The Virginian-Pilot.

Three fine museums are clustered within minutes of one another. The Peninsula Fine Arts Center has rotating exhibitions ranging from contemporary to classic.

The War Memorial Museum, which takes all of America's wars as its province, deals with war's every aspect, including its raw reality.

After World War I, when naval appropriations dried up, shipyard President Homer L. Ferguson persuaded Archer Huntington, the son of founder Huntington, to fund a museum devoted to the seas and those who sail them. He also envisioned a 550-acre park on the James River.

Thus, the Mariners Museum came to be. Landscaping the park kept 200 men busy. Archer's wife, Anna, a petite, dynamic artist, peopled the park with mammoth granite statuary.

Few museums have as many men and boys perusing the galleries as this one dedicated to the sea.

When naval business languished, Ferguson saved the shipyard by bidding abnormally low on a job to refit the captured *Leviathan*, a liner that Germany had used as a troop ship.

When a crowd of workers at the shipyard saw the battered *Leviathan* coming up the James River for the remodeling, many cried. For them, it was bread upon the water.

The job held the yard together, but it lost $1.5 million. When Ferguson went to present the news to Huntington, he carried a letter of resignation in his pocket. He never had to take it out. Huntington said to him, with a wink, "My wife owns most of the company's stock and she's not feeling well just now, so we'd better not say anything more about it."

HAMPTON

Driving east along Interstate 64, upon entering the City of Hampton, the traveler sees a beguiling building, the Hampton Roads Coliseum, the first one built in Virginia. The immense structure in cement is as beautiful as the day it opened, both bold and graceful, always there to delight the eye of the passerby.

The great round structure is rimmed by pointed, diamond-shaped panels, huge kites for flying or sails that grace the meandering Hampton River. It is a building that invites metaphor.

It is a gigantic coronet or, at night, when rainbows of lights flood the exterior, a setting of flamboyant jewels—a double vision by night and day.

The vast coliseum, half embraced by moated water, opened at a cost of $8 million—the buy of the year according to the American Institute of Architects. It symbolizes Hampton's get up and go.

It was to have been built together with Newport News, but when the design committee recommended the Hampton site, Newport News withdrew. Like the Little Red Hen in the fairy tale, Hampton forged on its own. The Coliseum came into being during the administration of Ann Kilgore, the city's first woman mayor, an individual of high humor, energy, and intelligence.

A mile or so farther on Interstate 64, looking down from a high-arching bridge, the traveler catches a tantalizing glimpse of another lovely vignette far below, a winding harbor, its blue water specked with white sails. From the viewpoint atop the bridge the billowing sails seem to be large, white, handkerchiefs. In the background looms Hampton's handsome City Hall, the color of natural granite, rock-shelved.

Catching that eyeful, many a driver, enroute to Norfolk or Virginia Beach, takes a sudden detour and descends at the next exit to see more.

He or she finds the magnificent Air and Space Center smack in the middle of downtown Hampton. When the city set about to build the museum, NASA agreed to integrate its museum with Hampton's and make an annual contribution for its operation and maintenance. It was a generous transaction.

The first seven astronauts trained at NASA Langley. The Air and Space Museum was done in conjunction with NASA, the United States Air Force, and the Smithsonian Institute. It is intriguing with eyes to the skies, to the future, as well as to the past.

Hampton's downtown on the waterfront is done in Colonial-style reminiscent of Williamsburg's a few

miles west off Interstate 64. But there is a different mood. In Williamsburg, one is apt to feel, now and then, a part of an artful staging. There's an edge at moments. In Hampton, one feels at home. The visitor may take a boat tour to a dozen or so fascinating points of interest anchored in the deep past, fronting the waters of Hampton Roads.

Television executive Thomas P. Chisman, a Hampton native, exemplified the best in regional cooperation by working equally hard for the advancement of both sides of Hampton Roads.

Only Hampton has a full-time arts director, Michael Curry, who arranges the television series of Great Performances. He presented in nearby Phoebus in June 2000, the New American Theater, a 1920s movie house transformed into an intimate 400-seat stage for the performing arts. A public fund-raising, staffed by Jay Joseph, financed its construction. Magruder Boulevard has long been regarded as Hampton's frontier of industrial and business development. In the middle of the corridor was the city's major landfill. The landfill was closed 25 years ago; on the site is a major 27-hole golf facility. Rimming it are headquarters for industries and businesses. One of the early settlers of Hampton Roads Center I is the Gateway Computer Assembly Plant, employing a force of 2,500.

Hampton Roads Center II will open in 2001. Hampton City Manager George Wallace pushed the installation of a 311-telephone call center on which people can call for guidance on non-emergency matters. In its first year of operation, the nine full-time operators and several part-time aides have handled 153,000 calls for help. It touches every department except fire and police.

Its manager, Liz Nisley, said calls range from a complaint about a pothole to a question about a house assessment. Another question is whether one may bury a dog in the back yard. Yes, the caller is told, but first check with Miss Utility to make sure no wire or pipe is in the way.

The information system has won two national awards and one from the Virginia Municipal League.

In neighborly Hampton, no task is too big or too little to put people at ease.

VIRGINIA BEACH

In recent years, Virginia Beach has had two, quite different, highly-effective, compelling leaders: shrewd, amiable Sidney Kellam and petite, quick-minded Meyera Oberndorf. Kellam, who died at 83 in 1986, was born into the thick of politics, the son of Abel Erastus Kellam, Princess Anne County Clerk for 23 years. Sidney was the seventh of 12 brothers.

An apocryphal story had it that Abel sat his sons on a wall and had them speak to anyone who came by. "He didn't sit us on the wall, but he did like for us

to speak to everybody," Sidney Kellam acknowledged.

When his mind wasn't on politics, Sidney Kellam watched what was going on about him as if he *were* on that wall, benign, bemused. In a relaxed mood, he said, "I've eaten so much crow it tastes like chicken." Asked what he enjoyed most about politics, Kellam answered, "Winning." He was one of the five top lieutenants in U.S. Senator Harry F. Byrd's organization, and its ablest strategist. Byrd reigned 40 years in Virginia and Kellam led Virginia Beach for nearly as long.

He was proudest of having created the modern city of Virginia Beach and of having helped avert a flare-up of racial violence in the 1960s. He persuaded owners of beachfront hotels and restaurants to admit all races. "We integrated our schools without any publicity," he said. "I suspect we were integrated the first year before anybody knew anything about it. We had some very fine black leaders. We worked together. We never had any problems."

In 1959, Norfolk, hungry to expand its eastern border, annexed 13.5 square miles of Princess Anne County. The bite included Janaf Shopping Center, the Norfolk Airport, and 30,000 county residents.

The legal process of growth was also occurring elsewhere in Virginia, but the wrath of some residents of Princess Anne and Virginia Beach was as if they felt they had received a personal affront. The land awarded to Norfolk was more of a nibble than a bite. Kellam feared that Norfolk would seek a larger portion of land in a second effort. To block the annexation, Kellam set out to devise a way to merge Princess Anne County and the tiny resort town of Virginia Beach.

And he did. He began to stall for time by proposing to Norfolk officials not to annex any of Princess Anne County for five years; in exchange he would not seek a change in annexation laws. The deal was struck. Kellam's maneuvering would make a casebook study for political science departments.

In September 1961, Princess Anne and Virginia Beach officials announced they would study a possible merger. What gave life to Kellam's strategy was a new state law allowing counties and cities to merge. That law was the hinge of the trap he snapped on Norfolk.

Some believe that Kellam was behind the adoption of the law. It smacked of his Machiavellian-style. Having managed political campaigns for Harry Byrd's organization many years, Kellam had friends throughout the Commonwealth and in the General Assembly who would do his bidding about a law that would appear to many to be a sensible, progressive one, anyway.

Residents in Virginia Beach and Princess Anne would be voting on whether to Merge, while Norfolk, on the sidelines, tried to hinder any merger.

The merger of Norfolk's two neighbors would

Above
After securing the merger of huge, rural Princess Anne County and the then tiny resort strip of Virginia Beach, Sidney Kellam set about shaping the new boom-town city of Virginia Beach. For nearly all of 40 years Kellam was the dominant figure in Virginia Beach politics and the foremost campaign strategist for U.S. Senator Harry F. Byrd's powerful state-wide political organization in Virginia. Courtesy, The Virginian-Pilot.

Left
Meyera Oberndorf, Mayor of Virginia Beach, led the 15-year, finally successful struggle to supply the city with water through a 75-mile pipeline from Lake Gaston in North Carolina. In her fourth term and 13th year as Mayor, she was the first woman elected to public office in Virginia Beach. In her revolutionary administration, Virginia Beach has advanced on many fronts. Photo by David B. Hollingsworth. Courtesy, The Virginian-Pilot.

Bottom
At age 90 in 2000, Elizabeth Sills is still vigilant and active in preserving environmental treasures in Virginia Beach. At word that she is in yet another crusade, a horde of her dedicated volunteers turns out for her command. She also founded the Virginia Beach Society for the Prevention of Cruelty to Animals and the Virginia Beach Little Theater. Photo by Mort Fryman. Courtesy, The Virginian-Pilot.

put Norfolk into a box that not even Houdini could get out of.

Any chance the merger would fail on December 5, 1961 faded, when the Norfolk City Council made a fatal blunder. It threatened to cut off the water to Princess Anne County within six months if the merger was approved. That was the worst tactic it could have taken.

Kellam called it blackmail. In comic disdain, he said, "They put a water pistol to my head." In an overwhelming vote, Beach residents approved the merger four to one. Princess Anne County voters favored it 5 to 1. Virginia would have a new city.

The coupling in Virginia Beach encouraged political leaders bent on merging South Norfolk and Norfolk County into the City of Chesapeake.

Still another success was the merging of the City of Suffolk with sprawling Nansemond County. In all three instances, the mergers helped avert annexation of territory by the older core cities.

In his strategies, Sidney Kellam had changed dramatically the map of Hampton Roads and affected the destinies of its cities. Hereafter, Kellam would be known as the Father of Virginia Beach or "Mister Virginia Beach."

Instead of the easy, unrestrained growth enjoyed by the major cities of North Carolina, with their access to ample land, the trio in Hampton Roads would have to grub for progress.

A further question was whether the parties in the dispute would be able to lay aside old grievances and cooperate on measures that would benefit them all.

Meyera E. Oberndorf's meteoric rise to mayor of Virginia Beach began when neighbors asked her to host a meeting to iron out differences between them and the city's schools. After the meeting, someone asked her mother if Meyera had ever considered running for public office. "Oh no," she replied, "Meyera likes to work behind the scenes."

But city council members George Ferrell and Al Bonney asked her to serve on the library board. At her first meeting, Meyera, then 24, was elected vice chair, then chairwoman.

In her more than nine years at the helm, the city built a model central library and several branches. It whetted her interest in how government works. In 1974, she ran for city council. "I fell in love with the city," she said. "I just wanted to work with people to make things happen."

She came in fifth in a field of 12. Only two years later she won, the first woman elected to public office in the city.

In her fourth term and 13th year as mayor she said, "I feel that if Virginia Beach had not been such a young and open city, I'd never have been given the opportunity to serve as early as I did and as long as I have."

The 1980s brought dynamic growth. The *Wall Street Journal* called it "Boom Town." City council built schools, roads and libraries, and began a 15-year struggle for a reliable water supply. The contract with Norfolk provided water from its surplus to Virginia Beach.

Meyera wanted a long-term guaranteed source of water that would supply Virginia Beach, if need be, as much as 60 million gallons of water a day. Two droughts in the 1980s dramatized the need. "We didn't ration water, and when we asked people to conserve it, we had to be judicious in the way we phrased it," she said.

"People were angered at seeing others washing a car or watering lawns. They called the city to turn them in. We had to impose a moratorium on new building. Every election campaign evoked ideas to

Willie Nelson performing to a packed beach at the Fifth Street stage. His concert, one of many that was part of the third Annual American Music Festival in 1996. He took the stage to a standing ovation. Photo by David B. Hollingsworth. Courtesy, The Virginian Pilot.

relieve the shortage. Two rows of books contain studies of them. It always came back to one conclusion. For a supply of 60 million gallons a day, we had to go to Lake Gaston."

That objective drew objections from Virginia towns and counties along the way and from North Carolina, home to most of the lake. It also aroused opposition from doubters in Virginia Beach. "None of the political power brokers tried to give me directions," Oberndorf said. "They left me on my own to do what I thought was morally right."

Early on, the only individual to offer substantive support was Governor Charles S. Robb. He conferred in North Carolina with Gov. Jim Hunt, assuring him that the pipeline would draw water only from the Virginia side. Sen. Jesse Helms, muddying the water, accused Hunt of trying to sell North Carolina's birthright.

Norfolk eventually endorsed the pipeline plan and entered into an agreement to treat and deliver the Lake Gaston water to the Beach. Chesapeake also became a partner in the pipeline.

But the Beach did most of the heavy work, with Councilman Liaison Louis R. Jones, City Attorney Les Lilly, and City Manager James Spore, working with Oberndorf as a team, seeing the $150 million project to completion in 1997. "The Gaston project marked a critical point in Virginia Beach just as it was about to emerge from its adolescence to young manhood," Mayor Oberndorf said.

Virginia Beach continues to be a caring community: 10,000 volunteers contribute 1.5 million hours annually. The volunteer program is a model for other cities around the world.

In blending a city with a county, Sidney Kellam left undone a central business district. Beach leaders moved to fill that gap early in 2000 in breaking ground for a 1.8 million square-foot Town Center. Clustered around two 22-story towers will be new hotels, apartment complexes, retail restaurants, movie theaters, and a park. It will cost $167 million.

The city keeps treasured farms in production with an Agriculture Reserve Program. It buys development rights from willing owners. They obtain their nest eggs without having to take their farms off the market.

The Hurricane Protection Plan has tripled the width of the sandy beachfront along the beach. Its cement boardwalk has been strengthened and widened. Atlantic Avenue has been restored as a place for families. Some 30 miles of waterfront are open from Willoughby Spit to pristine False Cape State Park bordering North Carolina.

A host of farms in and around the seven cities produce fresh fruits and vegetables that make for feastful springs and summers. There are 22 horse farms. Among other amenities are the Contemporary Art Center that keeps Hampton Roads alert to mocking, shocking, modern Art. The Virginia Marine Science Museum, already judged one of the 10 best museums in America, is adding a 1.2 million gallon tank for sea creatures.

For concerts there is the GTE Virginia Beach Amphitheater. The Sportsplex in Virginia Beach vies

A tall ship in the Chesapeake Bay seen from Fort Story in Virginia Beach when OpSail 2000 visited Hampton Roads. Photo by David B. Hollingsworth.

173

with Harbor Park in Norfolk where the Norfolk Tides play baseball. Hockey is played in Norfolk's Scope. Other sports are hosted at a dozen campuses at colleges and universities throughout Hampton Roads.

North Landing River in lower Virginia Beach is the site of lovely Munden Park.

Chesapeake and Portsmouth joined Norfolk in favoring a light rail line that will be needed to link Hampton Roads with a network of lines from Washington, D.C. It will speed traffic along the East Coast.

In an advisory referendum, Virginia Beach citizens opted out of planning for the light rail line. As Town Center nears completion, the laggards may see the line as being helpful in conveying visitors to its attractions.

They may yet have time to catch that train.

Among hundreds of treasures that have been here always is First Landing State Park, a secluded wilderness in the northend of Virginia Beach. Its huge, sun-baked sand dunes, three stories high, are ever on the move, growing by fractions of inches through eons of time.

Environmentalist Elizabeth Sills and her cohorts defeated a move by the state in the 1960s to privatize and sell the park. It fronts the beach on Chesapeake Bay where the first English settlers disembarked from three tiny sailing ships and set foot in the New World. They looked around, in awe, ate wild strawberries big as a man's fist, then moved up the river to found Jamestown.

Here is where at all began.

Thanks to Liz and her friends, we are not greeted on that hallowed land by a handy convenience store.

NORFOLK

If one of various calamities hits America's mid-sized cities, you can count on Norfolk rallying to overcome it. The city is quick to seize any opportunity to advance.

In 1963, Norfolk was denied annexing any more land to expand its borders. It toiled to make the best of what it had. Mayor Roy Martin, Jr. heard that Walter P. Chrysler, Jr. wished to move his art trove from Provincetown, Massachusetts to a larger locality. The mayor invited Chrysler to meet in Norfolk with 15 civic leaders. Chrysler did so, and they began negotiations for the transfer of the collection, the valued then at $85 million, to Norfolk.

When Larry Cox, Norfolk's lobbyist in Washington, D.C. reported that a pending bill would grant Denver funds to build an arena, Mayor Martin said, "Get us on board." Virginia Sen. A. Willis Robertson put a rider for Norfolk on the bill and Norfolk built its Scope arena, and the concert hall that it named for Chrysler.

Thousands of dollars flow to Norfolk from individuals. Former Gov. Colgate Darden, Jr. once observed, "Norfolk, unlike some other cities, loves people more than it does money."

Stanley Harrison loved his wife, Edythe, who loved him and opera. They joined with the city and the state in funding construction of the Harrison Opera House. In a night at the opera, people from throughout Hampton Roads enjoyed music. By day, they began working on boards for the opera and the other arts.

Yellow buses bring school children from the seven cities and beyond to hear maestro Peter Mark con-

The Harrison Opera House is home to the internationally-renowned Virginia Opera. The building originally served as a USO during World War II. Photo by Anne Peterson. Courtesy, Virginia Opera.

duct the opera. Super titles flash above the stage, and an entire generation is learning to like opera.

People in Hampton Roads may disagree at times on political issues; but they are able to take a regional view on the arts. In the Chrysler Museum is Tissot's large oil painting of "Artists Wives"— women in a busy outdoor Parisian cafe, smiling, self-absorbed in talk. Centered in the foreground, one looks over her shoulder toward you, laughing as if in recognition, her dark eyes inviting you to join the circle. That is the message of all the arts in Hampton Roads: "Come in!"

In the 1960s, the Norfolk Zoo was shameful in its tight confines. Margaret Falkiner, former *Virginian-Pilot* reporter, led in organizing Friends of the Zoo. They campaigned for funds and the city joined in making the Virginia Zoological Park a world-class zoo. Hefty private gifts for the zoo ensued, some large ones from Virginia Beach. Children donated dimes toward housing two Siberian tiger cubs in the first spacious natural habitat. The zoo now is part of a nationwide network to breed rare species.

The board of the Norfolk Botanical Gardens continues to assure that their garden grows ever lovelier amid canals, lakes, and tall pines.

Bewitching JoAnn Faletta leads the Virginia Symphony in more than 100 concerts a season throughout the region. The Symphony has won rave reviews at Carnegie Hall in New York and the Kennedy Center in Washington, D.C. An auxiliary of more than 100 women aid in the fundraising.

In the early 1960s, Norfolk suffered a flight of citizens to suburban shopping malls. It recruited developer Jim Rouse to design a festival marketplace by the Elizabeth River, as he had done for other core cities. He had pioneered in creating suburban malls that had wooed shoppers away from the core cities. Now he sought to lure them back.

With dozens of events, the new marketplace, Waterside, drew crowds to the Elizabeth River— and still does—but it did not reach downtown.

In the mid-1960s, Norfolk strove, but failed, to attract a mall to fill 17 undeveloped acres downtown. In a bold move, City Council invested $100 million in public funds to persuade Taubman Co. to build MacArthur Center across from the old City Hall, now a memorial to General Douglas MacArthur. Malls throughout Hampton Roads began remodeling—

a lifting of their quality. Even Richmond began angling for a mall anchored by Nordstrom. Norfolk also had a Dillard's flagship store.

The *Virginian Pilot*'s Jennifer Goldblatt caught the exuberance of the MacArthur Center's opening on March 12, 1999. It drew 72,000 people, most of them shoppers. By 9 a.m., responsible parties had invoked the name of General MacArthur. "Like the General himself who vowed, 'I shall return,' the city has returned to its historic and rightful role as role as the business, cultural, and retail hub of Hampton Roads," said Norfolk Mayor Paul Fraim.

By noon, mall officials estimated 30,000 people, including 140 reporters and managers from other area malls, had descended upon the Center. Customers didn't want to go home when closing time came, and managers were lenient in bringing down the gates.

Those who had put so many years and so much effort into MacArthur Center were awestruck at what they had created. The city had, after all, tried for 40 years to fill the land where MacArthur Center was finally built, with many proposed projects falling through.

In the words of Councilman Mason C. Andrews, who was the major force behind preserving the 17 acres for Norfolk's new mall: "It was a satisfying moment, but we've still got a lot to do." Andrews' friends, reading Goldblatt's report the next day, were not surprised that even in a moment of triumph he was plotting what to do next to assure Norfolk's progress.

In Norfolk, where Andrews started his medical practice, the first conditions that struck him as needing improvement were at Norfolk Community Hospital, which served the city's black population. "Somehow or other it just seemed necessary to go out there and help do something about it. We all just worked together in treating patients and began formulating a new set of procedures," he said.

One doctor had applied to other places for further training, but none accepted him. Andrews helped him find a place in Detroit. "They made me chief of services until he came back from Detroit. He is one of the best doctors in this area."

Andrews' concern about medical care for Tidewater Virginia culminated in a 12-year drive for a medical school. He consulted experts throughout the United States.

Foes came from the University of Virginia in

CHAPTER TEN

CHRONICLES OF LEADERSHIP

Surrounded on three sides by the world's finest harbor, Norfolk has had troubles as well as blessings from the water. The British bombarded the strategic gulf during the Revolution. Yankees occupied it during the Civil War. The Navy conscripted it during both world wars. Yellow fever came by ship. Norfolk's natural advantage as a port caused upriver planters and then upriver cities to band ogether to stifle it. The city's history has been one of starting over.

A business history of Hampton Roads must include a general background because so much of its commerce has been and continues to be dependent upon the harbor. Enterprises suffered when the area was bombarded, occupied, and conscripted. On the other hand, businesses have generally thrived during periods of peace and unhampered international trade.

Norfolk and its sister cities on the port have enjoyed a period of economic growth since World War II. Several of the companies whose histories are recounted in the following pages were originated after the war. Considering the age of the city, this may seem surprising. Actually, it is characteristic—these ventures were begun by people who were themselves starting over. Many of their stories are heroic.

There are also several biographies of organizations that have been around for a century or longer. In some cases these firms, while retaining their historic names, also had to be reestablished after the war.

In general, Hampton Roads' maritime economy derives from the late 19th century. The construction of major shipyards, some surviving today, dates from that time. The arrival of the Navy in 1917 as a major economic force accelerated the expansion of water-related industry, but the basis for it had already been well established. The Navy made an opportune choice.

With commerce development has come cultural and governmental growth. This too is described in the following pages.

But the constant throughout all the annals, the constant throughout the history of Hampton Roads, is the harbor. The area has experienced intervals of negating its heritage and denying its own nature, periods when lack of care let the waters be poisoned, the beaches fouled, the shoreline turned over exclusively to industry. Hampton Roads is flourishing because it is again taking pride in its natural glory.

CAPE HENRY COLLEGIATE SCHOOL

In the 1920s Virginia Beach was a sleepy East Coast ocean-side resort town where families came to spend their summers. The population was barely 800 (less than the current enrollment of Cape Henry School) and the street lights were turned off at 9:00 pm.

It was 1924 when Mrs. Helena Everett decided her four young daughters would receive a better education at home. Starting a school was not her intention, however four of her friends soon convinced her to teach their children as well, and that fall, with an enrollment of eight students, the "Everett School" was born.

The first classes were held in a summer cottage on the ocean, but

Helena Keville Allen (1885-1978).

enrollment grew and more room was needed. In 1930 Mrs. Everett built a colonial style home on Cavalier Drive and designated two rooms as the "school." Within a few years the need for more room was again apparent and additional classrooms were constructed at the rear of the home.

In the spring of 1959 Mrs. Everett, then in her '80s, wanted to retire and asked Grace Jordan and her niece, Dickie Jordan, to take over the School. Enrollment was at 100 students. After running the school for a year, Grace and Dickie

Helena Allen Everett, founder.

were given the option to buy the corporation, Everett School, Inc., which was owned by Mrs. Everett. In the '60s Everett School offered classes from kindergarten through 5th grade for girls and through 6th grade for boys; enrollment had grown from 100 to 170 students. The now 10-classroom school was staffed by 10 full-time teachers, with three part-time teachers for art, music and physical education. Most of the pupils were from Virginia Beach Borough, although some came from what was then considered "as far away" as Aragona Village.

It was during the '60s that the board of directors realized the need for a private school in Virginia Beach that went through high school and, in 1970 obtained 30 acres on Mill Dam Road. The first building fund was started, and the pre-kindergarten through 12th grade dream was becoming a reality.

The original founder, Mrs. Everett, was unhappy with the planned change of location for the School. She wanted Everett School to remain on Cavalier Drive. Since Mrs. Everett was in her '90s by this time, Grace and Dickie decided to change the name as well as the location to avoid any conflict. Many names

were considered but Cape Henry was the choice. Construction began, and over the Thanksgiving weekend of 1970, with the help of many parents, Cape Henry moved into the new facility on Mill Dam Road, consisting of just the gymnasium, separated by partitions for offices and classrooms.

Dickie was made headmistress in 1972 and Grace retired in 1973. The School went through two headmasters, Calvin Schutzman and Tom Smith, in three years, then Mr. N.W. Morris came in temporarily in 1974. Dr. Hugh Moomaw came in 1975 as head of school, and that year Cape Henry graduated its first senior class with four students. The following year, the board of trustees added "Collegiate" to the School's title in order to reflect its college preparatory mission.

During Dr. Moomaw's tenure, 1975-1986, the School grew from 157 students to an enrollment of over 400 students. Those 11 years were truly a period of rapid growth and development for Cape Henry Collegiate School. As enrollment grew, so did the campus. The auditorium and lower school building were added in 1978, and when the enrollment again grew beyond those boundaries, 13 portable trailers were purchased to temporarily accommodate the growth.

In 1987, when Dan Richardson became head of school, Cape Henry Collegiate School's campus facilities included one academic and administra-

The Everett School on Cavalier Drive was torn down in the 1980s.

Cape Henry today, The Perry Library.

tive building, the original gym, and 13 portable trailers. Cape Henry did not want to be "the best kept secret at the Beach" any longer. The community needed to know what a fine job Cape Henry was doing of educating young people, and the campus facilities needed to meet the increasing demands of the community.

The commitment to the School by its founders and board of trustees was strong, but the inadequacies of the campus facilities were hindering growth. From 1989 through 1999, with the support of many dedicated board members, Cape Henry continued to develop as a leader in the educational community. During that 10-year period, with the help of all Cape Henry Collegiate School constituents, a new two-story academic building was added, with 27 classrooms (Founder's Hall); a new gymnasium (the Alfred T. Taylor Fieldhouse); a new 7,800 square-foot library (Perry Library) with an additional six classrooms and administrative wing; a new cafeteria area and a new 5th grade wing. In addition, the athletic playing fields were significantly upgraded and expanded, and construction was completed on the Perry Family Auditorium, Fain Family Atrium and the 15,000 square-foot Arts Complex.

Cape Henry Collegiate School has traveled many paths since 1924 when Mrs. R.C. Everett taught those first eight students in her summer home. While each path has been marked by chal-lenges, Cape Henry has remained faithful to its stated goal of excellence.

Cape Henry Collegiate School welcomes students of all races, religions, national and ethnic origins, recognizing the educational benefits and personal growth that can be achieved by providing an economically and culturally diverse atmosphere for students. The environment provided for each student attending Cape Henry is one of support and challenge, with ultimate goals of developing self-esteem and critical thinking skills.

With a coed enrollment of nearly 1,000, Cape Henry enjoys a student/ teacher ratio of 10 to 1. One hundred percent of Cape Henry's graduating se-niors have traditionally been accepted into colleges that include Harvard University, Princeton University, Duke University, University of Virginia, Brown University, Johns Hopkins, Massachusetts Institute of Technology, The College of William and Mary, University of Southern California, James Madison University, Virginia Polytechnic Institute and many others.

Today Cape Henry is a vital and thriving educational complex, honored by the U.S. Department of Education as a National Blue Ribbon School and cited for excellence in every arena. Area business and community leaders have singled out Cape Henry Collegiate School as a dynamic alternative to traditional methods of education.

As Cape Henry Collegiate School passes its 75th anniversary, it is readily apparent that these are not the marks of an educational institution that lives in by-gone days or rests upon past achievements. Cape Henry is a beacon for learning that is vibrant, alive and eager to move into the 21st century.

In the '40s, the chidren found their stages all over town. If the weather was good, it was the Cavalier Gardens, as shown here.

THE CAVALIER HOTEL

The hotel that made Virginia Beach famous, The Historic Cavalier, or as many locals refer to her "The Grande Dame or Queen of the Hill," has a history so rich that most of the other oceanfront hotels pale in comparison. Her sturdy beginnings, lavish grand opening, famous guests, and her rise to national prominence gave way to the days of being leased by the Navy, and eventually becoming a private club in 1953. The Grande Dame of the resort strip in Virginia Beach closed her doors in 1973 amidst rumors of demolition only to triumph again and reopen in 1976 in time to meet the demands of the summer tourist season. This is a story of one of the nation's most magnificent hotels, The Historic Cavalier.

On May 9, 1926, the cornerstone of The Cavalier was set in place. It took 300 business-minded Norfolkians, $2 million, 225 men, 13 months of steady labor, 500,000 bricks, and tons of steel and cement, to build one of the first fireproof, high-rise, and one of the finest hotels on the East Coast.

The grand opening, a week-long event, attracted over 7,000 guests. Members of the community, regional businessmen, senators, and the national media converged on the 250-acre property and looked on in awe at the many

A photograph dating back to the 1930s depicting The Historic Cavalier on The Hill, the gardens, and the famous Cavalier Beach Club.

amenities that were unheard of then and remain so to this day. For example, each guest room had four water lines: hot, cold, saltwater and ice water. Saltwater was considered to have medicinal value, and the hotel went as far as to fill the indoor pool with seawater. Refrigeration was uncommon during this time so ice water was considered very posh.

In the early 1930s, the hotel gained the reputation as the "Aristocrat of the Virginia seashore." The hotel was considered by many to be a city within itself and by 1935 was hailed as Virginia's largest industry, paying more taxes and employing more people than anyone else. Every imaginable amenity was available for guests, including a commercial photographer, doctor, barber, ice cream parlor, beauty shop, drugstore, gift shop. Even a stock broker was available for transactions, with a ticker tape connected directly to the New York Stock Exchange.

Trains from the Midwest, and later from the Northeast, brought guests right to the front lawn of the hotel. The Midwest line even fashioned a slogan using the hotel's name, "The Cavalier to the Cavalier."

The Cavalier resort as it stands today, The Historic Cavalier on the Hill, the modern day oceanfront Cavalier, and The Beach Club.

Businessmen weren't the only guests to enjoy the many unprecedented amenities. Hollywood's elite, prime ministers, and high-level government executives of the day could be seen strolling through the sunken gardens, playing golf on the 18-hole course, horseback riding, and hunting. Other guests could be found savoring the sun and Atlantic Ocean from the hotel's private beaches.

When the sun went down and the stars came out, the place to be was "The Cavalier Beach Club." It stood seconds away from the Atlantic Ocean, where guests would dance to the sounds of the best big bands of the decade. Every big band that toured the country would ultimately play The Beach Club. Greats such as Benny Goodman, Glen Miller, Tommy Dorsey with Frank Sinatra singing, Cab Calloway, Guy Lombardo and Lawrence Welk, with his singing trio, the Rhythm Boys—one of whom was Bing Crosby—entertained hundreds of guests at the private club.

Locals who weren't members of the private Beach Club could hear the sounds of the big bands as the music drifted up and down the oceanfront. Dancing under the stars and by the sea during the hot summer months was a fond memory often recalled by local residents. After the bands called it a night, guests would hop into a limousine destined for nearby clubs offering verboten gambling and (during prohibition) drink.

Catering to a guest's *every* whim was the mantra at The Cavalier. During its heyday there were 435 employees to meet the needs of 367 guests. Guests' servants, horses and even hunting dogs all had special quarters, with one dining room catering solely to chauffeurs.

Word of the exclusive resort and its impeccable service quickly spread around the country, and soon the rich and famous of the day had made it their playground. Guests included F. Scott Fitzgerald, Rudy Vallee, Victor Borge, Bob Hope, Elizabeth Taylor, Betty Davis, Jean Harlow, Judy Garland, and the list goes on. Carlos Wilson, a present-day employee and a living historian on The Cavalier Hotel, has been a busboy, waiter and bartender and served many of these celebrities as a personal steward.

In fact, Wilson recounts the many times President Richard Nixon would come and insist on starting a fire in the Hunt Room—an exclusive "men's club,"—where he would sit reading for hours, staring into the huge fireplace that made the Hunt Room a "must visit" for all male guests. President Nixon wasn't the only President to visit The Cavalier. Over the years, seven United States Presidents have enjoyed the Hotel's abundant amenities. Other Presidents who have reportedly stayed at The Cavalier include: Calvin Coolidge, Herbert Hoover, Harry Truman, Dwight Eisenhower, John Kennedy and Lyndon Johnson.

In 1992, during the filming of the NBC-TV movie "Life of Jackie Kennedy," film crews came and filmed many scenes at the original Cavalier.

President Gerald Ford presented a speech before the Virginia Bar Associa-

Above
The Historic Cavalier lobby.

Left
A shady spot on the lawns of The Historic Cavalier on the Hill.

tion, President Jimmy Carter spoke at the hotel addressing the Southern Baptist Convention, and President George Bush, as the Ambassador to China, also delivered an address here to the Virginia Bar Association.

Norfolk, Virginia is known throughout the world as the headquarters of the largest naval base. During World War II, Navy personnel from around the country descended upon Hampton Roads. It was during this time (1942-1945) that the Navy leased the hotel, using it for a radar training school. Blackout curtains were placed over the ceiling glass and windows of the swimming pool area. The water was drained from the Olympic-sized pool to facilitate Navy training maneuvers. During 1944–1945 there was such a shortage of space that the stables were cleaned and turned into living quarters for sailors. Again, Carlos Wilson can recount the day the war ended. He was waiting on Lieutenant Bailey when he heard the sirens from the ships off the oceanfront and SOS signals that the war had ended. Never in his life had he experienced such joy and celebration. Lieutenant Bailey gave him a $100 tip and told him to forget the food, just bring on the drinks and let the celebration begin. That night Wilson was afraid to sleep because of all the money he had made in tips.

The war was over and the Navy left the hotel in ruins. The silverware was missing, there were holes in the walls, and even the bell from the bell tower was missing, never to be found again. It was restored, but it would never again see the brilliance of yesteryear.

Only three months after Hank Ketcham, his wife Alice, and his world-famous son Dennis were guests at the hotel on July 1, 1953 and for nearly a

The famed Hunt Room fireplace located in The Historic Cavalier is a popular night time gathering for winter guests of the oceanfront Cavalier.

A pictorial of activities that capture the Cavalier on the Hill from yesterday to today.

decade, the Historic Cavalier became a private club. Ketcham eventually drew several *Dennis the Menace* cartoons based upon his family's stay.

On December 31, 1959, Mr. Gene Dixon, Sr. and his partners purchased The Cavalier. On August 28, 1961, Dixon became the sole and current owner of the property.

In 1973 a newer, more modern, Cavalier Hotel opened only yards away from the Atlantic Ocean. It was at that time that the "Grand Dame on the Hill" closed. It was a sad day for historians and the news grew dim as rumors spread that the original Cavalier would be de-

molished. On October 9, 1974 a group of local children formed together and started a "Save the Cavalier" campaign. For three years the hotel remained closed, but in 1976 after numerous renovations, the hotel opened to meet the demands of the summer tourist season.

To this day, The Cavalier on the Hill reminds us all of the colorful and rich history of the Virginia Beach oceanfront, the military's part in the play, and how this grand and historic hotel put Virginia Beach on the map.

DOLLAR TREE STORES, INC.

Who says a dollar can't buy anything these days? At Dollar Tree Stores you can get anything from candy bars to luxury soaps, from calendars to hardback books—all for only a dollar.

Perhaps that's why Dollar Tree Stores, Inc. is the nation's leading discount retailer with a $1.00 price point. It has enjoyed consistent growth and impressive financial results since its inception in 1986, and today includes over 1,400 stores across the United States. "Our concept is essentially that of a modern-day variety store, filling the gap left by Woolworth's and other five-and-dime- type stores of yesteryear," explains the company's president and CEO Macon F. Brock, Jr.

Dollar Tree has its roots deep in the Hampton Roads community. Brock and fellow-founders J. Douglas Perry and H. Ray Compton, began their retail careers at a family-owned Ben Franklin's in Norfolk's Wards Corner area. Owned by Mr. Kenneth R. Perry, Sr., the Ben Franklin's grew into a 136-store toy chain before being sold in 1991. In those early years, the Wards Corner store was the K&K Toys flagship, complete with a lunch counter for the lunchtime regulars. Long-time Dollar Tree employees still recognize their roots in the K&K Toys-era

Dollar Tree's stores are located in the most convenient locations for the customer. A flexible format and size allows the stores to be tailored to their environment.

when they stop to chat at the soda fountain in their Chesapeake headquarters facility.

In keeping with the variety tradition, the stores appeal to a broad range of shoppers of various ages and income levels. But, unlike the dim, dusty five-&-dimes of yore, Dollar Tree stores have an upscale look (most with carpeting, music, and quality fixtures and shelving). The location of the stores is given great consideration. Most are located in power strip centers, regional malls and neighborhood centers, near major grocery stores or large discount retailers such as Wal-Mart, Kmart, and Target. "Right in the heart of Middle America," as chairman J. Douglas Perry puts it, "just like the variety stores that used to line Main Street, USA."

Part of Dollar Tree's success can be attributed to the rich variety of merchandise in its stores; they carry everything from food and party goods, to seasonal items, toys, housewares, and gifts. Also, due

Stores range from a smaller "boutique" size of 5,000 square feet to a larger "variety store" size of 10,000 square feet. The broad selection of goods fits a customer's needs and desires, from the kitchen to the bath, from gifts to school supplies, all at $1.00.

to its size, the company enjoys significant purchasing power, using an experienced buying staff and selecting value merchandise from all over the world.

Dollar Tree has five distribution centers strategically located in its geographic market areas: northern California; Chicago; northern Mississippi; Chesapeake, Virginia; and Savannah, Georgia. Clustering stores around these support centers is part of what gives Dollar Tree its edge. The Chesapeake facility, completed in early 1998, is a fully-automated distribution center encompassing 400,000 square feet. It is situated in an ideal location, with easy access to the Port of Hampton Roads as well as major rail lines.

Dollar Tree has great long-term growth opportunity, with plans for continued store expansion each year, increased coverage in existing markets, and the virtually unlimited availability of potential sites. The company looks forward to making history well into the 21st century.

EDGAR CAYCE FOUNDATION

Born on March 18, 1877 in Christian County, Kentucky, Edgar Cayce was known at the time of his death in Virginia Beach on January 3rd, 1945 as one of the most accurate psychic medical diagnosticians of all time. Nine thousand six hundred and three transcripts were given on a great number of diseases in which the cause of the disorder was cited and treatments were outlined in great detail. When the instructions were followed, the individual was helped. Cayce gave only verifiable physical readings for the 22 years, before other types of information were requested. He left behind over 14,306 copies of transcripts, which were meticulously recorded, indexed and cross-referenced by his lifelong secretary, Gladys Davis Turner, into the largest body of revealed information in the world.

The roots of the three Cayce organizations in Virginia Beach were planted in September 1925 when Edgar Cayce and his family moved from Dayton, Ohio to found the Cayce Hospital for Research and Enlightenment. Financial backers Morton and Edwin Blumenthal and David E. Kahn of New York; Thomas B. Brown and Madison B. Wyrick of Dayton, Ohio; Franklin F. Bradley of Chicago and F.A. Van Patten of Virginia Beach purchased what is today the Cayce Hospital. The hospital, designed by Rudolph, Cooke and Van Leeuween and built by the United Construction Company of Norfolk, Virginia, still stands on what was once an isolated sand dune overlooking the Atlantic Ocean. Other organizations followed shortly. Headed by Dr. William Moseley Brown, formerly of Washington and Lee University, sister organization Atlantic University was chartered April 30, 1930. In 1948 Cayce heirs Hugh Lynn Cayce, Edgar Evans Cayce and Gladys Davis Turner chartered the Edgar Cayce Foundation.

Atlantic University, located on Little Neck Road in Virginia Beach, offers a Masters of Arts in Transpersonal Studies. Transpersonal Studies encompasses a course of study designed to explore that which transcends the persona, or the five senses. The interdisciplinary nature of

Above

The Cayce family: taken in Selma, Alabama in 1922 by LB Cayce. Left to right: Edgar Evans Cayce Jr., Gertrude Cayce, Edgar Cayce, and Hugh Lynn Cayce.

Below

Gladys Davis Turner, 1905-1986.

the program offers both traditional and non-traditional courses at a distance and in-residence. Course concentrations include archetypal studies; consciousness and intuition; creative writing; holistic health and holistic living; sacred literature; visual arts and women and the transpersonal perspective.

Atlantic University students avail themselves of the ARE/AU Library, located at 215 67th Street in Virginia Beach, which has over 60,000 volumes topically concentrated in holistic health, metaphysics and parapsychology, as well as a published edition of the Cayce readings available to the public. This beautifully-appointed library includes the largest collection of para-psychological and metaphysical subject matter on the east coast of the United States. Students from nearly every country of the world visit to avail themselves of its resources.

The Association for Research and Enlightenment (ARE), chartered in July 1931 is an international membership organization with a mailing list of over 100,000. Conducting conferences and workshops, facilitating member activities and events organized through 10

regional offices in the United States as well as at the Conference Center in Virginia Beach, the ARE is a vigorous focal point for Virginia Beach. The Health and Research Center provides an opportunity to participate in both educational and experiential programs in alternate

The Cayce Hospital, circa 1928.

healing methodologies based upon the Cayce information. Other programs administered from Virginia Beach include ARE Camp for children and families, internationally-organized groups studying the Cayce material, an annual June ARE Congress, daily tours and free lectures at the Visitors Center and the Harold J. Reilly School of Massotherapy. The Reilly School, established in 1985 by founder Dr. Harold J. Reilly, certifies students in massage and the holistic health practices espoused in the physical readings. The ARE Health Services Department, open to the public, is a popular year-round attraction in Virginia Beach.

Chartered in 1948 to provide permanent legal and physical custody of the readings, personal papers and related memorabilia the Edgar Cayce Foundation also houses Edgar Cayce's personal correspondence with the 5,756 people who had psychic readings from him over a 44-year period. The Foundation provides

research and consultation support for many researchers, television and motion picture scriptwriters and authors. Among these is Dr. John O.A. Pagano of Englewood Cliffs, New Jersey, who has published a book based on his 20 years of clinical research entitled, *Healing Psoriasis–The Natural Alternative.* His successful treatment of this seemingly incurable disorder has focused international attention on Edgar Cayce and Virginia Beach. The Foundation also maintains Cayce-related exhibits at the Pennyroyal Area Museum in Hopkinsville, Kentucky and the Old Depot Museum in Selma, Alabama.

The Cayce information has always had good things to say about Virginia Beach, urging financial backers as early as 1925 to consider the area because of its nearly unlimited potential for future growth. Norfolk was included in this growth projection, and in 1936 Cayce's information stated that within 10 years Norfolk would be the "larger port on the Atlantic Coast," a statement which has indeed proven accurate.

Growing along with Virginia Beach, the Cayce organizations provide employment for over 125 people and utilize over 100 volunteers. The Cayce readings are available in their entirety on CD-ROM. Over 600 books have been written in 18 languages, beginning in 1943 with the publication of the first Cayce biography, *There Is A River*, published by Henry Holt and Company, written by Thomas Sugrue. Other significant titles include *Sleeping Prophet* by Jess Stearn and Putnam's latest biography, *Edgar Cayce-An American Prophet* by Sidney D. Kirkpatrick. Several major television programs have featured the Cayce information and from the four corners of the world over 40,000 visitors a year are drawn to Virginia Beach to learn more about this unique body of information.

In February 1944 an inquirer asked Edgar Cayce the following question, "Where should I live?" To which Cayce responded, "Wherever ye choose. Virginia Beach is a very good place." Indeed, it is.

Dr. Harold J. Reilly, 1895-1987.

CEDERQUIST RODRIGUEZ RIPLEY MADDUX—ARCHITECTS

Located across from the Harrison Opera House in Norfolk is one of the City's premier architectural firms, Cederquist Rodriguez Ripley Maddux. Based in Norfolk, with offices in Chesapeake, Virginia, the firm provides the highest quality architectural, planning and interior design services throughout the United States and the Caribbean.

The firm's success is attributed to exceptional leadership by its founders, and exceptional customer service from its diverse and talented staff. Founders David V. "Dave" Cederquist, Arnold C. "Rod" Rodriguez, William J. "Bill" Ripley and John B. Maddux, Jr. built their reputations on creative designs, doing their work right and putting their customers first. It was only natural that, as a team, they would nurture these very same qualities within their firm. They continue to handpick their staff and to help them develop their craftsmanship, interest in pleasing their customers and pride in the important work they do.

Today the firm thrives with an excellent reputation in the design of new and renovated facilities, and is known for its proven ability to create cost-effective solutions for major renovation and modernization projects. Cederquist Rodriguez Ripley Maddux plays a leading role in the public schools in this regard. It was among the first in the country to complete multi-school studies focused on bringing outdated facilities in-line with today's learning standards. Its work has contributed to helping keep the availability of quality classrooms in balance with the area's growing demands.

Delivering quality projects on time and within budget continues to be the key to keeping valued customers. Retaining those customers in today's dynamic marketplace also requires helping them outpace their competition. Cederquist Rodriguez Ripley Maddux continues to expand its satisfied customer base by doing just that. In the nationwide retail arena, for example, the firm is a major player in the timely opening of several hundred, highly-competitive retail stores each year.

It is not surprising that, with its dedi-

Above
First Virginia Bank Tower (right) in downtown Norfolk.

Below
Renovation of the historic N24 at the Norfolk Naval Base, which was a part of the original Jamestown Exposition.

190

In the late 1970s, founders Dave Cederquist and Rod Rodriguez distinguished themselves with the design of the First Virginia Bank Tower. This 17-story structure was the tallest building in Norfolk at the time and is still an impressive part of the Norfolk skyline.

The public spotlight focused on the firm in the early 1990s, when it won a major design competition to restore and renovate the former Wheat Building for Life Savings Bank (now BB&T Bank). As Norfolk's first "skyscraper," it took its place as a part of the City's skyline between 1897 and 1899. It became an architectural *"cause celebre"* among preservationists in 1989 when the previous owners announced plans to sell it as a development site for the construction of a modern high-rise. Fortunately, those plans never came to fruition and its new owners recognized it as one of Norfolk's true architectural gems. For its work, the firm received the Preservation Alliance of Virginia's *Virginia Preservation Award* for Restoration of a Historic Property, and the City of Norfolk's Design Review Award.

Cederquist Rodriguez Ripley Maddux continues to grow and attract the very best talent. As the firm expands its customer and project base, its strength in the design arena grows, as well. The firm is proud to have federal, state, municipal and private customers that value excellence in their work and who, in turn, give it a very bright future. Cederquist Rodriguez Ripley Maddux is equally proud to be a part of the Norfolk success story.

cation to providing maximum value to its customers, Cederquist Rodriguez Ripley Maddux received the U.S. Department of Defense's International Award for "Outstanding Value Engineering" in 1999. At a ceremony held at the Pentagon in Washington, D.C., the firm was singled-out for its ability to provide the highest-quality product while saving the U.S. Navy nearly $60 million.

Flexibility and the skill to anticipate changes have allowed the firm to become a major contender in today's design field. Seamlessly adapting from a manual design system to a totally networked and computer-based one was key to the firm's transition and growth during the '90s. Its ability to efficiently harness the enormous power of global networking and global commerce will continue to allow Cederquist Rodriguez Ripley Maddux to stay in the forefront during the new millennium.

Cederquist Rodriguez Ripley Maddux traces its roots back to a practice begun in the 1940s by architect Harry R.

Restoration of the historic Wheat Building, Norfolk's first skyscraper.

Dudley, Jr. The current name represents a 1988 reorganization of Morrisette Cederquist Bondurant, an architectural and engineering firm started in 1978; a merger with William J. Ripley, Architect, a firm started in 1983; and a merger with The Architectural Associates, a company started by John B. Maddux, Jr. in 1987. Today the firm is actively practicing in 40 states, and on the islands of Aruba, Curacao, Puerto Rico and Cuba. Its work has also extended to the Azores, Spain, Italy and England.

The new W. T. Cooke Elementary School in Virginia Beach.

CLARK NEXSEN ARCHITECTURE AND ENGINEERING

Clark Nexsen Architecture and Engineering is the largest design firm in the Hampton Roads area. This 80-year-old firm has deep roots in Virginia, but its reputation for excellence is known worldwide. Clark Nexsen projects have served clients in 20 states from Hawaii to Massachusetts and in 32 foreign countries from Panama to Nepal.

The firm's long record of success derives from the expertise and professionalism of its staff, which now totals 162 people, up from 43 in 1993. This success puts it among the largest 500 design firms in the U.S. Clark Nexsen's staff prides itself on the ability to adapt to the complex needs of an ever-changing business world and technical environment. It realizes that, beyond expertise and dedication, serving clients' needs requires the hands-on development of innovative and creative solutions to client problems.

Pendleton S. Clark, FAIA, set this tone in 1920 when he started the firm in Lynchburg. His growing reputation for professionalism with institutional projects across central Virginia carried the firm successfully through the Depression and World War II. In 1948, the Lynchburg firm accepted two new partners, Walter R.

Twin Oaks I office building on the site of Old Tidewater Tides baseball complex off Interstate I-64 on Norfolk. First of several buildings to be constructed in the 42-acre business park.

Nexsen, AIA, and John D. Owen, AIA. Clark also formed a partnership in 1950 with Navy Civil Engineering Corps Admiral Victor D. Buhr, P.E. and Norfolk engineer Myron Sturgeon. The new Hampton Roads design office was focused primarily on government clients. This Norfolk office, originally called Sturgeon, Clark and Buhr, became Clark, Buhr and Nexsen, when Walter Nexsen became the managing partner. From 1965 through 1978, the two offices operated under the title Clark, Nexsen & Owen. The name was changed to Clark, Nexsen, Owen, Barbieri & Gibson

Corporate officers (left to right): Carl E. Cholewa, P.E. senior vice president; Kenneth G. Stepka, P.E. executive vice president; Robert C. Gibson, P.E. chairman of the board; Christopher M. Stone, P.E. president; Thomas T. Winborne, AIA, senior vice president; Robert G. Kal, P.E. senior vice president.

in 1979, recognizing partners Robert C. Gibson, P.E. and Clifton L. Barbieri, AIA. In 1996 the firm's name was shortened to Clark Nexsen.

After 1950, the Lynchburg office concentrated on service to private and institutional clients for over 30 years; while the Norfolk office concentrated on serving governmental clients. In 1980, Clark Nexsen made a major commitment to overseas work, opening an office in Madrid, Spain to serve U.S. agencies in Europe, North Africa, and the Middle East. Completed projects include Embassy improvements in Germany, Turkey, Nepal, and Mali; cruise missile launch facilities in Italy, and abort-landing facilities for the Space Shuttle in Morocco and Gambia. The on-site manager in Madrid was Kenneth G. Stepka, P.E. This venture was directed from Norfolk by Robert C. Gibson, P.E., who succeeded Nexsen as president of the firm in 1985.

In 1994, another expansion resulted from a merger with the architectural firm of Gunn Hardaway in Charlotte, N.C.

COLONNA'S SHIPYARD, INC. 2000

One of the state's oldest family-owned businesses has been in continuous service for 125 years. It has grown slowly, but steadily from the small boat yard founded by Charles J. Colonna in 1875 into the 50-acre shipyard it is today. Colonna's is located at the confluence of the Eastern and Southern Branches of the Elizabeth River diagonally across the river from downtown Norfolk. The yard services commercial and military vessels from up and down the East Coast and around the world. It is a full-service ship repair and conversion shipyard with four marine railways up to 5,000 tons and two floating drydocks up to 18,000 tons. The shipyard workforce includes inside and outside machinists, shipfitters, metal fabricators, welders, pipefitters, electricians, docking crew, laborers, painters, carpenters and a gas free department.

Over the years, the shipyard has become known for its great facility, skilled and stable work force, fairness to customers and timely work.

The shipyard has recently purchased a small yard near its main plant and is

developing it into a repair facility for "mega" yachts from the United States and around the world.

Above
Aerial view of Colonna's Shipyard.

Below
Work being done on Gopher State *in 1992.*

EAST COAST ABATEMENT CO., INC.

Rick Webb was a teenager when he began working for his father's Chesapeake-based mechanical insulation company, installing pipe insulation on mechanical piping and boilers. Richard C. Webb Sr. began East Coast Insulation Company in March 1980, with the $17,000 he had earned from profit-sharing while working as a superintendent for a local insulation company for 17 years. He and his wife Annabell Webb, ran the office from their home. The company began as a sole proprietor business until it became well-established and was incorporated in the mid-'80s. By this time, Rick had become quite experienced with the insulation business.

When the federal government finally banned asbestos building materials as a potentially deadly carcinogen, Rick and his father did the only logical thing. They expanded their company to include asbestos removal. In 1983, at the age of 22 and newly married, Rick began running the asbestos removal operations. In August 1983 the company hired Mrs. Betty Hodge to handle the daily office routine, payroll which consisted of eight employees, and typing asbestos abatement removal plans for government, state and city projects. Mrs. Hodge is still with the company today. Betty said that her biggest challenge in the early years was acquiring liability insurance and bonding capabilities for the company in

East Coast's first asbestos Decon trailer and company truck in 1981 at the beginning of the asbestos removal business.

a high risk, competitive industry such as asbestos. In the beginning, an asbestos plan consisted of one page outlining the procedure for the removal operation. Today the average required plan is approximately 500 pages. With the increasing demand for asbestos removal as well as increasing cost for risk insurance and the liabilities involved, the Webb's decided to form a separate company to handle the hazmat removal demand. Thus, in 1986, East Coast Abatement Company was created.

East Coast Abatement was incorporated in February 1987, with Rick Webb as president. In 1987 the government passed the Asbestos Hazards Emergency Removal Act-AHERA. AHERA gave all schools, public and private, one year to devise an asbestos management plan and two years to begin implementation. As the demand to remove asbestos in-

creased, hundreds of contractors flooded the market. Through Rick's foresight, hard work, integrity, excellent reputation and determination to give his customers the best service possible, along with the hard work and dedication of employees Robert and Tyrone Fuller, East Coast Abatement grew into a thriving business. Today, East Coast is likely the last family-owned asbestos company remaining in the area.

In 1994, Mr. And Mrs. Webb, Sr. decided to take life easier and semi-retire. Rick took over the company in May 1994, owning 100 percent of the stock. Rick relocated the business to its present location in the Hickory Township of Chesapeake. Rick was full of visions and dreams for his future with his wife Phyllis and their young family, which by this time included daughter Kara Marie Webb and son Richard C. Webb, III. He wasn't satisfied to stay an asbestos abatement contractor; he wanted to move on to a more challenging career. By this time the company had several ongoing contracts with local municipalities for demolition and renovation projects for neighborhood revitalization, as well as government housing projects.

So often, asbestos removal and building demolition go hand-in-hand. For years Rick had been hiring subcontractors to perform all demolition operations. One day he thought to himself, "I can do that." He could and he did. He purchased two LN9000 Ford tractors, two dump trailers, and one 320 Cat Excavator in October 1994. At this time he had an existing contract with Department of Housing and Neighborhood Preservation for the City of Virginia Beach, and thus began the demolition business and East Coast Demolition. In one year sales exceeded $2 million.

Also during this same year, most cities in Hampton Roads had completed testing all city parks' playground equipment for lead paint. One-third of the playground equipment in 10 of Chesapeake's 28 parks had dangerous levels of lead-based paint on them. When East Coast Abatement was awarded the contract by the City of Chesapeake, they

The first fleet after the expansion of the company into the demolition business, in 1994.

Mr. and Mrs. Webb presenting Rick Webb with a congratulations cake when he became president of East Coast Abatement Co.

became the first contractor to commence the abatement of lead paint from the city parks.

East Coast Abatement and Demolition has been involved in many revitalization and modernization projects throughout the Tidewater Area since1995. After the Housing and Redevelopment Departments for the various cities condemn the blighted neighborhoods' drug-infested houses and dilapidated structures, East Coast Abatement demolishes the buildings and cleans up the site. Rick says, "It feels good to know we are 'making things better' by cleaning up the drug neighborhoods and converting them into parks and better living environments."

One large project was the demolition of Fairwood Homes in Portsmouth, Virginia. East Coast Demolition's government contracts involve the demolition of government housing and World War II buildings at local Army bases such as Fort Eustis and Fort Story, Virginia. The company has participated in many cleanups, including following hurricane damage in the area. One such project was the demolition of the Tradewinds Hotel. The oceanfront hotel, a landmark on Virginia Beach's resort row, had been damaged Labor Day Weekend 1998 by Hurricane Bonnie. Another oceanfront landmark, the old Seaside Amusement Arcade in Virginia Beach, was razed by East Coast Abatement. The 87-year old arcade was demolished to make room for a $45 million hotel and retail complex as well as a public park.

Rick has stated that his most memorable job was the "World's Largest Attic" and "World's Largest Wooden Structure" located in Elizabeth City, NC. The steel blimp hangar with a 100-foot ceiling consisted of another ceiling below, 22 feet above ground by one-inch cable suspensions. T-Com, L.P., a blimp company, bought the building and needed the newest ceiling removed. To complicate matters the hangar was open at one end, and when the wind blew the ceiling moved like a wave. Mr. Webb stated that this was a very dangerous undertaking and he was very thankful all of his employees walked away with no more than a cut finger. The "Worlds Largest Wooden Structure" was destroyed by fire in 1995, leaving the steel doors standing. Bringing down 300,000 pounds of steel by crashing them to the ground was one of the challenging projects of his career.

The demolition business has grown and prospered so well, along with the inventory of equipment and fleet of vehicles, that it became necessary in recent years to hire full-time mechanics for maintenance and repairs. The construction is completed on the new East Coast Equipment Repair building and

storage facility on approximately 18 acres in the Currituck Industrial Park in Moyock, North Carolina. Along with the growth of the business has come expansion of the office staff to 12 full-time employees and a field employment averaging 75 to 85 employees, and gross revenues for 1999 exceeding $6 million.

Rick has met the challenge and surpassed his expectations for the demolition division of his company. For the future, plans are in process to expand into the recycling and concrete crushing aspect of demolition disposal. By 2001, East Coast Crushing and Recycling should be in full operation.

Rick is very appreciative and proud of the great achievements his company has made and wants to thank the people in his life who have contributed to his success and been so meaningful to him and the company. "I can only say that God and my parents, wife, family and most of all my employees, have blessed me. Without the support of my valued employees—including Betty Hodge, Robert and Tyrone Fuller, Bob Slick, Dino Johnson, Bobby Vann, Carl Stallings, Jerry McPherson, Johnny Harper, Darren Clark, Joyce Webb and Connie LaCross—East Coast Abatement and I would not be what we are today. And from the bottom of my heart, 'Thank you all!'"

Demolition tractor and trailer inside World's largest attic (T-Com Blimp Hanger, Elizabeth City, North Carolina) loading out debris.

EASTERN VIRGINIA MEDICAL SCHOOL

Eastern Virginia Medical School holds an honored position in American history as the only school of medicine established by a grassroots effort of the local community.

The medical school traces its history to 1964, when the Virginia General Assembly passed enabling legislation that allowed planning for a new medical school to begin. The organization chartered by the General Assembly to oversee the medical school is today known as the Medical College of Hampton Roads, and its governing body is the Board of Visitors.

After nine years of planning for the proposed school, community leaders next turned their attention to raising the necessary funds. In 1970, the Eastern Virginia Medical School Foundation launched a three-year, $15 million campaign. At that time, this campaign was the most ambitious fundraising effort ever undertaken in Hampton Roads.

People throughout Eastern Virginia joined in this effort. Large corporations and small business owners; philanthropic organizations and ordinary citizens—thousands contributed in amounts large and small because they recognized that a medical school would vastly improve the community's quality of life. After three years of intensive fundraising, the EVMS Foundation surpassed its goal, raising more than $17 million by 1973 for the new medical school.

The success of this first campaign allowed EVMS to receive its first accreditation in June 1973 and matriculate its first medical students in October 1973. Graduate medical education began the following year, as the region's existing programs were brought under the medical school's umbrella. Over the years additional doctoral and master's degree programs in the health professions were developed, including programs in biomedical research, clinical psychology, art therapy, public health, and for physician assistants.

Today, the Medical College of Hampton Roads Board of Visitors continues to serve as the governing body responsible for all education, research, and

The original campaign to establish EVMS was one of the most ambitious fundraising efforts ever undertaken in Hampton Roads. Pictured are campaign leaders Porter Hardy, Jr.; Harry H. Mansbach; Dr. Mason C. Andrews; and Henry Clay Hofheimer II in 1971, celebrating having reached the $7 million mark in the $15 million campaign for EVMS.

patient care programs of Eastern Virginia Medical School, and the EVMS Foundation Board of Trustees continues to oversee the school's fundraising efforts.

Eastern Virginia Medical School's unique heritage as a regional success story is reflected in the membership of the school's Board of Visitors. Eleven of the 17 board members are appointed by the city councils of Chesapeake,

EVMS caught the world's attention in 1981 with the birth in Norfolk of Elizabeth Jordan Carr, the first child in America to have been conceived through in vitro fertilization.

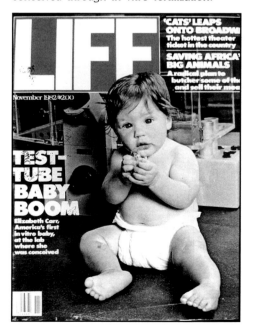

Hampton, Newport News, Norfolk, Portsmouth, Suffolk, and Virginia Beach, and six are appointed by the EVMS Foundation.

Eastern Virginia Medical School's first three decades have seen tremendous growth since the early days when classes were held in Smith-Rogers Hall, a building that originally served as a dormitory for Leigh Memorial Hospital's nursing students.

Construction on the school's first building, Lewis Hall, was completed in 1978. Designed to house the school's educational and research activities, this building was named for Richmond philanthropists Sydney and Frances Lewis, whose $1.5 million challenge grant in 1972 helped EVMS surpass its original $15 million fundraising goal.

Eastern Virginia Medical School caught the world's attention in 1981 with the birth in Norfolk of Elizabeth Jordan Carr, the first child in America to have been conceived through in vitro fertilization. This exciting breakthrough was made possible by the work of fertility experts Drs. Howard and Georgeanna Jones, who had joined the EVMS Department of Obstetrics and Gynecology after their retirement from Johns Hopkins. The success of the in vitro fertilization program led to the formal establishment in 1983 of the Jones Institute for Reproductive Medicine, which remains one of the world's leading centers for education, research, and patient care in reproductive medicine.

The school's growing clinical programs gained a new home in 1985 with the opening of Hofheimer Hall. This building was named for Henry Clay Hofheimer II, the founding president and chairman of the EVMS Foundation, and his wife Elise.

In 1987, a major gift from civic leaders Leonard and Joyce Strelitz allowed EVMS to establish an education, research, and patient care program in diabetes. Today, the Strelitz Diabetes Institutes is internationally-renowned for its work in the prevention and treatment of diabetes. In 1997, the Strelitz Diabetes Institutes announced the discovery of the

INGAP gene, which may hold the key to a cure for diabetes.

The medical school's growth as a center for biomedical research led to the construction of the next campus facility: a new building for the Jones Institute. With construction complete in 1992, this new building allowed the Jones Institute to house its growing team of physicians, scientists, and other specialists under one roof.

Two additional specialized programs were established in 1992—the Virginia Prostate Center and the Center for Pediatric Research. A joint program with Sentara Norfolk General Hospital, the Virginia Prostate Center provides education, research, and patient care for those struggling with prostate cancer.

The Center for Pediatric Research is a joint program with Children's Hospital of The King's Daughters. This unique research program joins basic scientists, practicing physicians, and community leaders to cure and prevent pediatric diseases.

The local community has continued to support the growth and development of Eastern Virginia Medical School. In 1993, the medical school and its

Completed in Spring 2000, the Edward E. Brickell Medical Sciences Library provides the EVMS campus with a new academic and architectural focal point.

supporters launched The EVMS Campaign for the Next Century, a $62-million effort to build the EVMS endowment and strengthen the school for the future.

As part of this effort, the school's geriatrics program received a major boost when local philanthropist Virginia Glennan Ferguson made a multi-million dollar gift to establish the Glennan Center for Geriatrics and Gerontology.

Major gifts to the campaign also established the Thomas R. Lee Center for Ocular Pharmacology and the Theresa

With the growth and development of Eastern Virginia Medical School, Hampton Roads has become a nationally-recognized center for medical education, research, and patient care.

A. Thomas Professional Skills Teaching and Assessment Center.

The support of the community also allowed EVMS to open its newest building—The Edward E. Brickell Medical Sciences Library—in spring 2000. Named in honor of Dr. Edward Brickell (EVMS President 1988-2000), the new state-of-the-art library provides an architectural and academic focal point to the EVMS campus.

The campaign also met its goal of increasing the EVMS endowment. Thanks to the generosity of the community, the total number of endowed faculty positions grew from five to 23, including 15 endowed chairs, six distinguished professorships, and two endowed professorships.

When it ended on December 31, 1999, The EVMS Campaign for the Next Century had raised more than $66 million, including $5.4 million for the Brickell Library. As Hampton Roads enters a new century, the community can take pride in having created a nationally-recognized center for medical education, research, and patient care.

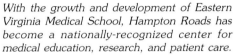

ECI SYSTEMS AND ENGINEERING

Founded in July 1980, Eastern Computers, Inc. (ECI) has become one of the major business successes in the Hampton Roads-area. Dr. Richard Cheng and his son James Cheng started this research and development company with one full-time employee and 120 square feet of office space in Virginia Beach.

Under Dr. Cheng's leadership and vision, ECI developed the first multilingual computers and peripheral equipment providing 26 natural languages. ECI marketed its multilingual technology products throughout the world, especially in Asia and the Persian Gulf countries. In 1983, ECI competed against computer giants such as IBM, Xerox, and Wang Laboratories, along with 38 other companies, to win a contract supplying the United States Information Agency's worldwide computer network. This multi-million dollar contract was the first major business breakthrough for ECI, leading to a string of U.S. government contracts with the Labor and Education departments, and the Pentagon. By then ECI had expanded its business in broadband computer networks, computer-based training systems, software development and telecommunications. Accordingly, the multilingual computing products became a very small portion of the company business. ECI is currently engaged in the business of computer simulation technology, telecommunications, multi-level secured networks, electronics manufacturing and e-commerce.

In 1990, ECI received the largest U.S. government contract ever awarded to a small business—a contract from the Internal Revenue Services to tend its Tax Processing Systems throughout the nation. The contract had a ceiling of $240 million dollars, which spanned six years. By 1991, ECI had approximately 500 full-time employees with operations in 30 different U.S. states and throughout Europe. Additionally, ECI expanded its business base into manufacturing of electronic components and systems, weapon simulation systems, telecom switches and import/export of general merchandise.

Above
Congressman Owen Pickett and Dr. Richard Cheng participate in "Ribbon Cutting" ceremony officially opening ECI's new headquarters in February 1989.

In 1991, ECI was recognized as Small Business of the Year by both the Hampton Roads Chamber of Commerce and the Commonwealth of Virginia. In 1991, President George Bush awarded Dr. Cheng the National Minority Small Businessperson of the Year Award on behalf of the U.S. Small Business Administration. In 1992, ECI received the High-Tech Business of the Year award by KPMG, and the High-Tech Business of the Greater Washington Region by Ernst & Young and Merrill Lynch. ECI has also been listed in the *Inc* 500 and *Washington Technology* magazines as one of the top growth companies in the nation.

The successes of ECI are the result of the excellence and dedication of the many outstanding people working in the company. The company was research-oriented in the very beginning, and that has set a defined direction for the future of the company. Committed to innovation, ECI has been a leader at the forefront of technology and has always been willing to take calculated risks in its investment into new ideas and new technologies. As a privately-held small business, the research and development expenditure to revenue ratio of the company surpasses that of many companies of similar size.

In the last decade of the 20th century, ECI invested into e-commerce for both the business to business (BtoB) and the business to consumer (BtoC) models. ECI is also diversifying into new businesses such as import/export of consumer products and subsequently marketing the products to large distribution companies. A new division has been established to manage real estate properties for the company in Virginia and the Washington, D.C.-area.

Looking forward into the 21st century, ECI will continue to develop new products and invest in new ideas. ECI has continued to expand its operations throughout the continental United States and other countries. Because of the favorable business environment Virginia has created, along with its mild weather, the convenience of the ports, and a significant military presence, ECI plans to continue its base operations in the Hampton Roads-area.

Above
Dr. Richard Cheng receiving the National SBA Small Business of the Year Award from President George Bush in September 1991.

Below
Photo of ECI's headquarters building in Virginia Beach, Virginia.

THE HAMPTON ROADS PLANNING DISTRICT COMMISSION

In 1969, Virginia was divided into 22 planning districts pursuant to the *Virginia Area Development Act*. Local governments embracing a majority of the population within the planning district were authorized to organize a planning district commission by means of a written charter agreement. As a result, planning district commissions were created throughout Virginia "...to promote the orderly and efficient development of the physical, social and economic elements of the district by planning and encouraging and assisting governmental subdivisions to plan for the future." (*Code of Virginia, Section 15.1-4207*). The existing Southeastern Virginia Regional Planning Commission became the Southeastern Virginia Planning District Commission, serving the southside area of the Hampton Roads. The Peninsula Regional Planning Commission became the Peninsula Planning District Commission, serving the Peninsula area.

The HRPDC serves as a resource of technical expertise to its member local governments, providing assistance on local and regional issues.

In 1990, the two commissions merged, forming the Hampton Roads Planning District Commission (HRPDC). The HRPDC represents over 1.5 million people in 16 jurisdictions: the Cities of Chesapeake, Franklin, Hampton, Newport News, Norfolk, Poquoson, Portsmouth, Suffolk, Virginia Beach, and Williamsburg, and the Counties of Gloucester, Isle of Wight, James City, Southampton, Surry, and York. Membership on the 44-member Commission is based on population, with each jurisdiction having a minimum of two members. The Commission has an executive committee, made up of one member from each jurisdiction. The executive committee provides policy oversight to the HRPDC's activities through monthly meetings held between the quarterly meetings of the full Commission. The executive director/secretary, selected by the Commission, manages the daily operations of the planning district's professional staff of more than 40 people.

The HRPDC is committed to providing leadership and support to other public and private, local and regional agencies in their efforts to improve the region's quality of life. The HRPDC has coordinated many regional milestones, including the formation of the Southeastern Public Service Authority for solid waste management, the establishment of a regional jail facility, the creation of the Hampton Roads Partnership, priority-setting for major transportation projects, and implementation of regional stormwater management, water conservation and groundwater mitigation programs.

Organization: The HRPDC serves as a resource of technical expertise and assistance to its member local governments. As a Virginia Planning District, the HRPDC is also the Affiliate Data Center for the region, providing economic, environmental, transportation, census, and other relevant information to businesses, organizations and citizens. The HRPDC provides regional vision, leadership, and innovation in transportation, physical and environmental planning, and economics.

The HRPDC is funded by annual contributions from its member local governments, by appropriations from the Virginia General Assembly, and by grants from federal, state and local governments.

The HRPDC's Transportation Department is the support staff for the Hampton Roads Metropolitan Planning Organization, the agency responsible for regional transportation planning. Assisting local elected officials and chief administrative officers in their efforts to improve the region's quality of life, the department conducts studies and produces information concerning transportation issues of local and regional importance. The department also provides technical support to member municipalities regarding transportation and emergency management and preparedness needs.

The HRPDC's Physical and Environmental Planning Department provides a forum for the local governments to exchange information and to develop cooperative initiatives that address regional environmental issues and opportunities, as well as state and federal regulations. The department conducts technical and policy studies, provides technical assistance to the member localities and others, and coordinates water resource management. The Physical and Environmental Planning Department staff performs general physical planning activities, as well as coordination with state and federal agencies and programs. The department manages community education and outreach programs, including regional efforts in water conservation, stormwater pollution prevention, and watershed protection.

The HRPDC's Economic Department serves as a resource for socio-economic data throughout Hampton Roads and provides member jurisdictions with ongoing information about the region's current economic issues. The department performs economic analyses on a large variety of regional topics, such as industrial targeting, economic growth, fiscal stress, taxes, and transportation. The staff gathers and maintains a large database from which regional trends are monitored to produce annual forecasts of business conditions in Hampton Roads. The department also includes a Human Services Planner who coordinates the Hampton Roads Loan Fund Partnership that provides low-income families with opportunities for home ownership.

The Commission represents over 1.5 million people in the cities of Chesapeake, Franklin, Hampton, Newport News, Norfolk, Poquoson, Portsmouth, Suffolk, Virginia Beach, Williamsburg and the counties of Glousester, Isle of Wright, James City, Southhampton, Surry and York.

HAMPTON ROADS SANITATION DISTRICT

The Hampton Roads Sanitation District (HRSD) can give credit to oysters for spurring its creation. HRSD traces its beginnings to 1925, when the Virginia Department of Health condemned a large oyster-producing area in Hampton Roads, bringing the question of sewage pollution to light. This closure resulted in the Virginia General Assembly creating a "Commission to Investigate and Survey the Sea Food Industry of Virginia" in 1927. Also of great concern was protecting the public from disease and the potential loss of recreational activities, real estate values, and natural resources. Other studies since 1927 recommended a public body to construct and operate a sewage system in the area. At the time, 30 million gallons of "raw" (untreated) sewage was being discharged daily into area waterways.

Virginia General Assembly legislation in 1934 created the Hampton Roads Sewage Disposal Commission, with a directive to draft a plan to eliminate pollution by sewage in the tidal waters of the Chesapeake Bay. Recommendations were made to the General Assembly, which resulted in the Sanitation Districts Law of 1938 along with an "Act

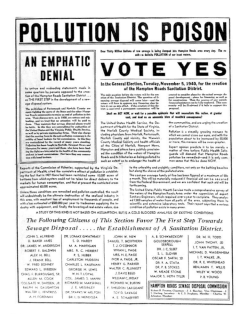

Above

To reduce water pollution from sewage, HRSD was created by public referendum in 1940.

Below

HRSD owes its creation to oysters, a robust seafood industry in the early 1900s. The Virginia Department of Health condemned a large oyster-producing area in 1925, bringing the question of sewage pollution to light. Courtesy, Norfolk Public Library

to provide for and create the Hampton Roads Sanitation District." The Act was later revised, and voters decided favorably for the creation of HRSD at a general election on November 5, 1940. The agency was named after Hampton Roads, a ship anchorage used for nearly four centuries at the convergence of the James, Elizabeth, and Nansemond Rivers before flowing into the Chesapeake Bay.

The 1940 Enabling Act permits HRSD to operate as a political subdivision of the Commonwealth of Virginia to provide wastewater collection and treatment. The agency is now governed by a commission of eight members appointed by the Governor for four-year terms. Administration is provided by the general manager, who is supported by five directors and their staff. The population served has grown from 288,000 in 1940 to 1.5 million in 2000, the 27th largest metropolitan area in the nation.

HRSD began operations on July 1, 1946, using facilities acquired from the Federal Works Agency. The Warwick County (now part of Newport News) trunk sewer line was HRSD's first construction project. The first treatment plant, the Army Base Plant, began operation in October 1947. Since then, the HRSD collection system has grown to more than 500 miles of interceptor pipelines and 80 pump stations. HRSD's nine major treatment plants in Hampton Roads and four smaller treatment plants on the Middle Peninsula have a combined capacity of more than 200 million gallons per day.

One of HRSD's greatest contributions to the wastewater treatment industry is the innovative Virginia Initiative Process. HRSD and the engineering firm CH2M Hill developed and patented this technology, used at both the Virginia Initiative Plant in Norfolk and Nansemond Plant in Suffolk. This biological process is a cost-effective, environmentally sound technique that removes most of the nutrients phosphorus and nitrogen from wastewater. The technology is offered free of charge to other wastewater agencies. It is key to HRSD's efforts to reduce nutrients entering the Chesapeake Bay.

HRSD's first treatment plant, the Army Base Plant, began operation in October 1947.

HRSD recycles biosolids, nutrient-rich organic matter resulting from extensive wastewater treatment processes. There are many beneficial uses for biosolids, which are proven safe to both public health and the environment. Biosolids can be processed into Nutri-Green® compost, applied as fertilizer, or incinerated into ash for construction uses. Recycling biosolids eliminates landfill disposal.

As a regional agency, HRSD not only works closely with cities and counties to meet the needs of the communities it serves, but also plays an important regulatory role. To protect the environment and its facilities, HRSD issues permits and monitors wastewater discharged from businesses and industries as part of its Pretreatment Program. The goal of the Pretreatment Program is environmental protection through the reduction of toxics and other pollutants entering the sanitary sewer system. The U.S. Environmental Protection Agency recognizes HRSD's program as one of the nation's best, using it as a model throughout the country.

HRSD's state-of-the art environmental laboratory uses the latest technology to monitor treatment processes, industrial discharges, and local waterways. This monitoring helps ensure that the agency maintains exemplary compliance of its regulatory requirements. Environmental monitoring and analytical services are also performed at cost for local government agencies, as part of the Municipal Assistance Program. More than 250,000 analyses are performed each year in the laboratory.

As the region has grown and its needs expanded, HRSD has become more than just a provider of wastewater treatment services. HRSD's mission is to prevent pollution, protect public health, and support community development by providing wastewater collection, treatment, and related services. The agency proactively seeks innovative services and programs to further support its mission. One such program, with support from an Environmental Protection Agency grant, unites HRSD's staff with faculty and students from Old Dominion University to provide free, nonregulatory pollution prevention assessments for selected businesses. This program has resulted in pollutant reductions in all media—air, land, and water—while saving business sectors such as shipbuilding and repair (so vital to the Hampton Roads economy) many thousands of dollars.

Another innovative program is boater education, conducted in cooperation with the Virginia Department of Health and funded by a Clean Vessel Act grant. Specially trained college students attend water festivals (such as Harborfest and Hampton Bay Days) and visit marinas to educate recreational boaters and provide free tank pumpouts. Boaters learn about the proper disposal of wastewater from sanitary holding tanks to prevent dumping into our waterways.

With over 60 years of service, HRSD has earned a reputation of environmental excellence and innovation. The agency has received national, state, and local recognition, including numerous awards for plant performance and outstanding regulatory compliance. HRSD is a progressive, environmentally responsible public utility working every day to protect and enhance the beauty and health of our natural resources.

The Virginia Initiative Plant features a patented biological process that removes most of the nutrients in wastewater, contributing to a healthier Chesapeake Bay.

HBA ARCHITECTS

HBA Architecture, Engineering and Interior Design began February 1, 1974, with two founding principals, William H. Hargrove III, AIA and Dan H. Brockwell, AIA and four employees. Today it is one of the most distinguished companies in its field. Founded on a principle of integrity and a standard of excellence, HBA committed itself to providing a realistic approach to architecture with an emphasis on quality service. HBA has spent more than a quarter-century pursuing its mission of excellence, and takes pride in the successes that have earned it a well-respected name in the region.

HBA has expanded its facilities four times since its inception. What began as a small office on Village Street in Portsmouth Virginia with four employees and two founding principals has grown to include two additional Partners, Bruce Prichard, AIA and C. Michael Ross, AIA, plus 45 individuals totaling a 49 person firm in Virginia Beach, Virginia.

In conjunction with HBA's growth has been its achievement of a reputation for a hands-on, proactive approach to consistently providing creative design solutions, on-time and below budget, and a customer service record built on a thorough understanding of the entire project. This has earned HBA a repeat client-base of 75-80 percent, as well as prestigious achievement awards from both local and state associations and other organizations.

Such a good standing is not built in a day, nor was HBA's resolute dedication to superior service. HBA began with a vision that incorporated the three disciplines of architecture, engineering, and interior design. The principals developed a team with the expertise to manage an entire project, offering services in architecture, planning, engineering, facilities, interior design, and design build. With their expansive professional resources, the HBA team is able to follow a project from design, through construction, to occupancy. This comprehensive approach enables HBA to help the client plan for the

future, and make design choices that will further his or her anticipated needs.

Although the firm is especially adept at designing new schools, it has graced landscapes with attractive banking, health care, and municipal facilities, offering aesthetic design that complements the environment in both domestic and foreign locales.

HBA has recently pushed the technological envelope with their Atlantic Division Naval Facilities Engineering Command (LANTNAVFACENGCOM) contract. HBA performs an intense two-week design charette, which the Department of Defense (DOD) calls a Facilities Assessment Concept Design (F.A.C.D.), with everyone from the base general to the janitorial supervisors to ensure the most encompassing project design possible. The HBA team utilizes the latest in graphics and estimating software during this charette. Because they cross-platform all their technology they are actually able to redesign, estimate and present a new concept every third day in both projector and paper format. LANTAVFACENGCOM was so impressed with their speed in presenting a finished package so rapidly they invited HBA to start a pilot program with them to develop a new way of transferring, reviewing, bidding and archiving their construction documents. HBA is very excited that they are on the

Chubb Rapid Response Unit, Chesapeake, Virginia.

forefront of this new technology, as they believe it will change the way all achitectural and engineering disciplines share information.

HBA's futuristic approach is evident in its involvement with educational facilities. The HBA design team does not approach a school facility design process in search of a static solution, but rather envisions the educational program as a master plan. Design solutions recognize and respond to the current criteria, while facilitating expansion and evolution. HBA assumes a responsibility to the community, spending public funds wisely as a partner with the school board.

One of HBA's more recent efforts is Antilles Intermediate School in Fort Buchanan, Puerto Rico, a new 600-student facility, featuring state-of-the-art technology applications and tropical courtyards. It is scheduled for completion in Summer 2002. Other well-regarded HBA projects include Jamestown High School in Williamsburg, Virginia; Currituck County High School in Currituck, North Carolina; Tallwood High School in Virginia Beach, Virginia; and Churchland High School in Portsmouth, Virginia. Among the features of these new school facilities are

mother's death, started Bay Disposal. He and Elliott bought a truck and 100 containers from Truxmore Equipment Company sales representative Bruce Armstrong, with whom he'd gone to school.

Starting service in January 1975, Bay picked up solid waste from restaurants and other commercial and industrial operations in the area.

The need to keep their restaurants in good condition led in 1978 to another venture: Bay Builders. Originally set up to augment Feather-n-Fin by building new restaurants and renovating existing ones, it eventually moved, under the management of Bob Wynberry, into building homes in the Suffolk area.

In 1985, Schaubach became aware of special needs developing for the removal of medical waste. He visited a plant with an incinerator while in Europe and, the next year he bought a 20-ton-a-day incinerator to burn medical waste in Norfolk. His and Elliott's new company, Incendere, was soon collecting medical waste in an area from New Jersey to Georgia. By 1988, the first incinerator was operating at capacity, and Incendere added two more units.

In 1987, Schaubach bought his brother's share of Feather-n-Fin. Three years later, he sold the restaurants to long-time manager Mark Roberts, who he had known since ninth grade.

In 1989, he and Elliott sold Bay Disposal to Chambers Development of Pittsburgh, and became affiliated with Smithton Sanitation Services of Washington, North Carolina, with Rob Cuthrell and Chester Smith. Smithton was named one of *Fortune* magazine's 500 fastest-growing companies in 1990.

In 1990, Incendere sought to expand its operations into Ohio. There, in Alliance, he bought municipal solid waste hauler Max Disposal and Recycling. This grew into a $5-million a year operation, which he sold to Laidlaw Environmental Services in 1995.

Back in Virginia, in 1994, Schaubach joined his son Jamie, and another father and son—Charles and Emmett Moore, to form Chesapeake-based Area Container, another municipal solid

Johns Brothers' variety of service trucks.

waste hauler. Schaubach merged into the operation another business he had held, BB Rentals, a portable toilet business.

Late in 1995, Dwight and Elliott split Incendere's operations, with Dwight taking the hauling operation and Elliott the incinerators. In February 1996, Dwight sold his waste disposal interests to Wayne Huizenga's Fort Lauderdale-based Republic Industries (later split into Republic Services Group and Auto-Nation).

In the same month he bought Johns Brothers, divided its operations into HVAC and security entities. On June 1, 1997 he moved it to modern quarters and he expanded its operations.

In 1998, with Hal L. Cole III, he founded Hal Cole Truck & Equipment Sales, Inc. in Richmond. On April 1, 1999, he acquired the assets of Suffolk Equipment Company, a Navistar truck dealership in Suffolk, and Hal Cole Truck & Equipment Sales of Suffolk, Inc. was formed. In March 2000, with additional changes in the area's waste disposal services, Schaubach decided to re-establish the Bay Disposal name as a locally-owned and operated Hampton Roads waste company. The company is run by the youngest of his three sons, Andrew.

Schaubach approaches all of his activities with enthusiasm and commitment, and has turned his long-standing interest in cars and racing into a business which has enhanced the sport in the area. In Spring 1997 he, Wayne Wyatt and Chuck Hall got involved with W.W. Motorsports, taking a 30-year lease

to operate and promote Langley Speedway in Hampton, a NASCAR-sanctioned Saturday night track. Wyatt handles business operations and Hall promotion.

Having earned Langley NASCAR recognition as one of the top five tracks in the Winston Racing Series, in 1999 they added Southside Speedway, a Saturday night short track in Chesterfield County (Richmond), to their operations. For Schaubach, it was a homecoming since his love of racing began as a boy, when the track was called Royall Speedway.

Schaubach, who says his goal is to "provide great competition in a good family atmosphere," sometimes drives in races at the tracks. He also collects, renovates and shows antique cars, particularly Duesenbergs and Buicks. One of his Duesenbergs, a 1929 model which was one of the first built, was nominated an outstanding vehicle in 1998 by the National Awards Committee of the Antique Automobile Club of America.

In what might remain of his spare time, he is an avid golfer with an eight handicap.

Family, too, is important to Schaubach. Married in 1962, when he was 20—"Jane and I were in school together from first grade," he says—he has three sons—Jamie, Stephen and Andrew, and two grandchildren. Jamie works in demolition and is a Legends Car driver at Langley, and Stephen designs computers and software.

After living in Norfolk for 30 years, in 1999 he and his wife Jane moved to a 76-acre farm in Suffolk, across the road from the 300-acre farm where son Jamie and his family live.

C. LLOYD JOHNSON CO., INC.

"The key to being a successful company is to make a commitment and live up to it."

This was the position Chuck Johnson took more than 50 years ago when he started the business that bears his name, and the position that remains at the heart of that Norfolk-based company today.

C. Lloyd Johnson Co., Inc. (CLJ) is the leading firm serving the $14 billion U.S. military resale market. It provides the vital link between manufacturers which market some of the world's top consumer brands, and the military stores that serve U.S. servicemen and veterans globally.

Born in Seattle in 1918, C. Lloyd Johnson Sr. first sold to the military resale system in 1936. During the early days of World War II, he was the first warrant officer appointed to the Navy Supply Corps from civilian life. Promoted to Lieutenant jg and assigned to the Brooklyn Navy Yard, he purchased supplies for ships in the 3rd Naval District.

In 1943, he was transferred to the Bureau of Supplies and Accounts in Washington, D.C., as the second officer in what would eventually become the Navy Exchange Service Command (NEXCOM). Later that year, to ensure that Navy units were being properly supported by the existing resale system, he was assigned to the Army/Air Force Exchange System in Jersey City, NJ, as liaison officer. After the war he completed his military duty at the Ship's Store Office in Washington.

On leaving the Navy in 1946 with both civilian sales and military purchasing experience, Johnson founded CLJ in shared office space on West 42nd Street in New York City. "I saw a niche in supplying goods to military resale organizations," he says.

At first, his was a one-person operation. The only account he represented was Waterman Fountain Pens, for the eastern half of the U.S. only. In the absence of a centralized exchange system, he spent his time visiting post exchanges of all four military services up and down the eastern seaboard. Soon he hired Bill McMonigle as a salesman

C. Lloyd Johnson, Sr., founder, now chairman emeritus.

to visit exchanges to the south while he visited those in the north.

"We would sit with the buyer, write up an order and send it to the manufacturer, who would ship," he recalls.

By 1948, CLJ had added such national firms as Tommy Traveler Leather Goods, Eaton Stationery, Dr. West Toothbrushes, and the American Safety Razor Corporation to the list of companies it represented. That year, Johnson took his first trip to call on Army, Navy and Air Force stores in Europe, and in 1949 he visited bases in the Pacific. In 1950, he made four trips to Europe, three to the Pacific, and one around the world calling on military accounts.

In 1949, CLJ added a leased warehouse and a second office in Norfolk to begin supplying Navy ships' stores based along the East Coast. In the early 1950s, the company added a warehouse and distribution center in Newport, Rhode Island, and began positioning people in

key market areas. In the second half of the decade, it added operations in San Diego, California, extending its services to the West Coast.

Along the way, the company established a reputation for reliability and integrity, and the number of manufacturers it represented grew.

In 1960, CLJ branched out to include service to commissaries. It formed its first division calling on a single, separate military resale activity. At first such sales territories covered between 13 and 15 states with sales associates traveling as far as 500 miles between appointments. This specialized approach worked, foreshadowing today's four divisions, serving commissaries, exchanges, ships, and the Veterans Canteen Service, which was added to CLJ's business list in 1991. Printing, accounting, art design, management information services, and

C. Lloyd Johnson, Jr., chairman and CEO.

corporate services departments support the divisions.

In the mid-1960s, CLJ added a civilian division, Carolson Commercial Corporation, which distributed Timex products to JC Penney stores in the East. Eventually, Carolson expanded to include JC Penney stores nationally and all Montgomery Ward Stores. It also built a civilian distribution and brokerage business in Hawaii and Alaska.

As computers became prominent, CLJ set out to be the industry leader in developing business applications. From the beginning, it hired its own programmers who tailored software to meet its needs faster and more accurately. This allowed it to offer services to its manufacturers and to the resale systems. By the time of its 50th anniversary, it was handling thousands of electronic orders each month, and taking a leading role in electronic commerce and category management.

"Whenever we see a technical oppor-

tunity, we want to be on the cutting edge," says C. Lloyd Johnson Jr., who took over as chairman and CEO after his father retired in 1996. Johnson, Sr. remains on the board of directors as chairman emeritus.

In 1974, CLJ moved its headquarters to its own building in Norfolk. Over the years, the military resale structure evolved into four separate exchange systems: The Army and Air Force Exchange Service (AAFES), NEXCOM, The Marine Corps, and the Coast Guard Exchange System. CLJ adapted to their differing procedures and methods of procurement. When the commissary segment changed dramatically with the introduction of the Defense Commissary Agency (DeCA), CLJ realigned its field sales and merchandising to DeCA's organizational structure.

CLJ's headquarters is close to the headquarters of all of its major military customers, except AAFES, which it serves from its largest regional office, in Dallas, Texas. Other offices are located in Frankfurt and Heidelberg, Germany,

and an office/distribution center exists in San Diego.

Throughout, service remains central to CLJ's operations, particularly when geopolitics requires fast delivery. "In the ships business, during emergencies, we need to deliver product within 24 to 48 hours," says Lloyd Johnson, Jr. During situations such as Operation Desert Storm, its warehouses and fleet of delivery vehicles work around the clock.

In 1996, CLJ initiated a merger with John K. Kealy Company, an exchange-focused firm, resulting in the Johnson Kealy Exchange Division of CLJ. At the time, military markets were shrinking, but this trend reversed in the last two years of the decade, restoring strength and momentum to the industry and the company.

CLJ is looking at diversifying within its core business by possibly operating retail ships' stores as well as supplying them. Outside, in-store merchandising services may soon be offered to the civilian market. Food service brokerage, an information technology service bureau, and the possibility of acquisitions are also being considered.

With nearly 300 full-time and over 400 part-time trained professionals, CLJ offers its trading partners a range of sales, marketing and merchandising services. These include theme-sale programs for commissaries, sophisticated electronic vendor-managed inventory systems for exchanges, and telemarketing services for Veterans' canteens. The staff uses its knowledge, expertise and training to build brand equity for client manufacturers, provide millions of dollars in savings for military shoppers, and raise hundreds of thousands of dollars in donations for non-profit and cause-related organizations.

CLJ's leaders have always been active in their industry. Chuck Johnson was a founder of the Armed Forces Marketing Council and served two terms as its president and one as co-chairman of its board. Lloyd also served as a chairman. Both have chaired the American Logistics Association and in 1993, Chuck received the ALA Lifetime Achievement Award.

JONES, BLECHMAN, WOLTZ & KELLY, P.C.

The law firm of Jones, Blechman, Woltz & Kelly, P.C., with offices in Newport News and Williamsburg, Virginia, has as its mission, "A firm commitment to excellence." That they are serious about that mission is evidenced by the firm's growth from its origins in 1905.

Jones, Blechman, Woltz & Kelly now has more than 20 attorneys on staff. But it wasn't always that way. The firm's current name represents the four lawyers who became partners between the early 1900s, when Allan D. Jones began practicing, and 1946 when Herbert V. Kelly joined the firm. Between that time, Franklin O. Blechman joined Mr. Jones in 1926, and Arthur W. Woltz joined the firm in 1942.

The original partner, Allan Jones, Esq., served as Assistant Attorney General for Maritime Affairs under President Franklin D. Roosevelt. He was known to be a very colorful individual, and was well-respected in the community of Newport News. Mr. Blechman, who had formed a partnership in 1932 with Mr. Jones, was a pillar of the community. He received many awards and honors, and was responsible for encouraging many young attorneys.

Herbert V. Kelly, who is still the driving force of this noted law firm, joined

Arthur W. Woltz in his office in downtown Newport News in 1978.

the partnership just four years after Arthur Woltz. Mr. Kelly has had a distinguished career as a former member of the Board of Visitors and past Rector of The College of William and Mary in Williamsburg, Virginia.

Today, 23 other lawyers practice along with Herbert Kelly. Among these is Thomas N. Downing who served as a member of the United States House of Representatives. Herbert H. Bateman, a former member and partner of the firm also became a member of Congress and continues to serve as such to this day.

The firm's former senior secretary Marguerite Bridges, who came to the firm in the same year as the only living original partner, Herbert Kelly, and who served as a secretary of the firm for 50 years, talked about how it was back in 1946. She reported that while she had a lot to learn professionally about law in Virginia, having moved there from Georgia, she also had to take in some of the idiosyncrasies of the

firm. One was that Mr. Blechman did not want a coffee pot in the office, so breaks were usually spent at Kresge's lunch counter, downstairs from the original office site. She said that all errands, such as banking, deliveries, etc., were done during your "lunch hour" on a daily basis. Ms. Bridges also said that a Western Union "boy" appeared within five to 10 minutes of her turning a little handle on the side of her desk, to fetch a telegram. She was only 30 years old at the time, and said she felt "really old" compared to a 17-year-old helper who treated her as though she would be in her grave any minute. She felt even older at times, going home with aching arms and wrists from having to produce four and five copies of every document on a manual typewriter.

Longevity seems to run high regarding staff at Jones, Blechman, Woltz & Kelly. The number of long-term employees, other than lawyers, testifies to the relationships between the employees of the firm. Today there are many differences, including the fact that the firm has grown

The partners in 1983, standing from left to right: John Tompkins, Harry Kostel, Herb Bateman, Bert Kelly, Buddy David and Conway Sheild; seated from left to right: Frank Blechman, Herb Kelly and Raymond Suttle.

Pictured in 2000 are Svein J. Lassen, managing partner (left), Herbert V. Kelly (seated) and Raymond H. Suttle (right) in Kelly's office.

substantially. Numbering more than 50 people, the support staff includes the personnel director, Ebbie Memory, who joined the firm nearly 40 years ago in 1962 for $65 a week, Ebbie took the job of firm bookkeeper, with only one week's training! Bookkeeping was apparently quite crude in those days, as Ebbie Memory reports that there were many "blank" stubs at the end of the month in the firm's two check books. She says that Mr. Blechman, to whom she reported, was always there when someone needed him. "He was a wonderful person and never too busy to open his door and speak with you about a problem," according to Ms. Memory. She further comments that this same consideration is continued with Mr. Kelly. She says that the family atmosphere at Jones, Blechman, Woltz & Kelly made her challenging career fun over the years.

Another long-term secretary, Margaret Hudnall was hired by Marguerite Bridges in 1963. As a youngster right out of high school, she was paid 50¢ an hour to start, which was raised to a "whopping" 75¢ an hour soon after. At the start she was the "runner" whose trips were "on demand," not just twice a day. She then started doing real estate work with Mr. Kelly and his secretary. Ms. Hudnall has enjoyed her long-term relationship with the firm, and reflects fondly on those early days. A further definition that the firm cannot ignore is the extreme comarderie among lawyers who not only work together, but who also play together. It is this relationship and the willingness to take part, to jump in on any occasion, that makes the firm what it is today.

Today, Jones, Blechman, Woltz & Kelly is one of the preeminent law firms in southeastern Virginia. The partners and members provide professional legal assistance in both individual and corporate areas, not only in the Commonwealth, but throughout the eastern United States. The law firm combines the qualities and vigor of a smaller group with the efficiency and resources of a larger firm.

As the largest law firm on the Virginia Peninsula, Jones, Blechman, Woltz & Kelly, P.C. offers a unique and ideal combination of talents and services. The partners and member attorneys have the expertise and experience expected of a well-respected law firm. JBW&K is structured into practice groups which focus on specialized legal areas including employ-

ment law, business and technology law, governmental law, personal injury and family law, real estate law, estate planning and taxation, and commercial litigation. Although a client usually works primarily with one attorney, the resources of the entire firm are available to ensure excellent support. The attorneys collectively embrace a philosophy of aggressive and innovative representation which is totally focused on resolving legal matters in the way most beneficial to the client.

The attorneys at Jones, Blechman, Woltz & Kelly, P.C. are involved corporate citizens who contribute their personal and professional time to charitable institutions, advisory committees, and at legal and business seminars. Members serve on various boards of private and public academic institutions and corporations; publish business and legal articles of both a scholarly and practical nature; and chair or serve as members on state commissions, boards of directors, and bar association committees. Their list of awards and recognitions is too extensive to list, but the attorneys in the firm are an asset not only to their profession, but to the community. Truly, a "firm commitment to excellence."

Pictured in 2000 are Raymond H. Suttle, Jr. (standing) and Herbert V. Kelly, Jr. (seated), both partners, with portrait of Allan D. Jones in the background.

LIFENET

LifeNet's mission is to improve the quality of human life through the provision of organs and tissues for transplantation and to serve the community by providing educational and support services which enhance the donation process.

The world is full of uncertainty. And while there's no question that death will touch each of us during the course of our lives, no one knows how or when it will cross our paths. Preparing for this certainty and finding meaning or purpose in it is up to us to decide for ourselves.

At LifeNet, their mission is preserving life and improving its quality. Each day they meet people dealing with death—reaching out for a way to meet it with dignity or searching for a way to cheat it.

Effectively helping in this area means presenting important donation options just as a bereaved family is trying to comprehend and accept their loss. It's a difficult and painful time for people to discuss organ donation, but unfortunately, this is when it's most critical to do so. Because organ donation is a gift

The Virginia Tissue Bank's original building in 1988.

Dr. Richard Hurwitz presents a plaque to Bill Anderson and Helen Leslie on opening day of the newly-built Virginia Tissue Bank in 1988.

that can benefit so many, including the grieving family, LifeNet offers whatever time or support the family needs. Donors and their families are its first priority. A family's single act of unselfishness can improve a life. Or save it.

LifeNet was founded in 1982 as the Virginia Tissue Bank and operates today as a model organ recovery program and one of the nation's largest full-service tissue banks. The processing of more than 25 percent of the human tissue used in the United States and more than 2,000

tissue donors annually has resulted in more than a million tissue grafts. In all, LifeNet has processed thousands of grafts for patients and hundreds of organs for transplantation in Hampton Roads and beyond.

Tissue recovery services are provided in Virginia, North Carolina, and metropolitan Washington, D.C., and tissue is processed in specially-designed and constructed operating suites. Modeled after those in the space and electronic industries, these facilities place LifeNet among the processing elite.

LifeNet provides tissue banking services for musculoskeletal and cardiovascular human tissue, while organ recovery services include hearts, livers, kidneys, heart-lung, lungs and pancreas. Human tissue for clinical use includes bone, skin, fascia, cartilage, ligaments, tendons, nerves, veins and heart valves.

LifeNet coordinates the recovery of organs for transplant centers in Virginia, including the long-distance recovery of extrarenal organs from other U.S. organ procurement organizations outside of the local LifeNet service area.

LifeNet has been designated an Organ Procurement Organization by the

Health Care Financing Administration (HCFA). As such, they supply not only organ recovery, but also tissue recovery, processing and distribution services. LifeNet is accredited by American Association of Organ Procurement Organizations (AOPO) and is an institutional member of the United Network for Organ Sharing (UNOS). One of its most exciting achievements is that it is the only organization of its kind in the world to be registered to the ISO (International Standards Organization) 9001 standard for quality. This measure of quality exists throughout the organization, in every aspect of its daily mission.

LifeNet adheres to the strict Standards of Tissue Banking as set forth by the American Association of Tissue Banks (AATB), believing that quality assurance originates prior to donation. As an institutional and accredited member of AATB, LifeNet is involved in every facet of its intensive donor screening. Transplant coordinators obtain detailed medical and social histories that are meticulously reviewed prior to donation. This screening is specifically aimed at identifying high-risk factors for disease transmission.

LifeNet is a nonprofit, independent agency. As such, its staff concentrates

LifeNet's staff flies throughout Virginia and surrounding states to recover organs and tissues.

on compassionately pursuing its mission. In this way, the precious organs and tissues that are recovered for recipients become a powerful symbol of the respect for the people they serve, and the gifts they provide to others.

LifeNet believes the ultimate success or failure of transplantation rests with education. Programs for continuing education are a consistent part of its efforts to increase public knowledge and awareness of medicine's need for transplantable organs and tissues. Included

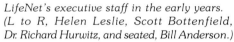

LifeNet's executive staff in the early years. (L to R, Helen Leslie, Scott Bottenfield, Dr. Richard Hurwitz, and seated, Bill Anderson.)

in these programs is a special emphasis on minority awareness, an area where the need is particularly great. Another area is in donor family services, one of the most effective in the country.

In short, without an enlightened population, lifesaving technology and transplant efficacy would mean nothing. That's why LifeNet actively promotes both public and professional education. LifeNet's public relations department provides informational materials, sponsors special events and actively seeks marketing and financial support from target audiences. By working closely with hospitals throughout its service area LifeNet can offer professional education programs donor evaluation and even counseling for families in all stages of the grief process.

Showing true generosity of spirit, special care is taken to help loved ones understand the donation process. These individuals are a crucial part of how LifeNet's organ recovery services provide lifesaving transplants to the community it serves. However, the final decision to

donate must be made by families quickly, as immediate removal is essential to the continued function of organs after transplantation.

Everything LifeNet does is accomplished through the work of dedicated employees. They come from a variety of medical and business backgrounds. Medical processes aside, LifeNet's primary purpose is to increase the number of high-quality organs and tissues donated for transplantation. In the real world of injuries, illnesses, hospital waiting rooms and death, that means offering families a compassionate opportunity to make and receive donations.

LifeNet was founded by two committed individuals—Bill Anderson and Helen Leslie. Anderson and Leslie began their careers working with kidney dialysis patients, later becoming employees of an Organ Procurement Organization now serving the western part of Virginia. They began coordinating organ recovery in eastern and central Virginia, but soon learned of the tremendous need for human tissue. At that time—the early '80s—clinicians had to go as far as Miami, Florida to obtain tissue for their

SCHEMATIC ELEVATION FOR
LIFENET - BAYSIDE
VIRGINIA BEACH,   VIRGINIA

LYALL DESIGN
ARCHITECTS

1/16" = 1' - 0"   10-30-99

A conceptual drawing of the new LifeNet administrative headquarters in Virginia Beach.

LifeNet pays tribute to all organ and tissue donors with "Reflections," a memorial garden on its property.

patients. Anderson and Leslie wanted to make a difference in their community. They began learning tissue processing and banking from the Navy Medical Facilities in Bethesda, Maryland. They perfected their skill and sought to create an organization in Virginia to provide citizens with much-needed human tissue. Their first office was in a rented space in a small office complex in Virginia Beach. They quickly grew and saw a need to expand. They later built a processing and office facility in the Norfolk Airport Industrial Park in Virginia Beach and dedicated it 1982.

Staff grew from 10 to 50 over the next eight years; today LifeNet employs nearly 300 people. The leaders of the organization, Bill Anderson and Helen Leslie, with tremendous support from Richard L. Hurwitz, M.D., a local transplant surgeon, successfully created a thriving business whose purpose was, and still is, to serve the community with organs and tissues that improve the quality of human life.

As LifeNet enters the 21st century the organization looks toward an exciting future. LifeNet has purchased and plans to build a new corporate center

located on nine acres of land in the same industrial park where it is housed today. The existing building will remain as a technical center, housing the highly-sophisticated equipment and technology used to process human tissue. The new corporate center will house the administrative, financial and business aspects of the company. The grounds will pay tribute to donors and their families with a special memorial garden dedicated to the precious gifts of life donated through organ and tissue donation. LifeNet has developed many exciting relationships with other organizations to provide enhanced services to its community, as well as with other countries to develop similar tissue banking facilities.

In the final analysis, LifeNet's role is really a matter of public trust. In reality, they are in the business of helping people live better lives. High technology just happens to be the way they enhance the healing process.

W.F. MAGANN CORPORATION

As a frogman in the U.S. Navy during World War II, Wilferd F. Magann was part of an underwater demolition team stationed in the South Pacific. His unit tackled the difficult and dangerous job of clearing the beaches by detonating explosive devices.

After his discharge in 1945, he turned his talents to construction and spent the next half-century in Portsmouth building the W.F. Magann Corporation. The diversified general contractor for heavy, marine and industrial construction has completed projects ranging from small repair jobs and expansion in operating facilities and $30-million projects throughout the Middle and Southeastern Atlantic states.

Although the company's founder retired as president in 1996, his son William S. Magann, now president, retains the company's focus on safety, quality and top performance on every job, large or small. "My father is from the generation that wanted to keep on building and achieving, always bigger and better. He used his 'muster-out' pay from the Navy, bought a government surplus truck, hired a couple of guys and started by building curbs and gutters."

With a focus on concrete work in the booming postwar construction market, the company steadily expanded into more complex and diverse heavy construction. In 1956, W.F. Magann Corporation moved from its original location on High Street in Portsmouth to its current location at 3220 Mariner Avenue, where it now employs 140 people.

During the mid-1970s, William S. Magann steered the company into marine construction, starting with coastline and offshore protection work in heavy stone and timber structure. The company continued to expand with experienced marine crews and specialized equipment ranging from small boats to custom built material-handling barges. The company has performed major repairs and new construction work on inlets from Portsmouth to Puerto Rico. When Murrells Inlet was created by a storm along the South Carolina coast, the U.S. Army Corps of Engineers contracted W.F.

W.F. Magann, founder.

Magann to construct a permanent inlet, using 300,000 tons of rock and dredging one million cubic yards of sand.

The company's largest and most complex project to date was its $29.2 million contract for the Interior Drainage-Northside Alignment portion of the Richmond Local Flood Protection Project along the James River. After developing cost and time-saving engineering proposals and completing the

project on-time in 1993, the company was commended by the U.S. Army Corps of Engineers. Other company awards include one from the U.S. Department of the Navy for its role as general contractor for a floating dry-dock mooring facility project at the Norfolk Naval Station. Working on land, the company combined its heavy and industrial capabilities for the turnkey construction of two satellite communication antennas at the Northwest Naval Radio Station near Norfolk.

From small projects to large, "…our most important resource continues to be the experienced, innovative and dedicated people of the Magann construction team," says Wilferd F. Magann. "Low employee turnover is a major factor in the company's success," agrees second-generation William S. Magann.

One of the newest employees at the Portsmouth company is William S. Magann, Jr., a project engineer in charge of quality control and a third-generation Magann continuing the tradition of a family that likes to "build it big."

Manitowoc 4100W (200-ton capacity crawler crane driving 54" and 66" diameter cylinder piles for bulkhead replacement at Newport News Marine Terminal and Pier IX.

LYON SHIPYARD

Lyon Shipyard was established in 1928, when three partners, including Guy H. Moon and George C. Lyon, Sr. bought out the facilities of the G.T. Taylor Marine Railway. Originally known as Moon Shipyard and Repair Corporation, the yard was situated on the eastern branch of the Elizabeth River at the foot of Brown Avenue, where it remains today. Shipyard facilities consisted of a frame machine shop with offices and storeroom on the second floor, and a carpenter shed located at the head of two marine railways. They were one of several small marine railway and repair companies located on the Norfolk waterfront, and provided dry-docking and repair services to the harbors' many wooden barges, fishing vessels, and steam powered tugs. Craig Brothers Marine Railway, for whom George Lyon worked prior to joining his partners in the buyout of Taylor, continued to operate immediately to the east at the foot of Willoughby Avenue. Wood Towing Company, a predecessor to Curtis Bay Towing Company and now Moran Towing Company operated a small fleet of tugs and had a marine railway of its own immediately to the west

Above
Moon Shipyard and Repair Corporation (now Lyon Shipyard). Old machine shop and NBC Lines tug "Martha M," on old Railway #2, late 1960s.

at the foot of Lovett Avenue.

As the principal seaport of the Mid-Atlantic States and the head of the Intracoastal Waterway, Norfolk provided a prime focus for shipbuilding and repair activity. Norfolk's harbor was the distribution point for break-bulk cargo from overseas, as well as the consolidation point for Virginia's bounty of seafood, forest and agricultural products. As harbor and coastal vessels made the transition from wood to riveted iron to welded steel, Lyon Shipyard upgraded its facilities and the capacity of its railways to accommodate the growing size of its customers' vessels. Nevertheless, as late as the early 1980s the rhythmic thump of the caulking hammer could still be heard as some of the fishing fleets' few remaining wooden hulls came to be repaired and re-caulked.

Few records remain from the '30s and '40s, but it is known that Guy Moon sold his interest to pursue other business opportunities. During World War II Lyon Shipyard undertook work on small naval and military vessels. Following the war, operations returned to an emphasis on commercial customers, supplemented by repair contracts from the military and other government agencies. Principal customers included NBC Lines, Curtis Bay Towing Company, and the CG Willis Barge Line.

In the late 1950s George Lyon, Sr. bought out the last of the remaining partners and became the sole stockholder. In addition to managing and developing the business of the shipyard Mr. Lyon

Below
Lyon Shipyard-C&P Towing tug "Sea Level," fishing trawler "Sea Rambler" and NBC Lines container barge #2 at Lyon Shipyard peirs, late 1970s.

was active in civic and community affairs. In his neighborhood of Ocean Park he led the effort to create a volunteer fire department, and served as chief for many years. He was an active member of the Lion's Club, and was a long-time member and chairman of the school board of the City of Virginia Beach. He also served on the Vestry of Old Donation Church.

In 1972, George C. Lyon, Jr. joined the company as vice president. Employment at the time was approximately 25 people. In 1977, George Lyon, Sr. died, and control of the company passed to George C. Lyon, Jr., who continues to manage and oversee its growth today.

Also in 1977, Craig Brothers Marine Railway, which had been a competitor for decades, was sold to a new owner. The new owner encountered financial difficulties shortly thereafter, and in 1979 Lyon Shipyard was able to purchase its neighbor and former competitor. The acquisition of the Craig Brothers' yard more than doubled the land and waterfront area of Lyon Shipyard, and provided an additional railway to increase the working capacity of the

Allied Transportation Company tug "Sea Robin," at Lyon Shipyard bulkhead, Fall 1999.

facility. In 1981, the shipyard officially changed its name to Lyon Shipyard, Inc.

During the recession of the early 1980s shipyards and their customers both experienced difficult economic times. While these cyclical downturns were stressful, they provided opportunities that were advantageous in the long run. The company initiated ongoing marketing efforts and, driven by the barge and towing industry's need for competitive service and pricing, Lyon Shipyard was able to introduce itself to previously unavailable customers.

Over time, as new contracts were successfully completed, Lyon Shipyard gained the confidence of its new customers, subsequently broadening and diversifying its customer base.

In the early 1990s the Shipyard leased a dry-dock, giving it the capacity to dry-dock inland and coastal barges up to approximately 350 feet long and 85 feet wide. The size and lifting capacity of this dock gives the company the ability to keep pace with the increasing size and complexity of the commercial tug and barge fleet.

Salisbury Towing Company tug "Capt. Henry Knott" drydocked at Lyon Shipyard Railway #3, Spring 2000.

MOON ENGINEERING COMPANY, INC.

Moon Engineering Company (MECO) is a long established, highly-experienced Hampton Roads shipyard and industrial service company that has been engaged in the business of marine and industrial repair, conversion and alteration since its founding in 1920. During its 80+ years of operation, MECO has built a well-deserved reputation as the "can do" company.

MECO's current business base includes shipboard work performed for the U.S. Navy, the U.S. Military Sealift Command and the U.S. Maritime Administration, as well as a host of other government and commercial marine customers. The company also does work for a variety of industrial customers such as utility providers and manufacturers.

The company's successful development can be principally attributed to one man and his family, and the corporate vision and business skill that turned a small "downriver" repair shop into a complex operation that now ranks among the area's top shipyards. Mr. William E. Thomas Sr., along with sons Bill, Jim and Wayne, combined efforts to transform MECO into one of Hampton Road's most prominent and respected shipyards.

MECO was founded on 4½ acres of Elizabeth River waterfront in Norfolk on Front Street. The founding partners, Guy Moon (from whom the fledgling company took its name), William F. Jordan and Paul N. Gibbings, initially

MECO's Norfolk shipyard on Front Street. Pictured are the Victory ships Lawrence *and* Selma, *and the U.S. Navy "yard derrick" No. 169, in 1969.*

specialized in commercial ship and industrial repair services. When first opened, MECO's primary assets were two 400 foot berthing slips and a well-equipped machine shop.

Guy Moon left MECO in 1922 to pursue other interests, leaving ownership to Jordan and Gibbings.

In 1943, the company realized the first significant expansion of its business base when MECO broadened its services to include work for the U.S. Government's Merchant Marine fleet of World War II. Mr. William E. Thomas Sr. established the modern operation of the company in 1958 when he joined the firm as vice president. Mr. Thomas brought to MECO the rich heritage of three generations of ship repair experience dating back to the U.S. Civil War. Mr. Thomas' great-grandfather was a ship's carpenter and operated Thomas Railway in

Portsmouth during the 1800s. His grandfather continued operation of the yard, relocating the business to the Berkley section of South Norfolk in the early 1900s. Mr. Thomas and his father operated the business until 1947.

Mr. Thomas worked summers in the yard while a student at Norfolk's Maury High School. Following a hitch as a lieutenant in the Merchant Marine during World War II, Mr. Thomas opened his own ship repair shop, Thomas Marine Corporation, on Boush Street in downtown Norfolk. Mr. Thomas operated Thomas Marine until the time he joined MECO.

Gibbings died in 1959. That same year, Mr. Dana F. Gray joined MECO as general superintendent. Mr. Gray, a graduate of the Maine Maritime Academy, had spent 11 years with the Merchant Marine as a chief engineer before joining the American Bureau of Shipping.

Following the death of Jordan in 1972, Mr. Thomas assumed the presidency of the company. In the reorganization of corporate leadership, Mr. Gray became executive vice president.

The reorganization marked a major milestone for the company, and set MECO on a path of growth and expansion care-

MECO's Portsmouth shipyard on Pinners Point at the start of construction, in 1985.

fully planned and executed by Mr. Thomas with the assistance of Mr. Gray.

Until this time, the most complex contract completed by MECO was its first "in yard" availability for the U.S. Navy in 1962. Tasks on the destroyer escort USS Darby (DE-218) included galley work that required the ship's crew be messed off board the vessel. Ingenuously, MECO provided messing facilities aboard Norfolk & Western Railroad diner cars that had been moved into the yard.

In 1983, MECO joined the Portsmouth Partnership, a group of business and civic leaders working to promote economic development in the city. The Partnership was one among many community organizations in which Mr. Thomas would invest considerable time and energy.

One of the most significant milestones in company history occurred in 1984 when MECO purchased 70 acres of Elizabeth River waterfront property on Pinners Point in Portsmouth. The property,

The Pinners Point shipyard nearing completion of construction for "Phase One." Pictured is the USS Barney (DDG-6), in 1986.

MECO's Portsmouth Shipyard in full operation. Pictured are the M/V's Cape Race, Cape Rise, Cape Ray *and the* USS Peterson (DD-969) *and* USS Carter Hall (LSD-50), in 2000.

adjacent to the mouth of Scott's Creek, had most recently been the site of an abandoned ship breaking operation.

Construction of the entirely new, state-of-the-art shipyard proceeded on schedule, including completion of MECO's new 650 foot concrete pier in 1985. The *S.S. Lone Star Mariner* and *S.S. American Courier* became the first vessels to tie up to MECO's new pier.

Formal dedication of the facility took place on November 1st, 1986. Among many notable guests in attendance were the Honorable Norman Sisisky, U.S.

House of Representatives; the Honorable James Holley III, mayor of Portsmouth and Capt. Richard Westbrook, Supervisor of Shipbuilding, Conversion and Repair, USN.

The *USS Barney* (DDG-6) became the first U.S. Navy ship to be overhauled at the new shipyard. MECO was awarded its first multi-year contract in 1987 by the Naval Sea Systems Command for the five-year "Phased Maintenance" of the LSD/LPD class of amphibious vessels.

At this writing, MECO's Portsmouth yard boasts over 50,000 square feet of covered shop and storage. In 1993, the company completed construction of a second concrete pier which measured 799 feet in length. The first ship to tie along MECO's newest pier was the *Cape Henry* (AKR-5067). Combined with modifications to the original pier that extended its length to 799 feet, the facility now has over 3,200 feet of deep draft berthing to 35+ feet.

In 1992, after 32 years of dedicated service, Mr. Gray retired from the company. Later that year, on November 10th, Mr. William E. Thomas Sr. passed away at the age of 69. Upon the occasion of his passing, the Commonwealth of Virginia General Assembly passed Joint Resolution No. 416 in celebration of his achievements.

Corporate management of the firm continued in Mr. Thomas' tradition under the direction of sons Bill, Jim and Wayne. Mr. William E. Thomas Jr. retired from the company in 1999 after serving as president. Today, company leadership resides with Mr. Wayne G. Thomas, president and Mr. James M. Thomas, executive vice president.

R.G. AND DONALD MOORE

You are standing at the first rough lip of a parcel of untamed acreage, dotted with stately old trees, rolling gently down to a natural creek. To one side stands the building legend R.G. Moore, to the other side, his sons Donald and Robert Ray. You close your eyes and see small children running barefoot though the wildflowers, kites trailing high above. And, the Moores? Yes, they see those same children, but inline skating down manicured sidewalks past a row of sparkling, new, single-family homes. You, my friend, have seen the future. And it is Moore Country.

The Moore building dynasty is a well-documented entity in the development annals of Hampton Roads. Between father and sons, nearly 20,000 families have been able to claim a brand-new, Moore-built residence as home, almost all in master designed communities created in the spirit of the old-fashioned neighborhood. And, while father R.G. created most of his legendary communities with affordable, single-family homes for growing families, son Donald is making his mark by creating a new genre of lifestyle housing for the opposite buyer profile—private estate condominiums for the mature, move-down buyer. Whether the

Donald L. Moore.

R.G. and Frances Moore.

buyer is moving up or scaling down, however, one indisputable fact cannot be ignored. R.G. Moore and Donald L. Moore have indeed changed the residential landscape of Hampton Roads.

Many empires are built from the most humble origins, and never has that been truer than the chronicle of R.G. Moore's rise as one of the most powerful influences on home building in the region. As the youngest of six boys growing up on a 200-acre spread of corn and soybeans in northeastern North Carolina, Robert Gilliam Moore suffered the loss of his mother at age 14 and his father when he was just 21. From those early tragedies came a fierce independence and unrelenting drive to succeed, catapulting him on a road that would bring him in a truck cab to a young Virginia Beach. Steering his Carolina-Norfolk tractor-trailer to the recognition of the owners, R.G. was recruited in the early 1950s to run the company's warehouse in Norfolk. In he steamed, with his beloved wife Frances and two young sons in tow.

The Moore's first home was a tiny, four-room structure in Norfolk, and not at all to R.G.'s liking. Having learned critical carpentry skills from his father, he set out to build his own home, a 900-square foot frame unit near Newtown Road and Virginia Beach Boulevard on the Virginia

Beach side of the Norfolk line. Even though he still worked full time for the trucking line, the building bug took hold, and he sold this first house, took the profits and built another. And another. And another, eventually nudged by co-worker O.J. Sprott with a $39,000 loan to start home building full-time. The Moore kingdom had begun.

From his earliest full-fledged subdivisions—Kings Grant and Level Green—smack in the middle of Virginia Beach, Moore's commitment to creating environments conducive to raising a happy, healthy family reflected his dedication to his own family. Recognized as one of the first to design curved streets and court areas in his neighborhoods, many of Moore's innovations sprung from his focus on keeping young children and families safe. And, in the early years of his business, when he could be hands-on with every phase of construction, he was not beyond climbing aboard a bulldozer in a three-piece suit to ensure that his land was being treated with the proper respect.

R.G's developments continued to shape the region, from the Virginia Beach oceanfront to Chesapeake, the Peninsula to the North Carolina line. Moving vans by the thousands have pulled into

Royal Court Condos.

Brigadoon, Kempsville Meadows, Ocean Lakes, Red Mill Farm, Salem Woods, Sajo Farms and so many more, into at least one-half of all single family homes built in Virginia Beach in the 1980s. In fact, statistics tell that in 1992, R.G. Moore was the single, largest landowner in Virginia Beach, with $144 million in holdings.

From his original vision of simply building a solid, affordable home where his own family could grow and thrive, R.G. Moore has irrefutably shaped the city of Virginia Beach, determining new school and road improvement locations, and precisely where new neighborhoods would embrace a whole generation of new homeowners. In doing so, R.G. nurtured the ambition of his own sons—Robert Ray, into an accomplished construction field supervisor, and Donald, into an owner of a successful company built on the foundation of the same high standards and commitment to quality as was his father's.

After his 1971 graduation from Virginia Commonwealth University with a degree in business, Donald Moore made a fateful decision—to start his own building company, putting into action all of the on-the-site construction lessons he had learned over summers of working in the field for his father. While he shared offices with his legendary dad, Donald showed the same Moore streak of fierce independence and set out to build his own legacy, starting with individual, custom single-family homes in Norfolk. Having enlisted a private sponsor to underwrite these modest beginnings, Donald began to formulate a bankable history of successful projects and satisfied customers, a track record that would allow him to expand his horizons into multiple dwelling development. Like his father, Donald had the exceptional vision to quickly identify opportunity in the marketplace, and possessed the skill and focus to take untapped resources and mold new communities that responded directly to consumer demand.

Indeed, building lifestyle residences has been the governing trademark for Donald Moore. Since the mid-1980s developments like Aeries on The Bay, an enclave of beachside townhomes nestled along the shores of the Chesapeake Bay, have emerged, as well as award-winning golf course communities of Centre Green at Cypress Point and Grand Bay, Glenwood Greens on the Honeybee Golf Course, Willow Point and Players Choice at Kiln Creek in Newport News. While vastly different in appearance, density and price point, all share a common bond as distinctive reflections of the greater community in which they were built. The Moore mission remains, "build to the buyer's dreams... lifestyle is king."

These first communities did a great deal to define the future of Donald Moore's development focus. By listening to his customers, Moore found an untapped niche in the marketplace, the need for upscale, maintenance-free residences crafted for the sophisticated urban lifestyle. Thus was born the concept for Royal Court Estate Condominium, a breakthough development in the prestigious Great Neck corridor of Virginia Beach, blatantly aimed at the well-heeled society couple ready to divest themselves of the old family home without sacrificing a "respected address." The project was an overwhelming success, and was followed by equally-successful upscale offerings at Haygood Estates and Chancellor Walk.

Donald Moore's responsiveness to the marketplace has been rewarded not only in multi-million dollar sales figures, but also in the respect of the Hampton Roads building industry. His homes and communities have garnered almost every award given by the Tidewater Builders Association, and his own former beachfront home earned the Laslo Aranyi Memorial Design Award for Excellence in Architecture and Landscape Planting Design. Even the Virginia Beach Planning Commission has been impressed with his contributions, honoring Royal Court Estate Condominiums with the Design Award for Outstanding Residential Development.

While Donald has been able to keep a much lower public profile, both he and his father have been praised for their unselfish contributions to the communities they serve. R.G. and Frances Moore are widely-recognized for their generosity to Virginia Wesleyan College, Old Dominion University, the Virginia Museum of Marine Sciences, Children's Hospital of the Kings Daughters and especially Eastern Virginia Medical School, with donations totalling well beyond hundreds of thousands of dollars. Donald has been honored for his contributions to United Way, Eastern Virginia Medical School and his avid support of junior golf in

the Hampton Roads region. Both father and son have built Scholarship Houses for the Tidewater Builders Association, profits from which have grown into one of the largest sources of scholarship funding in the area.

Both father and son have also demonstrated their appreciation for the complex demands of a tightly-knit community, and have taken individual, extraordinary measures to communicate openly and honestly with Civic Leagues and Coalitions of Civic Leagues that have appropriately challenged new Moore projects planned for their own backyards. Through a tire-

less work ethic, willingness to address tough opponents and personal obligation to stand firm to their beliefs, both R.G. and Donald Moore have been able to build far more than brick and frame structures. They have built life-long friendships and the respect of colleagues and customers alike.

And lastly, both entrepreneurs share one more common thread in their ability to attract the most experienced and talented designers, master craftsmen and sales professionals... and to maintain the same, loyal team for decades. It is with the unwavering support of these finely-tuned armies of supporting players that many of the Moore's innovations have sprung, been meticulously developed and finally, executed with class and confidence.

Along the way, both men have learned a few things. Number one is respect for their customers. No builder—in fact, no company—can survive, much less thrive, without a thorough understanding of and appreciation for its customers. By keeping homebuyers, their dreams and their aspirations as the singular guiding beacon, R.G., Frances, Robert Ray and Donald Moore have built a powerful legacy of reliability, quality and service. In doing so, they have changed the residential landscape of the proud region of Hampton Roads.

Centre Green.

MEDICAL CENTER RADIOLOGISTS, INC.

Medical Center Radiologists, Inc. (MCR) was founded in 1955 by Dr. Carl B. Wisoff who had completed his formal radiology training under the famous Dr. Benejamin Felson in Cincinnati, Ohio. Prior to this time, and for years after in many areas, radiology was practiced by physicians with little or no formal training in the discipline. This commitment to the developing specialty and Dr. Wisoff's philosophy that his practice would provide state-of-the-art imaging to his patients has continued with Medical Center Radiologists. The group, now with some 40 diagnostic radiologists and over 120 employees has grown by providing a practice which attracts the best and brightest radiologists and provides the tools necessary for growth and development of the specialty. Though Dr. Wisnoff is now retired, his counsel remains valued by Dr. Sture Sigfred, MCR's current president. "Those basic values of patient care, education and public service continue to guide MCR as it rounds out its first 50 years," according to Sigfred.

MCR is largely built from subspecialty trained radiologists including pediatrics, gastrointestinal, bone and joint, chest, interventional, neuroradiology, body imaging, nuclear, and women's imaging. The group also provides the only neurointerventional service within southeastern Virginia. This commitment to patient care has set the standards of care in radiology for the entire region. In addition Medical Center Radiologists is the dominant teaching arm of the Eastern Virginia Medical School in Norfolk and runs a highly competitive residency program.

Since the availability of CT scanning and MRI, which are digital images, radiology had become the lynch pin in providing timely and accurate diagnosis and often treatment. This led MCR to diverge from the traditional practice of radiology in 1997 by developing a local and wide area computer network linking its hospitals through high speed transport lines to near real-time interpretation, provided by board certified radiologists around the clock. MCR's

innovation did not stop with this network development and coverage, but was extended by allowing the seamless transfer of images throughout its system for appropriate subspecialty review and interpretation.

As its network has matured, MCR has made coverage available to rural hospitals throughout the state and region. This coverage links vital imaging modalities to MCR's central reading site for near real time interpretation as well as subspecialty consultation on complex cases. Affiliated hospitals can now enjoy the depth of coverage made possible only by a group this size while maintaining its own identity with its local radiology group.

Future direction will include expansion of the network, addition of Picture Archiving and Communication Systems (PACS) and information systems.

Dr. James Mosure of Medical Center Radiologists provides a subspecialty consultation on a challenging case referred from a rural Virginai hospital.

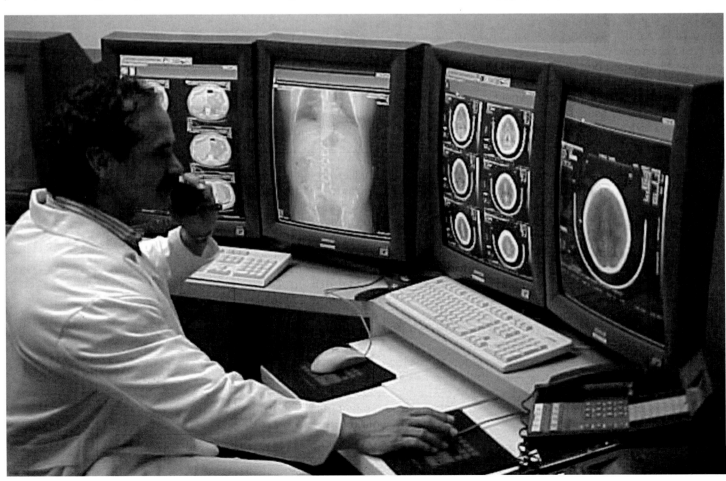

H. D. OLIVER FUNERAL APARTMENTS, INC.

H.D. Oliver Funeral Apartments was established in 1865. Their advertisement in an 1874 publication read:

"STERLING T. OLIVER, UNDERTAKER, is now prepared to execute any Jobs in the Cabinet Making or Undertaking line, (and also Repairing to Furniture, etc). *The FINEST HEARSE in Tidewater Virginia. Agent for Fisk's Improved Self-Sealing Metallic Burial Cases. Any styles of Coffins furnished at the shortest notice..."

Already in business at that time for nearly 10 years, the Oliver family was not only building cabinets for the early settlers in Norfolk, a trade which later evolved into the making of caskets, but was also burying the Confederate dead.

It all began in 1865 with the great-great-uncle of the present owners of H.D. Oliver Funeral Apartments Sterling T. Oliver who, while in the cabinet-making business, also built a tradition of excellence in funeral service. The family has continued this custom of excellence for over 135 years and five generations. H.D. Oliver Funeral Apartments has served the needs of families in distress with a dependable, caring, multi-generation family-owned business. The present owners, John and Martin Oliver, are proud to share in the reputation and dedication of their predecessors as they provide the highest quality of personal and community service to Norfolk, Virginia Beach, and now Chesapeake.

H. D. Oliver.

Originally named after the founder, it became Harry D. Oliver Undertaker in 1888, before becoming known as H.D. Oliver Funeral Apartments. As to the reference to the word apartments, it seems that the custom of the day was to offer small rooms (or apartments) for the deceased. Hence, they aptly named it funeral apartments. In addition, and as was also the custom of the time, they provided an on-site apartment for out-of-town funeral guests.

Norfolk Chapel.

Having started in the mid-19th century as a cabinetmaking shop in downtown Norfolk, the business became an undertaking establishment during the Civil War. In those days, it was a natural transition for a furniture maker to "get into" caskets. Much of the Norfolk deceased population was buried by H.D. Oliver because they loaned the families their horse-drawn carriages with which to carry their loved ones to the cemeteries. Mr. Harry Oliver was described in a publication called *Pictures in Maritime Dixie* as a "skillful embalmer by the arterial process who had vast experience as a funeral director, numbering as he does among his patrons the best people of the city and vicinity." Members of the local Jewish faith gradually allowed the funeral facility to make their caskets and conduct the funerals, something the Jewish temples had done for themselves prior to that time.

Martin V. Oliver.

As the Tidewater area grew, so did H.D. Oliver Funeral Apartments. The original business moved once before locating in the current facility at 1501 Colonial Avenue. It was built in 1936, being the first to have been constructed exclusively for funerals; most funeral parlors had tended to be converted homes. Two more locations in Virginia Beach and Chesapeake were built later, in 1964 and 1999, respectively.

Today, H.D. Oliver offers spacious viewing and receiving rooms. They conduct traditional funeral services in

the deceased family's church or in large on-site non-denominational chapels which feature modern sound systems and pipe organs. At the family's request, they can provide a memorial service or arrange for no service at all. Because of the availability of refrigeration, embalming the deceased is not necessary at H.D. Oliver's. A formal burial service or onsite cremation is available. Each option is planned to meet the personal taste, the emotional wishes, and the financial decision of the family. Other services provided by H.D. Oliver include handling all aspects of arrangements including grave purchases and filing for veteran and social security death benefits, at no cost. They offer a comprehensive aftercare program to assist the family with their grief, and have an extensive bereavement library.

In this time of ever-changing business practices, many local funeral homes have been sold to large, out-of-town companies or conglomerates. H.D. Oliver still values the principles of family ownership, and its dedicated staff, 35 strong, share in its success with the five-generation family management. They employ the customs of traditional dignity, including maintaining a close relationship with

Chesapeake Chapel.

local clergy and churches to assure proper customs for all faiths. These locally-owned and managed funeral services often also mean lower costs.

Payment choices at H.D. Oliver include an affordable pre-payment program, protecting family funds against inflations. Pre-arrangement of a funeral at no cost is available for those wishing to place their desired options on file. With intact records dating back to the 1800s, the firm now employs a state-of-the-art computer system for safekeeping of information and accurate billing.

Laskin Road Chapel.

John P. Oliver.

As for being a "little old-fashioned," with their now over 100 years of service, H.D. Oliver is proud of opening doors for clients, being dressed impeccably, and handling the deceased with dignity and respect. They treat the family as if they were members of their own. The owners, who are ethical, experienced, trusted, and honest professionals, are involved in the community through the church and civic and fraternal organizations. They consistently strive to uphold the same degree of excellent professionalism that was inspired by their predecessors. Their compassion and service to their clients, built upon the foundation established generations ago, continues today.

RIVERSIDE HEALTH SYSTEM

The Peninsula's leading provider of quality health care services is Riverside Health System. Riverside is an integrated health system, providing a wide array of medical and health care to the citizens of eastern Virginia.

Riverside Regional Medical Center is the 576-bed flagship of the organization, anchoring over 100 different locations extending from Richmond to Hampton and from Isle of Wight to Tappahannock.

Also at the core of Riverside are two of the most technologically-advanced rural hospitals in the Commonwealth—Riverside Walter Reed Hospital in Gloucester and Riverside Tappahannock Hospital in Tappahannock. Riverside Rehabilitation Institute is the largest physical rehabilitation hospital in Virginia.

Woven among these institutions is a comprehensive network of outpatient, home care, wellness, physician care services and convalescent centers that now total over 7,000 employees with annual revenues of over a half-billion dollars.

Yet this progressive, non-profit organization was born from humble beginnings.

The Riverside organization of today was born from the efforts of two physicians who operated a hospital in a former private residence beginning in 1904. This facility was then known as the St. James Sanitorium.

Dr. Quinton Legg with patient in X-ray at the old hospital.

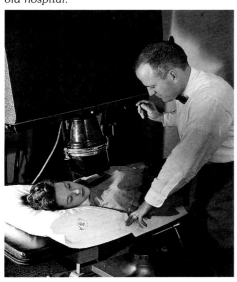

Hospital staff of original Riverside Hospital in 1918.

By 1908, that hospital had been abandoned and a new, expanded facility opened, then known as St. Frances Hospital. From its beginning, St. Frances Hospital's affiliated school for nurses was the forerunner of the Riverside School of Professional Nursing.

This 25-bed hospital soon became too small to meet the demands of the rapidly-progressing city. Physicians practicing there began discussing the building of a new hospital with the Newport News Chamber of Commerce.

Between 1911 and 1913, the Chamber solicited voluntary contributions from the citizens of Newport News and vicinity for the proposed new hospital. By January 1913, $25,000 was raised by the physicians and Chamber for the purpose of establishing the new hospital.

In May 1913, a corporation was formed as the Riverside Hospital Operating and Training Association, Incorporated. It was to be located in Newport News and its purpose was to establish, maintain and operate a hospital as a benevolence. The hospital, known as the Newport News General and Non-Sectarian Hospital, was to be under the trusteeship of three laymen. These three

comprised the central governing board which became known as the board of managers of the organization.

The new hospital was formally established in 1915; its charter was granted on December 15. There were now 18 physicians involved with the new hospital, each of which contributed to the funding needed for its operation. Provisions were made for 50 beds in the new facility, which was now located on Huntington Avenue north of 50th Street. The three-story facility was officially opened for the admission of patients and student nurses in January 1916.

At the height of World War I in 1917, the hospital was overwhelmed with pestilence and disease. There was a typhoid epidemic that year, and not a single hospital patient was lost. But, the great influenza epidemic the following year claimed the lives of many patients and left the medical staff and nurses severely overworked and physically exhausted.

Conditions at the hospital gradually grew worse during the war years. Physicians were unable to meet their financial obligations. In early 1921, the hospital closed for repairs, renovation and re-evaluation.

A new system of management was organized, with a new lay board to guide

Riverside Hospital in the 1950s.

and direct the hospital. A contract of reorganization was made between the three original trustees and the newly-appointed Board of Managers. During this period the hospital's name was changed to Riverside Hospital and continued to be general and non-sectarian.

When Riverside Hospital reopened on July 1, 1921, the bed capacity had increased from 50 to 70. In 1929, a new nurse's home was constructed and opened, bringing the total capacity to approximately 240 beds. After the war, further minor alterations were made and several key areas remodeled.

There was further construction near the hospital site in 1951 when a new three-story nurse's home was constructed across 51st Street, named Beavers Hall in honor of Riverside's first superintendent, Dr. John Beavers.

The 1950s was a period of tremendously-increased demand for Riverside Hospital. A fundraising brochure published in 1959 described the situation, "This hospital is now constantly overcrowded. One out of every three non-emergency patients seeking admission has had to take his place on the waiting list." In the brief five-year span of 1954-58, tests performed in the hospital laboratory rose from 62,000 annually to nearly 178,000. Major operations increased by 56 percent.

The planning and decisions made during the decade of the '50s were expected to determine Riverside Hospital's history for the next half century.

Riverside's School of Professional Nursing has been a major strength of the organization since the original hospital was founded.

During these difficult years, a long range plan was conceived by the Board of Managers. A hospital consultant was hired by neighboring Dixie Hospital and Riverside to conduct a comprehensive survey of the expansion needs for lower Peninsula hospitals. Since both hospitals required new facilities, it was mutually agreed that the need was more desperate for Dixie Hospital and that Riverside would defer expansion plans temporarily.

On March 1, 1959, after several years of formal and informal negotiations with the Board of Trustees of the Mariners Museum, a 30-acre tract was leased from the museum fronting on J. Clyde Morris Boulevard near Route 60.

In March 1959, the Board of Managers had finalized plans for a new $7 million hospital on J. Clyde Morris Boulevard. Hill-Burton funds would provide $3 million, $1 million would be drawn from the hospital building fund and the remaining $3 million would be raised through a capital campaign.

The campaign began, and its progress was both rapid and encouraging. During 1959, employees at the Newport News Shipbuilding and Drydock Company subscribed over $726,000 to be paid through deductions from their weekly pay for a period of three years. Within a few short weeks of the campaign's beginning, the area physicians had already exceeded their goals of $300,000 in pledges. By October 1959, 90 percent of the goal had been met, and by early 1960, the goal was achieved.

The beginning of what is today a 576-bed comprehensive medical center occurred on July 8, 1960, when bulldozers cleared the land to make way for the new 323-bed hospital. Construction progressed ahead of schedule and first patients were admitted on February 8, 1963.

The success of the new hospital at this site was immediately apparent. A prolonged period of expansion occurred throughout the remainder of the 20th century.

The phenomenal growth in facilities

The "new" Riverside Hospital in 1963.

during the '60s was matched with an equally dramatic growth in services and programs.

For many years, Riverside had been approved by the AMA for rotating internships and residencies in surgery, medicine, Ob/Gyn, general practice and pathology. Approved training programs were now underway for x-ray technicians and laboratory technicians, in addition to the Professional School of Nursing and the Licensed Practical Nursing program.

In 1965, a full-time director of medical education joined Riverside, leading to the establishment of a relationship with the Medical College of Virginia for medical education. This subsequently led to MCV's Family Practice Residency Program at Riverside.

This momentum did not slow in the 1970s. Formal programs were established for cardiology, cardiac catheterization and kidney dialysis. Outpatient surgery procedures were initiated utilizing areas set aside in the Emergency Room. And the first Open Heart unit on the Peninsula was opened in January 1973.

In mid-1975, Riverside Hospital assumed management of Patrick Henry Hospital for the Chronically Ill, a 385-bed long-term care facility in Newport News. During this same period, the state

Riverside Regional Medical Center provides state-of-the-art medical technology.

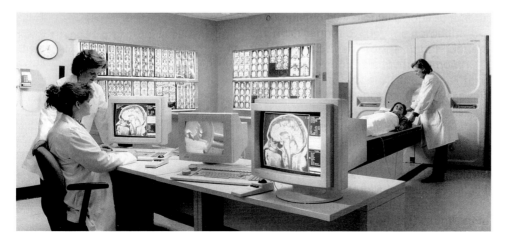

of Virginia turned over control of the Mental Hygiene Clinic at the Community Mental Health Center to Riverside.

By the mid-1970s, the hospitals on the Peninsula all shared a common problem—each institution faced large renovation and equipment replacement expenses for their laundry facilities. A consultant was retained and as a result of a detailed study of the common needs of Hampton General Hospital, Patrick Henry Hospital, Williamsburg Community Hospital and Riverside, a non-profit corporation was formed called Peninsula Hospital Services. A shared laundry facility was built and placed into operation in July 1976.

Two satellite facilities were in the embryonic stages of development at this time. Plans were being readied for a 71-bed satellite of Riverside in Gloucester, Virginia. Patrick Henry Hospital was preparing to begin construction of a 60-bed satellite nursing home in Saluda, Virginia.

With the two satellite facilities in the process of development, Riverside Hospital began studying the dietary needs of a rapidly expanding system. It was determined that a central food production center could provide these services for all facilities in the Riverside Hospital System. Construction of the Food Production Center began in June 1976.

This approach to food service has saved each hospital thousands of dollars in renovation, equipment and personnel costs. It has enabled the two satellite facilities to be constructed with minimal dietary facilities. Greater purchasing power and lower overall expenses have resulted.

The first satellite to be completed was the 60-bed nursing home for Patrick Henry Hospital. Located in Saluda, Virginia, the $13,389,000 facility was made possible by a donation from the Edmund J. Smith Foundation. The new nursing home began admitting patients in June 1977. Also in June, Riverside Hospital became the first hospital in the state of Virginia to acquire the full-body computerized axial tomography scanner.

One of the fastest growing segments

Riverside Regional Medical Center, flagship of the Riverside network.

of the Riverside service area is the Gloucester-Mathews-Middlesex County area north of the Peninsula across the York River. In the early 1970s, a committee of concerned citizens had been meeting to investigate the possibility of constructing a general hospital to meet the needs of their community. In 1974, Riverside Hospital was approached concerning the proposed hospital.

The project was planned as a 71-bed satellite hospital, to be located on a 20-acre site on US Route 17 in Gloucester. It was decided that the satellite would be named Walter Reed Memorial Hospital, in honor of the conqueror of Yellow Fever, who was born in Gloucester County.

A capital campaign resulted in over $400,000 in contributions from the citizens of the Middle Peninsula, and ground was broken in May 1976 for the $5,250,000 facility.

On September 11, 1977, over 10,000 enthusiastic citizens gathered at the hospital seat for the formal dedication ceremonies, and the hospital began operation two days later. This was the largest, single gathering of citizens in the history of Gloucester County.

Riverside's quilt image describes how the organization "covers all your healthcare needs."

The Riverside Wellness and Fitness Center–Peninsula became the first of six pioneering hospital-based fitness facilities Riverside would develop. A replacement facility for Patrick Henry Healthcare Center opened in 1985.

The Rehabilitation Institute of Virginia opened in 1986, being the largest physical rehabilitation hospital in Virginia. In 1988, as each division accelerated their growth, Riverside consolidated the corporate identities of all affiliates under one name–Riverside–a name which today has deep and abiding roots in the history of Eastern Virginia.

In the 1990s, Riverside welcomed over 150 physicians into the organization, established a joint venture HMO with Trigon Blue Cross and Blue Shield, and experienced a huge growth in demand for home care and outpatient services.

The tiny hospital, built with the commitment and energy of Peninsula citizens, has evolved into one of the most successful health systems in America.

ROOF SERVICES CORPORATION

Roof Services Corporation began operations on April 13, 1989, by founders John B. Babcock, II and Gary M. Rogacki, in Virginia Beach. With little more than a dream and their collective years of experience, they took the principles of integrity, quality and service and turned them into one of the most successful and respected commercial roofing contractors in Virginia.

While each were working for other roofing companies, their paths crossed, and when John and Gary decided to start their own business, they wanted it to be a new type of roofing company. They envisioned one dedicated to quality workmanship and customer satisfaction; those qualities have been the cornerstones of their success.

Each man brought his own special roofing background to the company and each complimented the other's. John's background had been primarily in sales, estimating and project management. Gary had begun his roofing career as an apprentice roofer, working his way up the ladder to eventually becoming a partner in Roof Services.

Those first years were lean. Sales for the first month totaled only $1,400. However, because of John and Gary's

Above
John Babcock, seated and Gary Rogacki, standing.

Below
Dollar Tree distribution center and corporate headquarters, Chesapeake, Virginia.

drive and determination, they finished their first year with over $2 million worth of business. Over the next 10 years, Roof Services Corporation achieved an annual growth of 25 percent. The bulk of this business—approximately 90 percent—has been from repeat customers; both John and Gary are proud of this statistic.

One of the area's largest commercial property managers and owners, S.L. Nusbaum, has chosen Roof Services Corporation exclusively for the past six years to perform repair and maintenance work on their commercial properties. This has been no small undertaking; those properties total over 5 million square feet of roof area. Additionally, some of the area's largest general contractors, including Hathaway Duke Construction Co., Hourigan Martone Construction Corporation, and Clancy & Theys Construction Co., consistently request Roof Services when selecting tradesmen for their projects. Work provided for these and other general contractors and customers has resulted in over $85 million of business over the last 10 years.

Some of Roof Services Corporation's largest and most noteworthy projects are the Panasonic Corporate Headquarters, Chesapeake, VA; QVC Distribution and Warehouse, Suffolk, VA; various Hannaford and Harris Teeter Food Stores; and GEICO Insurance Headquarters, Virginia Beach, VA; to name a few. In addition to these projects, Roof Services has been involved in roofing projects for several of Hampton Roads' schools, including Seatack Elementary School, Virginia Beach; Windsor Elementary School, Suffolk; W.T. Cooke Elementary School, Virginia Beach and more.

In addition to its operations and sheet metal departments, the backbone of Roof Services Corporation has been its repair and maintenance department. Many of John and Gary's competitors have had to close their doors during construction slowdowns because they did not have a strong enough maintenance department to carry them through lean times. Having witnessed this, both men agreed that their repair and maintenance department would be strong enough to provide work for their employees and revenue for the company during these slow periods. One of Roof Services Corporation's most ethical traits is its commitment to its employees, and likewise its employees' commitment to Roof Services.

With over 150 employees in both the Virginia Beach and Richmond locations, Roof Services offers its employees one of the highest qualities of life enjoyed by commercial roofing personnel in the area. With unheard of benefits such as paid vacation, profit sharing, health and dental insurance, and more recently, a company 401k plan, Roof Services Corporation exceeds it competitors in employee benefits.

Another trait Roof Services Corporation is proud of, is its policy of promoting from within. Because of its high personnel standards, Roof Services can draw from a vast pool of talent when expanding its management staff. This allows both field and office personnel to see "one of their own" succeed. Additionally, John and Gary pride themselves on their ability to listen to their employees. This not only fosters team spirit on the job, but also allows each employee to feel valued. These are the qualities that promote the loyalty that Roof Services employees have for their company.

Committed to the community, Roof Services Corporation and its employees are involved in several local and national charities. In Fall 1999 the company sponsored a team of its employees for a walk-a-thon which raised more than $2,000 for the Seton House, a local shelter for runaway teens. In addition to this contribution, Roof Services donated labor and materials for the complete reroofing of their main building, which was beyond repair.

Other charities Roof Services and its employees are annually involved in are the "Mayflower Food Drive," sponsored by one of the local radio stations at Thanksgiving, and the U.S. Marines' Toys for Tots Program at Christmas. In all instances, John and Gary generously give of their personal assets, as well as encourage their employees to do the same. Their enthusiasm for giving is infectious. In 1999 alone, Roof Services and its employees donated two tons in canned food to the Mayflower Food Drive and $2,000 worth of toys for Toys for Tots. All proceeds benefited local families in need. In addition, June 2000 will mark the first year that Roof

Roof Services Corporation corporate headquarters in Virginia Beach.

Services will sponsor a team of its employees in the American Cancer Society's Relay for Life. As always, John and Gary are enthusiastically donating their resources and assets to ensure the success of their announced goal of $25,000.

Over the last 10 years, Roof Services Corporation has been recognized for its commitment to quality standards through various awards. One of the most prestigious of these awards was being named as a Firestone Master Contractor for the past five consecutive years. Points are awarded based on the quality of workmanship during the installation of Firestone Roof Systems. The fewer installation defects found by the Firestone inspector, the higher the overall inspection grade. With a Master Contractor, a Firestone customer can be assured that their roof installation or repair will strictly meet manufacturer's guidelines, and because this title is so prestigious, Roof Services finds itself in a very select group of roofing contractors.

Along with being named Firestone Master Contractor, Roof Services is proud to have received the Stevens Silver Alliance Award for 1997, 1998 and 1999; the Stevens Roofing System Hall of Fame Award, awarded consecutively to Roof Services since 1993; and the Associated Builders and Contractors' Paragon Award for excellence in safety. Additionally, Clancy & Theys Construction Co. has awarded Roof Services their company's Award of Excellence for work performed on the Avis Rent a Car Telecommunications and Processing Center in Virginia Beach; UPS Customers Service Telephone Center in Newport News; and the Dollar Tree Stores Corporate Office and Distribution Center in Chesapeake.

What does the future hold for Roof Services Corporation? In the last 10 years, John Babcock and Gary Rogacki have seen their small home-based business grow into a multi-million dollar corporation. Looking forward to the 21st century led Roof Services Corporation to open a branch office in Richmond, Virginia in 1998. With this new branch, Roof Services was able to introduce itself into a market that has never seen the quality of service nor the customer satisfaction on which John Babcock and Gary Rogacki have based their business principles. Roof Services Corporation is rapidly gaining the same respect and customer loyalty, in this new arena, that it has enjoyed in the Hampton Roads area for the last 10 years.

Hickory High School, Chesapeake, Virginia.

THE TAF GROUP

One of the worst things that can happen to people as companies and individuals, is to see all of one's efforts "go-up-in-smoke." To experience a fire can be one of the most devastating experiences mankind can have. Lightening never strikes twice in the same place...or does it?

The TAF Group was developed in 1994 through a series of mergers and acquisitions between some very well-known and respected architectural, engineering, survey and construction companies. Created by its chairman Oliver P. Farinholt, The TAF Group offers total facility solutions under one roof, with the ablity to take total responsibility for transforming an owner's needs from concept to reality. The TAF Group can assist an owner in locating and evaluating sites, arranging financing, zoning, design and construction. The company can conceivably include in that overall plan the furnishing of the project, and subsequently, management of the facility. The TAF Group is the only firm in the Hampton Roads region to offer full services under one roof.

Shortly after the mergers of 1994 were completed, Farinholt received a call at 3:30 a.m. on January 6, 1995, informing him that there was a fire at The TAF Group offices. Upon arriving at the site it was immediately apparent that one third of the office was totally destroyed and the balance suffered very heavy smoke and water damage.

The fire occurred on a Friday morning; clearly the goal had to include being

The TAF Group's new facility located at 100 Landmark Square in Virginia Beach, VA.

The dynamic new entrance lobby.

up and running by Monday morning. With the help of our entire staff we made it happen," said Oliver Farinholt. "Everyone pitched in and by Monday morning the firm was working, but in the worst conditions anyone could imagine."

Three days after settling with the insurance company, lightening struck again. On July 3, 1999, at 2:30 a.m., an act of arson was committed and the building was totally engulfed and destroyed in 30 minutes. With the exception of the survey equipment, there was nothing salvageable from the entire facility.

Monday, after the fire, the entire team assembled in the parking lot underneath a tree, where Oliver Farinholt used a picnic table to set up his field office. The group of nearly 100 people had come together determined to overcome this adversity.

In a matter of days The TAF Group was up and running again. Office space was located within Virginia Beach. The space, less than half of the space they

were used to working in, was adequate to keep the team together and with the help of Gateway Computer Company, The TAF Group was fully-operational on July 9, only six days after the second fire.

After looking for alternate sites to rebuild the company offices, it was apparent that the office should be reconstructed on the original site at Landmark Square. The TAF Group, with all of its tenacity, proceeded, and subsequently moved into its new facility on December 17, 1999. Truly, "The Phoenix Had Risen."

The TAF Group's new home, a high tech, modern building, is a facility in which people can be creative and can emulate the mindset that enables The TAF Group to watch "the phoenix" rise from the ashes.

Someone once said that great strength comes from adversity and The TAF Group is truly an example of how factual that statement is.

239

SENTARA HEALTHCARE

Sentara Healthcare is a not-for-profit, diversified health services organization whose unique integration of people, processes and technologies has made it the number one health care provider in the greater Hampton Roads region and a nationally recognized leader in the health care industry. Sentara has been named one of the Top 10 Integrated Health Care Networks in the United States by SMG Marketing Group, a Chicago-based health care and information marketing company who ranks the Top 100 Integrated Health Systems nationwide.

"We feel it's our obligation to the community to provide leadership in health care," said David L. Bernd, Chief Executive Officer. "The point of doing so is not for our own success, but to make good on the trust the public has invested in us. If, along the way, we attract attention and net awards, we're honored. But the purpose of doing good work is to refine our abilities, improve our capabilities and then apply those efforts right here at home, to improve the health of our community."

Overseen by a volunteer board of community leaders which includes area physicians, Sentara features more than 70 care-giving sites. Among these are: six hospitals with a total of 1,832 beds; two outpatient health care campuses; seven nursing centers; three assisted living centers; 38 primary care practices; a full-range of health coverage plans; home health and hospice services; physical therapy and rehabilitation services; urgent care facilities; ground medical transport services; mobile diagnostic vans; and a health and fitness facility. Sentara also provides the region's only air ambulance and organ transplant program.

At the heart of Sentara is its founding institution, the Retreat for the Sick, a 25-bed facility established in 1888 in downtown Norfolk. This facility has evolved into today's Sentara Norfolk General Hospital, a 644-bed tertiary care facility recognized as the area's only Level I Trauma Center. Sentara Norfolk General Hospital earned national recognition in the 1999 *U.S. News and World Report* ranking of America's Best Hospitals, and is known for providing excellence in cardiac care, performing the region's first open heart surgery in 1967. In 1970, the facility unveiled a state-of-the-art open heart surgery center, known today as the Heart Pavilion.

Through the years, Sentara has grown to include five other hospitals in

Just as it was more than 100 years ago, Sentara is still dedicated to making the communities it serves healthier places to live, work and play...one person at a time.

Hampton Roads. Sentara Virginia Beach General Hospital, a 274-bed acute care facility and Level II trauma center specializing in cardiology, cardiac surgery, women's and infants' health, oncology, orthopedics and neurosciences, has been recognized as one of the nation's top regional hospitals. Also in Virginia Beach, Sentara Bayside Hospital is a 158-bed primary care facility specializing in outpatient diagnostic and surgical services. Sentara Leigh Hospital, a 250-bed facility located on the Norfolk-Virginia Beach border, specializes in orthopedic, gynecological and urological services. On the Virginia peninsula, Sentara Hampton General Hospital, a 358-bed facility, has been serving acute care needs since 1892. Sentara Careplex, an outpatient care campus offering emergency care, outpatient surgery, diagnostics and rehabilitation, will be the site of a new hospital in 2002. Williamsburg Community Hospital, a 139-bed facility, provides residents with emergency, surgical, cardiac and cancer services.

The Sentara network also includes the region's first health care plan, Optima, founded in 1984 and the region's first HMO. Sentara's products provide health coverage to more than 300,000 people,

Above
Sentara is an innovative, integrated health care organization that cares for patients through all the stages of their lives.

Below
Sentara knows that even the most humble beginning can inspire great things.

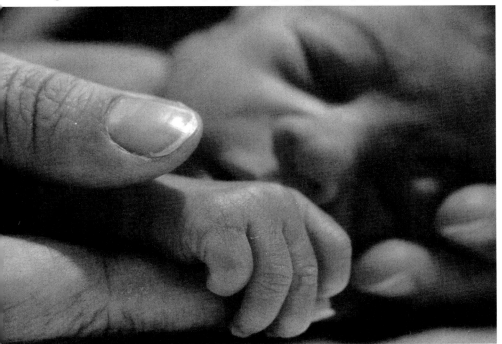

tapping into a provider network of nearly 2,000 affiliated physicians. The caliber of its plans has been recognized by the National Research Corporation, which named Optima Health Plan a Quality Leader, and by the National Committee for Quality Assurance who gave Sentara its highest rating of "excellent" and named it one of the top health maintenance organizations in the nation.

Since its inception Sentara Healthcare has made a tradition of giving back to the community. Each year, the organization donates approximately $69 million in charitable care, medical education and innovative outreach programs. The Sentara Health Foundation, a board-designated endowment fund, was established in 1998 to fulfill Sentara's mission of expanding community-wide efforts to promote health maintenance and disease prevention.

As it enters the new millennium, Sentara continues to be on the cutting-edge of the health care industry, continually seeking new and innovative ways to provide members of the greater Hampton Roads community with complete, integrated health care services—quality health care for a lifetime.

STEELMASTER BUILDINGS, INC.

Virginia Beach conjures up visions of surf, sand and sun, not "arch steel buildings," yet a group of distinguished, successful business people from the beach established what is today SteelMaster Buildings, Inc., the world's leading steel arch building manufacturer. The group included George and Marjorie Crump, founders of WCMS, the oldest country western radio station in the United States; John Waller, founder of the architectural firm of Waller, Todd & Sadler, in 1956; and Rhae Adams, Sr., recognized as Virginia Beach's first citizen in 1952 and founder of Beach Ford, Inc.

Originating in the southeastern United States, Southeastern Steel Buildings, Inc., as it was known then, spent its early years developing designs and specifications that would satisfy the agricultural market, i.e., animal shelters, grain and hay storage as well as small shops and garages. Rhae Adams, Jr. sold the company's first building to the Roanoke Island Steel and Boat Works, located in Wanchese, NC. The building, 25 feet by 30 feet, was sold for use as a portable welding cover for fabrication of steel trawlers. The building was able to be lifted by cranes and located throughout the boatyard as needed. The company quickly recognized the need for a wider range of buildings with more sophisticated applications, and its growth began.

Soon SteelMaster buildings could be seen throughout Hampton Roads. From

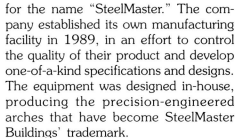

Rhae Adams, Jr., president of SteelMaster Buildings, Inc.

ships to surfboards, they were used to provide protective shelters for nearly everything. The company learned early on to adapt to the requirements of its customers. This led to the development of buildings able to withstand hurricane force winds on the Outer Banks of North Carolina, crane-liftable shelters to satisfy the very demanding and unique requirements of most of Hampton Roads shipyards and the ever-stringent regulations and specifications of the U.S. Military.

In November 1985, the company received the trademark registration from the U.S. Trademark and Patent Office

for the name "SteelMaster." The company established its own manufacturing facility in 1989, in an effort to control the quality of their product and develop one-of-a-kind specifications and designs. The equipment was designed in-house, producing the precision-engineered arches that have become SteelMaster Buildings' trademark.

In 1992, the factory invented the "A" model, which has redefined the public's thinking of steel buildings. With a unique pitch-style roof and straight walls, the A model offers a more traditional look with the same legendary quality of a SteelMaster building, and has become a huge success as a backyard garage or shop for thousands of American homeowners across the country.

The first "A" model ever erected was in Dillwyn, Virginia, on the Adam's family farm. Rhae Adams, Sr. erected the building in the paddock as a shelter for his horses and a llama named George, who had been a gift from his dear friend George Crump. The llama, unaccustomed to steel buildings, liked to kick the side of the building to hear the sound of his hooves against the steel. Soon the horses had picked up George's bad habit of kicking the sides to make the steel ring. Although George the llama has passed on, the building still stands, and the horses continue kicking their hooves against the steel to this day.

The company has passed from father to son and is now owned and operated by Rhae Adams, Jr. It has become the industry leader for economical, high quality, arch style steel buildings throughout the world. Rhae Adams, along with a younger brother David Adams and a core SteelMaster management team, have led SteelMaster buildings for the past 20 years, and have been the driving force behind its growth and success. With headquarters located in Virginia Beach, SteelMaster Buildings has expanded from two employees in the first year to over 100 employees today. There are now regional offices across the United States and representatives throughout the world including in

A typical "Q" model designed to house hay.

Twin 45x30x120, Naval launch/barge sand-blast repair facility designed to accommodate waterfront rail system.

Korea, Japan, Israel, Italy, England, New Zealand and South America.

The main office in Virginia Beach houses a central phone center, three sales departments and the accounting and marketing departments, along with the industrial/commercial and construction departments and various support teams.

SteelMaster Buildings' space age design and technology not only provide 100 percent open, useable interior space, but also amazing versatility. So versatile in fact, that Rhae Adams was contacted by 20th Century Fox to create a 1,400 foot tunnel posing as a New York aqueduct in the Bruce Willis movie, "Die Hard III, With A Vengeance." "Our engineers did a double take when we explained how we had to run two dump trucks through the SteelMaster tunnel while the bad guys fired automatic weapons at Bruce during the high speed chase scene which ended with a flooding of the tunnel," recalls Rhae Adams. "I think we added a few white hairs to our engineers, but we got the job done safely, in time, and on budget."

This was not the first such strange request the company has received. SteelMaster provided a temporary shop for the America Team car in the salt flats of Nevada and was hired by the Depart-

ment of Commerce to provide the entrance cover for the USA Pavilion at the 1990 Air Show in Paris, France. Its military and government customers around the world have come to depend on SteelMaster to meet their stringent requirements and specifications for everything from housing U.S. Marine Harrier jets at Cherrypoint, North Carolina to containing hazardous waste for the Department of Energy.

The requests aren't always for the "strange" or "unique." When First Colonial High School in Virginia Beach was looking for a batting cage, they turned to SteelMaster. "We needed to provide a building that could resist direct hits from baseballs and provide an indoor batting and pitching practice facility for year round training." Together with coach Norbie Wilson and the local parents and players who held raffles to raise money, the high school and the school board, the SteelMaster team contributed their time and materials to provide a wonderful facility. "It was an old fashioned barn raising where the community all pitched in and worked together to provide a great facility for the kids," said Steve Rankin, general sales manager of Steelmaster.

Whether it be inventing new designs or re-engineering the specifications and the manufacturing of the buildings, the SteelMaster team has provided leadership and innovation in the arch steel building industry. Rhae Adams still believes that maximum economy, superior quality and world-class service are what set companies apart. This is why SteelMaster continues to grow and prosper in an increasingly competitive world. It's also why today the company still follows the mission statement of its founders: "SteelMaster provides the highest quality steel arch buildings in the world. Leading the industry in customer service and value, we are committed to satisfying the challenging demand of the global market. Customer satisfaction and excellence is the cornerstone of our continued market leadership."

Batting cage built for First Colonial High School in Virgina Beach.

TIDEWATER COMMUNICATIONS AND ELECTRONICS, INC.

In 1959, Claude L. Hinkle, Jr. and his wife Peggy founded Tidewater Communications and Electronics, Inc. (TCE) to become the local Motorola Service Center for customers in Princess Anne County and the town of Virginia Beach.

Claude got his start in electronics when he served as an electronics technician in the Navy in the mid-1950s. After retiring from the Navy he started a TV repair business, but switched to the two-way radio business when Motorola asked him to help service radios for the Virginia Beach Police Department. Virginia Beach was a small oceanfront community with only six police cars in 1959. Forty years later, Tidewater Communications is still relied upon to maintain Virginia Beach's much larger public safety communications system.

Claude still goes into the office every day, but it is the second generation Hinkles, Marcus and Eric, who are now leading TCE toward its next 40 years of success. While still in high school, Marcus began installing radios for his father in 1976 and worked his way to vice president by 1982. After graduating from James Madison University in 1987, Eric pursued a career in the computer industry before finally joining the family business in Fall 1992.

The Hinkles take both their own reputation and that of their suppliers seriously. As they look to grow, both Marcus and Eric are adamant about maintaining and building on the reputation their father established for representing only the highest quality products and providing the best posssible service to their customers. "Motorola has a strong reputation," says Marcus. "But we earn a lot of repeat business and customer referrals because of our focus on service." Motorola also recognizes TCE's reputation. TCE was featured in a video used to promote Motorola's emergency response capabilities to public safety customers throughout the country. Eric feels so strongly about "doing the right thing" for customers that he has been serving on the Better Business Bureau of Greater Hampton Roads Board of Directors since 1996.

Left to right: Eric Hinkle, Claude Hinkle, and Marcus Hinkle.

TCE's first employee, Wally Burkett, is still there today. "Everybody in the radio business has heard of Wally—he's one of our greatest technical assets," notes Marcus. Other key players have included Robert Rockefeller ("Rocky") and Steve Toth. When Rocky, now retired, was TCE's service manager, he

244

served as a technical advisor for ITT Technical Institute. As the company's current service manager, Steve serves on a technical advisory board for ECPI.

For the first 30 years, the Hinkles operated the family business strictly as a service center, leaving the selling to Motorola's direct sales force. In 1989 however, Marcus led the company into the competitive world of sales. It was at this time that Motorola allowed their service centers to become dealers for their low-tier two-way radio product line. By 1992, Motorola recognized the Hinkle's growing success in sales by authorizing their dealership to represent the full line of Motorola products.

By 1994 TCE was recognized by Motorola again—this time for being the fastest growing dealership in Virginia. Since 1992, TCE has won numerous performance awards and has repeatedly earned a place in Motorola's prestigous Pinnacle Club, which recognizes the top 20 dealers in three divisions across the country.

Marcus discovered his talent for sales in a roundabout way, as the result of a family vacation. Soon after their first snow skiing trip in the mid-1970s, the Hinkle family helped one of Marcus' high school teachers open a new ski shop in Virginia Beach. Marcus quickly became an eager salesman for the store. Marcus now works closely with TCE's sales manager Gary Orosco, to offer direction to their professional sales staff.

"That our family business has not only survived in the competitive telecom industry, but is poised to take on new challenges is due largely to dad's foresight," says Marcus. "Wireless and telecom are the hot buzz words right now, but we've already been doing both for 40 years." The younger Hinkles continuously look for new "windows of opportunity" in their fast-paced industry. They're currently taking a serious look at what role "convergence" should play in their business future. Convergence allows users to access multiple technologies from a single device. "Everything is coming together. The trend toward 'convergence' could lead us to become a much

more broadly focused telecom company," says Eric.

As they consider new products and technologies, Marcus and Eric will remain focused on serving the commercial, industrial and government markets their company has been serving since the beginning. TCE has no plans to open retail stores or target individual consumers. "We're focused on helping business people. Our job is to help them

Eric and Susan Hinkle accepting Motorola's Pinnacle Award for Outstanding Performance.

choose the best solution for their unique situation," says Marcus. "Individual consumers simply don't need our level of expertise." TCE's sales people are trained to serve as consultants and to develop professional relationships with their customers.

TIDEWATER CONSTRUCTION CORPORATION

Travel by land or water anywhere in the Hampton Roads area, or anywhere along the eastern seaboard, and you will undoubtedly travel over, walk into, navigate by, or use something constructed by Tidewater Construction Corporation. Whether it's a bridge, tunnel, pier, wharf, industrial facility, light tower, or other heavy construction project, Tidewater was most likely involved. In the Hampton Roads area alone Tidewater has played a leading role in all of the major bay and river crossings and has been the primary contractor along the waterfront of the Chesapeake Bay.

Founded by John S. Gregory and S.E. Liles, Jr., in May 1932, during the depths of the depression, Tidewater Construction Corporation began operations as a marine and pile driving construction firm owning one derrick boat, a pile driver, and a few other pieces of small construction equipment. From that small beginning Tidewater and its subsidiaries have grown to a position of prominence among the country's major construction companies.

Tidewater's original large project was the first Campostella Bridge over the Eastern Branch of the Elizabeth River. This project launched Tidewater on its way to becoming the East Coast's premier marine and heavy construction contractor. Included in the list of the many bridges built by Tidewater in the Hampton Roads area are the James River, London Creek, 26th Street, Mill Creek, North Landing, Nansemond River, Thalia Creek, Hampton River, Route 13 Wayside, both the old and new Berkely bridges, and numerous highway bridge overpasses.

Tidewater's award-winning nine-day replacement of the George P. Coleman Bridge over the York River is a major innovative engineering accomplishment. More recently Tidewater has completed many significant highway projects in the area, including the Oak Grove Connector, and the HOV lanes and major bridges and overpasses along the I64/264 and Military Highway corridors.

Tidewater has also played a major role in bridge-tunnel projects in the Hampton

Roads Area. The Downtown Tunnel under the Southern Branch of the Elizabeth River that connects Norfolk and Portsmouth was the first such crossing. The second—the Hampton Roads Bridge Tunnel—connects Norfolk and Hampton. The project for which Tidewater is best known is the 17.6 mile Chesapeake

Above
Tidewater's Construction's Rig #1 installs piles for the first Campostella Bridge over the Eastern Branch of the Elizabeth River, 1993.

Below
Aerial view, looking north from Virginia Beach, of the Chesapeake Bay Bridge-Tunnel under construction, 1963.

Bay Bridge-Tunnel that connects Virginia Beach with the Eastern Shore of Virginia. It was named by the American Society of Civil Engineers as one of the seven wonders of the modern world.

The early experience in pile driving and heavy rigging for bridges and marine work provided the platform for expansion into the heavy industrial construction market and gained Tidewater the reputation as a lead contracting firm in construction of chemical, pulp and paper, cement and other manufacturing and heavy industrial projects.

Tidewater's subsidiary Tidewater Equipment Corporation (TEC), founded in 1959 and located on the Southern Branch of the Elizabeth River, specializes in the design and fabrication of barges, equipment, and heavy steel structures for the maritime industry. Barges and floating equipment built by TEC can be seen working along Hampton Roads waterfront and the inland and offshore waters of the East Coast. Commercial and military ships from all over the world are welcomed into the entrance of the Chesapeake Bay by the 135 foot Chesapeake Light Tower, one of the many

Above
One of the sections of the second Berkely Bridge being moved into place, 1990.

Below
Aerial view of the I-264/Military Highway overpass completed in early 2000. Photo by Advertising Visuals, Gene Woolridge photographer

towers and navigational aids built by Tidewater Equipment.

Another TCC subsidiary, Bayshore Concrete Products Corporation, is the premier East Coast supplier of a wide variety of precast prestressed concrete structural materials. Established in 1961 to produce the precast components for the Chesapeake Bay Bridge Tunnel, Bayshore has expanded production capacity and diversified its product line. Bayshore, with plants in Cape Charles and Chesapeake, Virginia, is the recognized leader in production of high-quality precast prestressed concrete products. Bayshore takes particular pride in its ability to fabricate unusually long, unwieldy, or massive precast items that are most economical if marine transportation and erection are feasible.

Tidewater and it's subsidiaries are now a part of Skanska USA, Inc., one of the top 10 largest construction firms in the United States. Skanska USA is one of the four business units of Skanska AB, an international construction company based in Stockholm, Sweden. As part of Skanska, Tidewater enjoys the benefits of a worldwide network of expertise and knowledge in virtually all facets of the construction industry.

VIRGINIA WESLEYAN COLLEGE

Virginia Wesleyan College, located on Wesleyan Drive astride the Norfolk/ Virginia Beach city line, was founded by The Methodist Church and chartered in 1961 by the Commonwealth of Virginia. The denomination, which is known for its strong commitment to education, saw a need to establish a church-related, residential, undergraduate, liberal arts college in the Hampton Roads area, where none existed. As the College approaches the 40th anniversary of its charter, the past reflects an era of tremendous growth and development and the future a myriad of opportunities.

The College opened its doors in September 1966 to a freshman class of 75 representing seven states, a faculty of 11 and an administrative staff of five under the leadership of President Lambuth M. Clarke. The entire campus was housed in one academic village, a cluster of seven interconnected buildings that included four dormitories, a dining hall, classrooms, faculty offices and lounges. With no administrative office space available, one of the dormitories served that function. Full accreditation was received in record time, prior to the graduation of the first class in 1970.

Location has always been an asset for Virginia Wesleyan. When property was purchased in the early '60s, the College replaced a cornfield in an area of Hampton Roads for which the definition of the term "suburban" would have been a stretch. While still on a relatively tranquil site, the original seven-building academic village has grown into a physical plant. The site includes over 30 buildings, including an award-winning library, science building, dining center, theater, chapel, additional academic village and a total of 11 residence halls, situated on 300 acres in the heart of the Hampton Roads area.

Virginia Wesleyan's mission is to engage students of diverse ages, religions, ethnic origins and backgrounds in a rigorous liberal arts education that will prepare them to meet the challenges of life and career in a complex and rapidly changing world. A wide range of approaches to teaching and learning

Growth continues to be a major part of Virginia Wesleyan College. In an effort to create the best possible atmosphere for its community, the College continues to upgrade its facilities and academics. Friends of the College continue to provide financial and emotional support as it grows in size and reputation. The ground breaking ceremony for the Jane P. Batten Student Center signified the addition of yet another outstanding facility which will serve as a hub for the entire campus community.

provides opportunities to connect the study of the liberal arts with practical learning experiences on campus, in the Hampton Roads region, and throughout the world. In accord with the heritage of The United Methodist Church, the College aspires to be a supportive community that is committed to social responsibility, ethical conduct, higher learning and religious freedom (*Academic Bulletin 1999-2000*).

Current President Billy Greer fervently believes that Virginia Wesleyan is in the business of shaping lives. A rigorous academic program and committed faculty are the forces that drive that endeavor. The caliber of the teacher/scholars on the College faculty is exceptional. Small class sizes and access to professors allow relationships to foster between teacher and learner. The college also strives to incorporate the surrounding community in its commitment to a well-rounded education. The PORTfolio program links the liberal arts curriculum and the world outside of the classroom. It can augment any major by

providing opportunities for students to apply their knowledge to a variety of experiential opportunities in the Hampton Roads area.

Virginia Wesleyan College continues to be recognized in several significant ways for its effort to shape lives. Recently, the John Templeton Foundation issued the first edition of *The Templeton Guide: Colleges that Encourage Character Development*, in which Virginia Wesleyan was cited in two separate categories for its "commitment

A strong part of the history of Virginia Wesleyan College is its relationship with the United Methodist Church. Construction of the Monumental Chapel and Bell Tower provided both a visual landmark and a place of worship. The College is proud of its well-established relationship with the church, and continues to recognize and foster the partnership.

to inspiring students to lead ethical and civic-minded lives." The first was for the College's Academic Honesty program. The second was in Spiritual Growth for providing, through the Office of the Chaplain, "opportunities for students to develop a coherent vision of moral integrity that connects believe to behavior."

The establishment of the endowed Birdsong Office of Community Service in 1997 brought focus to the College's efforts to encourage students to give back more than they receive during their college career. Throughout the school year Wesleyan students are out across Hampton Roads involved in tutoring, disaster assistance and programs for the elderly, and in building homes with Habitat for Humanity.

Virginia Wesleyan continues to emphasize the value of a well-rounded education that reaches beyond the walls of its campus. A student team from Virginia Wesleyan coached by Philosophy Professor Steven Emmanuel took top honors in the inaugural *Virginia Foundation for Independent Colleges* Ethics Bowl moderated by newscaster Roger Mudd, competing against all 15 VFIC schools that participated. The Bowl provided a forum for students to tackle difficult moral questions and consider their stand on real-life cases in

topics such as science, politics, religion, bio-engineering and human rights.

The establishment of two centers during the last decade has brought depth to the College's programming efforts for both the campus community and the community at-large. The Center for Sacred Music offers stimulating performance opportunities and educational programs to foster and encourage an appreciation of diversity and excellence in the sacred arts. The Center for the Study of Religious Freedom promotes the education and foundation needed to meet the challenge of fostering religious freedom in a diverse world, and was selected by the Virginia Foundation for

Virginia Wesleyan College, which straddles the line between Norfolk and Virginia Beach, has access to the major metropolitan area of Hampton Roads. At the same time it provides a small intimate campus nestled within the trees grown as part of the original farmland on which the College was built.

the Humanities and Public Policy to receive its 25th Anniversary Award for Religion and the Humanities. The Center was chosen from among 40,000 programs sponsored by the Foundation since 1974.

The Consider the Harvest campaign of the 1990s raised over $36 million for scholarships, increased endowments and building funds to accommodate the needs of a student body numbering over 1,400. That figure includes 350 students enrolled in the Adult Studies Program established in 1982, that provides a venue for adult learners to return to school and complete their degree.

Lambuth M. Clarke Hall opened in August 1998 as a technologically advanced classroom building. Katherine B. and Mills E. Godwin Jr. Hall was completed in 1999 and provides space for administrative offices that were housed in the library for 30 years, returning portions of that facility to its intended use. The Jane P. Batten Student Center, the latest and largest building project on Wesleyan's campus, will be complete in September 2001. The 138,000 square-foot facility will house athletics (including a competition gym and an eight-lane, 25-yard swimming pool) recreational activities, academic space, student support services, bookstore and food court.

Since its founding, Wesleyan has prided itself upon its heritage with both the community and the United Methodist Church, and it maintains those values and tradition to this day. The College continues to grow physically and academically, while continuing to provide the personal one-on-one education for which it is known. Virginia Wesleyan College is proud of its accomplishments and honored to be considered a part of the history of Hampton Roads.

THE VIRGINIAN-PILOT

In 1993, Frank Batten told Landmark Communications' managers that its people had been asking him, "Why are you shaking up the company? Aren't we making enough money?"

The bottom line is just fine, Batten told them, "but the competitive trends are tough! Newspapers and TV stations are no longer protected monopolies," he noted, "and if Landmark's media are not going to become endangered species, we must learn to become superior competitors."

Batten aimed to make Landmark "...the leader in all our markets. We will have to focus on delighting customers, improving productivity, creating better products and developing our people. To develop skills in innovation, we must be willing to experiment and take risks."

The dynasty began when Samuel L. Slover, son of a court clerk in East Tennessee, helped a candidate win a seat in the state senate. The senator hired Slover at age 19 to sell ads for *The Knoxville Times*.

Slover became manager. Circulation doubled, but the debt-ridden *Times* failed. Slover wasn't to blame, but over time, he repaid its $36,000 debt.

Selling ads for a trade paper, he visited Joseph Bryan of *The Richmond Times* and asked for a loan with which to buy a paper in Norfolk. Bryan declined.

"I didn't think he would lend me the money," Slover said later. "But I knew he wouldn't forget me."

Bryan hired Slover to sell ads on commission. Slover out-earned everybody. Then he roved Virginia buying and selling six newspapers. Once he held control of *The Richmond Times Dispatch*. He saved and sold *The Newport News Times* and bought *The Norfolk Ledger* in 1905. He suggested to James Thomson of *The Norfolk Dispatch* that they become partners. Thomson refused.

Often, Slover ran on borrowed funds, One day the foreman told Slover, "We can't deliver some of the papers. The mule died last night."

Slover went to the bank to borrow money to buy a mule to pull the delivery wagon.

One evening in a Norfolk theater, Thomson saw Slover in a box with Fay Martin, his fiancée. Thomson couldn't look at the show for watching Slover laughing and carefree. The sight took the fight out of him.

Next day he met Slover and told him, "I'll say it to your face. You licked me."

They became friends. Slover bought the *The Dispatch* from Thomson, who later termed him "one of the ablest publishers of the last half century."

Newspapers captivated Slover. A pioneer when papers were consolidating, Slover, buying and selling, set the footings for modern journalism throughout Virginia.

Col. S. L. Slover, founder of the newspaper dynasty and the ensuing development of Landmark Communications.

A big man of great assurance, his straight back and steady gaze made him a commanding figure. He treated his partners and associates with generosity. A bit shy at times, he tended to brush aside the thanks of those he helped.

"He was absolutely rigid in his belief that people should tell the truth no matter how painful it might be," Frank Batten Sr. recalls.

In 1933, Norfolk faced a fiscal crisis. City Council, without notifying Slover, elected him mayor. He agreed to serve a year, took no salary and put his own money into the task. Having saved the city, he resigned.

Friends called him Colonel as a mark of affection after he served two years as an aide to Governor Westmoreland Davis.

From age one, when his father died, Frank Batten and his mother Dorothy lived with her sister Fay, the wife of Slover.

In 1932, at age 5, Batten saw his uncle at work. "I remember a big man, Harry Goodrich, came to the house," he said. "He and the Colonel talked. After Mr. Goodrich left, the Colonel told Mrs. Slover, 'I just bought WTAR for $15,000.'"

Slover's finest service to Virginia, according to the late Gov. Colgate Darden Jr., was preparing young Batten to succeed him.

"He loved the business," Batten says. "He just wanted me from my childhood to carry on and to have the same fun and bigger opportunities.

"He raised me as a son. He was bigger than life to me. I looked up to him in awe. As a teenager I doubted I could live up to his standards. He was so successful as a self-made man."

At Culver Military Academy Batten found that achievers were those respected by their peers. He captained a company of 80 cadets. The track coach showed him that if he persisted in a sport, he could achieve.

"We boxed every day. I was sort of a punching bag for the guys on the first team, but I figured I should learn to fight."

As a reporter one summer, he took his car to 14 garages to test the new state inspection system. He found wildly differing reports on violations and cost estimates. One irate car dealer threatened to go to his "friend" Colonel Slover.

"He'd be happy to see you," Batten replied.

At the University of Virginia he found Dr. A.K. Davis, "the meanest man I ever met and a wonderful teacher. He would read to the class what you had written—or have you stand and read it—and he'd ridicule it line by line. It was painful!"

Batten took *The Virginian-Pilot's* helm in 1954. Slover was adviser-in-residence for two years.

The Battens, Frank Sr. and Jr., who expanded the newspaper into a multi-media conglomerate. Photo by Lawrence Jackson

Col. Slover died July 27, 1959 at age 86, having seen, a year before, the third link in the family dynasty with the birth of Frank Batten Jr.

When Frank Batten, at age 27, became publisher, he found a company in disarray. It was similar to some of the troubled firms he had studied in the Harvard Business School.

He infused cooperation among department heads and, drawing talent from universities and industry, he built a team open to change. He began developing enterprises that came under the umbrella of Landmark Communications.

Among them were the Weather Channel, TeleCable Corp., half ownership of Trader Publishing, two television stations, and 70 community newspapers. Two early purchases were newspapers in Greensboro and Roanoke.

"Newspapers are my first love," Batten says. *The Virginian-Pilot*

continues to be Landmark's flagship.

Its ancestor, *The Norfolk Virginian*, was born November 21, 1865, seven months after General Lee surrendered the Confederacy. No paper survived the city's occupation by Federal troops. At its dawning, *The Norfolk Virginian* was the only kid on the block. It urged Norfolk "to stimulate immigration and to awaken the enterprise" of its 15,000 citizens.

When the Wright brothers' plane flew three miles over the dunes of Kitty Hawk, NC in December 1903, a *Virginian-Pilot* reporter recorded it.

Most newspapers ignored the feat. *The Pilot's* editors ran a double-deck banner across the top of the front page.

Its editorial page was among the best. In 1929 editor Louis Jaffe won a Pulitzer Prize for an anti-lynching series. It prodded Gov. Harry F. Byrd to push to passage the nation's strongest anti-lynching law.

Anyone in a mob was deemed as guilty as those who had their hands on the rope.

In 1969 editor Lenoir Chambers won a Pulitzer Prize for editorials opposing the state's policy of massive resistance to the Supreme Court's school desegregation decree.

When a state fund-cut law closed public schools in Norfolk for the 1958-59 semester, Batten and Pretlow Darden persuaded 100 civic leaders to sign a full-page ad urging the city to reopen schools.

The Pilot was Virginia's only major newspaper to attack the policy. Batten was among business leaders who tried to persuade Gov. J. Lindsay Almond Jr. to open the schools. Almond erupted in anger. Red-faced, glaring at Batten, he denounced "that paper of yours."

Landmark's philanthropic foundation contributes to a host of causes and Batten directs his energies to civic activities.

He was rector of Old Dominion University for eight years. His wife Jane Batten chaired for three years the board of trustees at Virginia Wesleyan College. Landmark employees enlist in public service throughout the region.

Batten and Josh Darden established the Tidewater Scholarship Foundation that offers to help high school students through college if they maintain a record of good conduct and a C-plus average.

"I have thought all along that the strength of American democracy was that we had been a classless society, and that was largely because education had enabled people to overcome barriers," he said.

"Our hope is that this fund and the counseling we offer would be just one more incentive for students to stay in school and graduate."

Landmark Communications is a holding company and each business within it is self-contained with its own president and finance officers.

In training and promoting employees, Landmark's management may move them among the businesses. Fair treatment and the appreciation of employees are consistent themes emphasized by the Battens.

Louis Jaffe, Pulitzer Prize winner for anti-lynching editorials in 1929.

People are encouraged to apply for jobs in different areas under the theory that a good manager can learn a new business in a reasonable time and bring a breadth of experience to bear on a different context.

The idea is to hire the best, treat them well, give them challenges to grow and provide the support they may need.

Frank Batten, who had headed Landmark Communications and *The Virginian-Pilot* for 43 years, turned its chairmanship over to Frank Jr. on January 1, 1998.

Frank Sr. remained chairman of the board's executive committee and continued to chair Landmark Foundation.

"It's a new generation, but I don't think the company is going to change," Frank Batten Jr. said. "The company will continue expanding and looking for new opportunities, but we've been doing that for decades."

Frank Batten Jr., his associates say, has a way of visualizing matters past the details to a more profound understanding. Drawing on a background of voracious reading and varied experiences in moving through the organization, young Batten arrives at a view of how something new will turn out.

Teachers at Norfolk Academy smile over the purposefulness he showed as a first grader. During an emergency, a new bus driver, taking the children home, got lost. Batten eased up to his side and gave directions the whole way. In classes, he gave his best to any task.

Reminded of those early years, Batten smiled and said, "I guess I'd not be a very good sprinter, but I am a good sort of long distance walker."

The quiet humor understates his determination. He admits to sticking with a problem and "going at it from several angles."

As a copy boy at *The Virginian-Pilot*, he taught himself to type and learned to lay out pages, skills he later used editing the campus paper.

After graduating from Dartmouth College, he earned a master's degree at the Colgate Darden School of Business. A year in advertising at *The Roanoke Times* gave him "a little understanding of the jobs and a lot of respect for those who do them."

As a police reporter, he hesitated to intrude on grieving parents whose teenage son had been killed by a drug dealer.

Lenoir Chambers, Pulitzer Prize winner for editorials to keep schools open in 1969.

"Their boy had been an informer for the police department, which was not supposed to use under-age kids. They were glad to tell that the police had used their son unfairly."

He worked two years in London with the Associated Press followed by four years with the *News Enterprise* in Elizabethtown, KY. He worked first as general manager and then as publisher, where he had a broad array of employees testing his ideas.

"'It was a wonderful place to learn," he said. "One rewarding result was to be succeeded by people who did a fine job and built on whatever I had done and took the newspaper to a higher level."

He returned to Norfolk in 1990 as marketing director and worked through several levels to become publisher of *The Pilot* and then executive vice president of Landmark. He stays abreast of developing technology and is quick to spot new ventures.

In Fall 1990 Batten stopped in the hallway to comment to home editor Aimee Cunningham about a story on the Weyanoke Sanctuary.

The talk broadened into a mutual interest in gardening and a first date. They were married in 1992.

Now and then, Frank Jr. appears with their two sons in the building, a sight that would surely win the blessing of Col. Samuel L. Slover.

LILLIAN VERNON CORPORATION

Lillian Vernon is an entrepreneurial success story. In 1951, Lillian was a young housewife expecting her first child. She lived in a small apartment in Mount Vernon, New York, and wanted to supplement her family's income at a time when women rarely had careers. With $2,000 of wedding gift money, Lillian carried out an idea she was nurturing since she was a teenager. Using her kitchen table as an office, she placed a $495 ad in Seventeen Magazine to sell handbags and belts to young women. She offered a unique service: free personalization with her customers' initials, a trademark her catalogs and web site still offer today. To her surprise, $32,000 in orders poured in and Lillian's mail order company was launched.

Lillian Vernon Corporation now has annual revenues of over $240 million and a one million square foot state-of-the-art distribution center and annex on 62 acres in Virginia Beach. The centers employ over 5,100 people at the height of the Christmas season and are the size of 21

Lillian Vernon Corporation publishes nine catalog titles, mailing 165 million catalogs annually to a customer base of 22 million people nationwide.

Lillian Vernon, founder and chief executive officer of the Lillian Vernon print and on line catalogs.

football fields. Lillian Vernon also operates outlet stores in Norfolk, Virginia Beach, Williamsburg and Prince William.

Over 22 million customers nationwide have ordered from Lillian Vernon. The specialty retailer publishes nine catalog titles that market gift, household, garden, kitchen, Christmas and children's products and is well known for offering unique merchandise at exceptionally good values. With the dawning of the e-commerce revolution, Lillian Vernon Online, www.lillianvernon.com, was introduced in 1995. The web site features most of the company's 6,000 products, as well as customized gift services, an online newsletter and

lifestyle tips from Lillian. The company will also have a business-to-business web site to complement its wholesale division that serves more than 2,000 businesses including many Fortune 500 companies.

Lillian Vernon is a philanthropic leader who believes in giving generously back to her community. She has never forgotten her family's flight from Germany to the United States when she was a small child be-fore the onset of World War II. Lillian has donated considerable time, money and merchandise to over 5,000 charities. She provided sheets and blankets to families in Franklin, Virginia, who were displaced by Hurricane Floyd. She serves on the board of several nonprofit organizations, including the Virginia Opera and the Girl Scout Council of Tidewater. Lillian has received numerous honors and awards including induction into the Direct Marketing Hall of Fame, Hampton Roads Woman of the Year, Virginia Press Women Newsmaker of the Year, and Big/Brothers Big Sisters National Hero Award. She strongly supports women in the workplace and encourages the advancement of women at Lillian Vernon Corporation. The company has the distinction of being the first company founded by a woman to be publicly traded on the American Stock Exchange.

Lillian Vernon Corporation looks forward to a bright future in Virginia.

VOGEL LUBRICATION, INC.

Vogel Lubrication, Inc. provides 70 Hampton Roads residents with employment with the industry leader in lubrication devices and system technology. Originally owned and established by Joe Ahrens in 1982, the company was at that time the sole North American distributor for the territories known today as NAFTA. The first few years of the corporation's existence were spent creating product awareness.

Centralized lubrication, Vogel's core business unit, is a technology designed to reduce wear on mechanical components with a dynamic function. Typically, automatic lubrication extends the useful life cycle of lubricated wearpoints by 300-400 percent. This extended resource life is quite a contribution to society when one considers the amount of energy and raw materials utilized in the manufacturing of machinery. Presently, Vogel provides its centralized lubrication technology for applications within the following industries: machine tools, printing presses, cranes, food processing equipment, paper making machinery, locomotives and on-and off-road vehicles.

Vogel's first true success came when Con-Rail, one of eight major railroads in this country, decided to test a Vogel wheel flange lubricator. During field tests this product proved that it could reduce Con-Rails energy consumption by up to 10 percent. After successful conclusion of the test period, Con-Rail purchased the Vogel flange lubricator for most of its fleet of engines, ultimately realizing a savings of almost $30 million per year. This success provided the company with the impetus and recognition necessary to move forward.

Over the next few years Vogel shifted its marketing focus to Detroit, where it targeted the Big Three automotive manufacturers. Vogel was able to demonstrate to GM, Chrysler and Ford, both in theory and then in practice, that the Vogel method of lubricant delivery was technically superior to that being used by Detroit manufacturers at that time. These proofs were so successful that in 1995, Vogel was chosen as the single-source

Joe Ahrens, president and CEO of Vogel Lubrication, Inc.

supplier to the General Motors Power Train and Daimler-Chrysler CTC projects. In 1999, the company was also awarded sole supplier status for the Ford 1-4/15 project.

Vogel has grown from the entrepreneurial organization originally created by Joe Ahrens to the internationally recognized supplier of lubrication technology that it is today. It is a company that cares for its employees and is proud of its history on the Peninsula. Vogel looks forward to contributing to the overall well-being of society at the local, national and international levels.

FURTHER READING

On the one hand, Robert E. Lee said that a gentleman ought to be willing to forget an old offense. Let him summon the strength, General Lee said, "to let the past be but the past." And on the other, there is the cartoon of the Confederate soldier with the caption: "Forget, hell!"

This is Virginia, where the past is companion to the present, where it often seems to be the proud staple of today. Family, habit, history, and a sense of tradition urge Virginians to hold on to the past, to cherish it, commemorate it, improve it, institutionalize it-and to commercialize it for the tourist.

Indeed, it is quite a past. It is not surprising, then, that the libraries are bulging with histories of Jamestown and the settlement of Virginia, histories of the Revolutionary War and the Civil War, histories of the times when history was made in Virginia, as well as biographies of the great men who were given to history by the state.

I shall skip them; they are easy to find. I have mentioned many of the travelers who came to Norfolk and recorded what they saw and thought at the time. Among the histories of Virginia, the first to be written by a native Virginian, Robert Beverley's *The History and Present State* of Virginia (1705), is available in a convenient paperback and readable still. *The Hornbook of Virginia History, Fourth Edition* (1983), edited by Emily J. Salmon and Edward D. C. Campbell Jr. and published by The Library of Virginia, captures 400 years of Virginia's history in a nutshell, and is an indispensable reference tool for researcher and lay person alike. *Virginia: The New Dominion* (1971) is a big book, reverent and thorough. As an antidote I suggest Marshall Fishwick's Virginia: A *New Look* at the *Old* Dominion (1959). To anybody who is looking for a good place to start, I recommend *What Is It About Virginia ?* (1966), by Guy Friddell, who in the best tradition of American humor is serious about his subject. Two more specialized works are Ivor Noel Hume's Here *Lies Virginia: An Archaeologist's View of* Colonial *Life and History* (1963), which is an altogether delightful book, and Arthur Pierce Middleton's rich *Tobacco Coast: A Maritime History of Chesapeake Bay in the Colonial Era* (1953).

The 19th century histories of Norfolk, William S. Forrest's Historical and *Descriptive Sketches of Norfolk and Vicinity* (1853) and H.W. Burton's History *of Norfolk, Virginia* (1877), are entertaining and remain surprisingly topical. Good general histories from the 20th century include Thomas J. Wertenbaker's *Norfolk: Historic Southern Port*, published in 1931 and updated by Marvin W. Schlegel in 1960; and *Norfolk: the first four centuries*, by Thomas C. Parramore, with Peter C. Stewart and Tommy L. Bogger (1994). The best general history is still Thomas J. Wertenbaker's *Norfolk: Historic* Southern Port, published in 1931 and updated by Marvin W. Schlegel in 1960. The History *of Lower Tidewater Virginia* (1959), by Rogers Dey Whichard, is a valuable work. Not to be overlooked are *Salt Water & Printer's Ink: Norfolk and its Newspapers, 1865-1965*, by Lenoir Chambers and Joseph E. Shank; and Henry Lewis Suggs' *P. B. Young, Newspaperman: Race, Politics and Journalism in the New South, 1910-1962*. Both are excellent social histories as well as accounts of the city's newspapers. Schlegel's *Conscripted City: Norfolk in World War II* (1951) was written for the Norfolk War History Commission, and a similarly useful work is *The Road to Victory: A History of Hampton Roads Port of Embarkation in World War II* (1946), edited by Major W.R. Wheeler. For the first steamboats John C. Emmerson's "logs" of the newspaper stories that were printed between 1815 and 1836 are invaluable to the researcher, and Alexander Crosby Brown's books are essential to the later story of these waterways. Finally, I recommend the picture-books of Aubrey Bodine, which are a bit dated today, and the excellent pictorial histories put together by the late Carroll Walker, who was a bear at identifying old pictures. Walker's priceless contribution to Norfolk's recorded history is recognized in Amy Waters Yarsinske's delightful *Norfolk, Virginia: the Sunrise City by the Sea: a Tribute to Photographer Carroll H. Walker Sr.*

There are many others, such as Charles Cross in Chesapeake or George Holbert Tucker in Norfolk, lifelong devotees to keeping the historical record alive. I am pleased to be in their company.

INDEX

General Index
Italicized numbers indicate illustrations

266